ECONOMICS OF OCEAN RESOURCES

A Research Agenda

Proceedings of a national workshop
Sponsored by Office of Ocean Resources Coordination and Assessment,
National Oceanic and Atmospheric Administration

Orcas Island, Washington · September 13–16, 1981

Gardner M. Brown, Jr.
and James A. Crutchfield,
Editors

A Washington Sea Grant Publication
Distributed by University of Washington Press
Seattle and London

First published in 1982 by
Washington Sea Grant Program
University of Washington

Distributed by University of Washington Press
Seattle, Washington 98195

Support for this workshop was provided by the National Oceanic and
Atmospheric Administration under grant number NA80AA-D-00121,
project R/MS-19. Publication was accomplished by the Washington
Sea Grant Program under NOAA grant number NA81AA-D-00030, project
A/PC-5.

Library of Congress Cataloging in Publication Data

Main entry under title:

Economics of ocean resources.

"Proceedings of a national workshop sponsored by Office of Ocean
Resources Coordination and Assessment, National Oceanic and
Atmospheric Administration, Orcas Island, Washington, September 13-16,
1981."

"A Washington Sea Grant publication."
Includes bibliographies.
1. Marine resources--Congresses. I. Brown, Gardner Mallard.
II. Crutchfield, James Arthur. III. United States. National
Oceanic and Atmospheric Administration. Office of Ocean Resources
Coordination and Assessment. IV. Washington Sea Grant Program
GC1001.E27 1982   333.91'64   82-17471
ISBN 0-295-95982-7

Contents

Foreword

Before stating the broad purpose of this workshop on ocean resources economics, I would like to provide a context by describing the mission of its sponsor, the Office of Ocean Resources Coordination and Assessment (ORCA) of the National Oceanic and Atmospheric Administration. Within NOAA we are responsible for identifying and evaluating the impacts of alternative resource uses in intensely used coastal and ocean regions. We develop and recommend management strategies or policies for the use of resources of these regions which will result in maximum benefit to the Nation. We have the responsibility for development of NOAA-wide policy positions in two important areas: (1) outer continental shelf oil and gas exploration and development; and (2) marine transportation.

To improve our ability to carry out this mission, ORCA sponsors projects to develop and apply new methods for projecting and evaluating both the short-term and long-term environmental and economic impacts of coastal and ocean resource use decisions. We have initiated a series of five regional strategic assessments of the entire U.S. coastal and 200-mile fishery conservation zone to identify significant resource use conflicts before they occur.

We also give technical assistance to states and other federal agencies on a wide variety of coastal and ocean resource issues, ranging from special area management to evaluating the onshore impacts of marine mineral mining. We administer the Office of Coastal Zone Management's responsibilities for compliance with the National Environmental Policy Act with respect to both state coastal zone management programs and proposed marine and estuarine sanctuaries. We are one of the few--perhaps the only--federal offices attempting to develop in a strategic manner the necessary data base and methods for analyzing national policy on programs for coastal and ocean resource use on a comprehensive scale and within an explicit analytical framework.

The purpose of this workshop is to serve as one departure point for a modest program of economic and institutional research related to

the management of ocean resources that will be undertaken by ORCA
later this year. The oceans represent a set of resources for which,
in fact, very little management currently exists. An important objective of this program will be the development and use of data with
which to consider explicitly the benefits and costs to the nation
and its coastal regions of alternative ocean resource uses. Since
ORCA is concerned with the multiple use of ocean resources, the
problem of identifying and evaluating the costs and benefits of conflicts and compatibilities among these uses is of greatest importance to us.

Our coastal and ocean waters provide a wide mix of products and services to the nation. They are the incubators and life support systems of living resources which have been an important source of protein for centuries. They provide a relatively inexpensive source of
transportation and an attractive place for recreation. They have
also long been used as a place to dump the waste materials of our
economic activities.

All of these uses had little effect on either each other or the
natural environment when activities were widely scattered in time
and space and when levels of use were low. But this is no longer
the case. People and their activities continue to move to the coast
in increasing numbers. We now expect the oceans to provide increasing amounts of the energy and materials to drive the economy and to
yield not only sand and gravel, but also strategic minerals. The
assimilative capacity of the oceans will continue to be used heavily
as a sink for our wastes.

As economic activities increase in the oceans, interactions among
different uses are inevitable. While occasionally these interactions are compatible or even mutually beneficial as when domestic
sewage increases fish production in some areas, more often the
interactions conflict. That is, the production of one output of
the ocean has an adverse impact on the production of another. What
has traditionally been a relatively simply decision process--orient-
ed toward developing a single product or service from the ocean--
has now become a highly complex one of deciding what mix of products and services should be produced from any given ocean region
over time to maximize benefits to the nation.

What role can economists play in sharpening the issues of ocean resources management? What can economists tell us about the best
mix of products and services and the proper rate of development of
ocean resources and their uses? How can the benefits and costs of
multiple use be assessed? How can economic incentives be used to
minimize the extent of real conflicts among uses? What economic
incentives can be used to ensure efficient development of resources,
minimum damage to the natural environment, and an equitable distribution of the benefits and costs of ocean resource uses? What
changes in institutional arrangements might be desirable?

Timing of this workshop is fortuitous. Not only has it been almost
ten years since some of the early work in ocean resources economics,

but we now have a new Administration. Already some discussion has taken place about rethinking development of a national ocean policy. What do economists have to tell us about how to formulate such a policy? What results of economic research can be used to develop this policy?

These are some of the general questions we should address during the workshop. The need for improved scientific and economic information with which to manage the resources of the ocean is obvious to all of us who have had to deal with the practical problems of making decisions about their use. All too often decisions affecting multi-million dollar investments are made, at least in the public sector, with only the sketchiest information and analysis of economic and environmental consequences. The recommendations of this workshop on an agenda for ocean resources economics research should help to build a basis for improved decision-making on these valuable national resources.

Charles N. Ehler
May 1982

Preface

In September, 1981, a workshop on the economics of marine resources was convened at Orcas Island, Washington. The meeting was sponsored by ORCA, funded through the Sea Grant Program of NOAA, and arranged by Professors Gardner Brown and James Crutchfield of the University of Washington's Department of Economics.

The workshop reflected a perceived need to establish a more rational economic framework for research in the development, utilization, and management of marine resources. This is not to say that good economic analysis of marine resource usage has not been undertaken; but with the possible exception of fisheries, it has been fragmentary and of widely varying scope and quality. In its present state the field of marine resource economics does not provide a defined agenda for future research of the types required either by ORCA or by the academic community.

Dr. Crutchfield was asked to contribute a general overview paper while a selected group of experts was commissioned to prepare studies dealing with living resources, oil and gas, other marine minerals, marine recreation, and management of the marine environment. Discussants were requested to prepare written comments on these papers to stimulate discussion at the workshop. Dr. A.D. Scott was assigned the formidable task of summarizing the proceedings in a Capstone paper. Although the general theme--the need for an analytical framework that would provide an integrated set of research priorities--was stressed in our invitations, the authors were free to approach the issues in their own way. The result was a lively, productive, and wide-ranging discussion and a series of papers that appear to warrant wider distribution through publication of this volume.

We are particularly grateful to Drs. Charles Ehler and Daniel Basta of ORCA for their support and active participation in the project, and to the authors and discussants for their thoughtful and provocative contributions.

Credit for arranging the conference goes to Nadine Flaherty, Marge
Caddey and Kersti Stern. Drafts and revisions of the manuscript
were very ably prepared by Marian Bolan. Cathy Carruthers and
Richard Jacobson provided excellent research assistance and Victoria
Brown edited and orchestrated its final preparation. Coordination
with Washington Sea Grant was pleasantly and agreeably arranged
through Patricia Peyton.

Gardner M. Brown, Jr.
James A. Crutchfield

Seattle, Washington
May 1982

A Perspective on Ocean Resources

James A. Crutchfield

The purpose of this paper is to update the "state of the marine resources world," with only limited discussion of the institutional
and technical changes that account for observed and prospective
changes. No attempt is made to categorize or rank order research
needs, since that task is addressed by the authors of the commissioned papers.

Living Resources

In recent years there has been a major change in estimates of the
potential supply of the economically recoverable living resources
from the sea. It now appears that earlier estimates based on broad
productivity factors were grossly overoptimistic, and that limits on
production--i.e., levels at which further increases in output can
be obtained only at sharply rising marginal costs--are much tighter
than previously envisaged.

World Landings

This change stems from the discouraging behavior of world landings
during the past decade. From the end of World War II to 1970 there
was an almost continuous increase in fish and shellfish production,
world wide, from a level of about 20 million metric tons in 1948 to
more than 70 million tons in the early 1970s. Thereafter, however,
there has been little significant increase in total landings. Landings have been virtually stable for the past 5 years and declined
in 1980 (Table 1).

The internal composition of these total figures provides ground for
further misgivings. Much of the increase in the 1960s was a result
of the spectacular growth of catches for oil and meal, particularly
in Peru. Further impetus was provided by the rapid growth in deep
sea harvesting capacity in the Soviet Union and other east bloc
countries. Finally, geographic expansion, particularly along the
west coast of Africa and South America provided an additional boost
which has now peaked out. There is growing evidence that much of

TABLE 1

FISHERY PRODUCTS: WORLD CATCH OF AQUATIC ORGANISMS[a]

	Average 1970-73	1974	1975	1976	1977	1978	1979	1980b Prelim.
	000 t							
WORLD TOTAL	64,200	66,592	66,479	69,863	69,164	70,544	71,253	70,292
Developed Countries	34,386	36,736	37,178	38,575	37,982	37,432	37,323	37,097
North America:	4,022	3,821	3,835	4,152	4,216	4,783	4,843	4,850
Canada	1,212	974	993	1,102	1,235	1,366	1,332	1,260
United States	2,810	2,847	2,842	3,050	2,980	3,418	3,511	3,590
Western Europe:	11,073	11,295	10,989	12,030	12,038	11,440	11,134	11,089
EFC:	4,635	5,121	4,856	5,023	4,810	4,844	4,623	4,800
Denmark	1,384	1,835	1,767	1,912	1,806	1,740	1,738	2,000
France	772	793	784	787	744	777	732	700
Germany, Fed. Rep. of	505	526	442	454	432	412	354	315
Italy	406	426	406	420	380	402	427	457
Netherlands	329	326	351	285	313	324	324	328
United Kingdom	1,099	1,079	969	1,026	997	1,030	905	817
Others	140	136	137	139	139	158	140	183
Portugal	456	430	375	346	310	255	242	260
Spain	1,530	1,498	1,512	1,469	1,389	1,373	1,205	1,250
Iceland	762	945	995	986	1,374	1,567	1,645	1,510
Norway	2,985	2,579	2,481	3,361	3,402	2,587	2,650	2,417
Othersc	705	722	770	845	793	814	769	792
Eastern Europe and USSR:	8,829	10,596	11,493	11,509	10,562	9,977	10,259	10,118
Poland	528	679	801	750	655	571	601	640
USSR	7,735	9,256	9,970	10,132	9,351	8,915	9,114	8,910
Others	566	661	722	627	556	491	547	568

(Continued)

TABLE 1 (Continued)

	Average 1970-73	1974	1975	1976	1977	1978	1979	1980[b] Prelim.
				000 t				
Oceania:	176	203	172	187	210	223	237	237
Australia[d]	114	134	109	110	128	123	127	120
New Zealand	62	69	64	76	83	100	110	117
Other Developed Countries:	10,286	10,821	10,687	10,697	10,915	11,010	10,852	10,862
Japan	9,497	10,101	9,895	9,994	10,123	10,184	9,966	10,000
South Africa	597	592	600	595	550	600	659	635
Israel	27	24	24	26	24	26	27	--
Others	165	104	168	82	218	200	--	--
Developing Countries	29,814	29,856	29,302	31,288	31,181	33,112	33,930	33,195
Africa:	3,618	4,025	3,700	3,533	3,533	3,634	3,526	3,219
Morocco	278	285	224	281	255	287	280	--
Ghana	228	220	255	238	268	264	230	--
Nigeria	385	473	466	497	504	519	535	451
Senegal	259	357	363	362	348	359	308	--
Tanzania	173	171	196	239	288	295	344	240
Namibia	634	840	761	574	404	418	327	211
Others	1,661	1,619	1,435	1,342	1,466	1,492	1,502	1,499
Latin America:	10,462	7,447	6,604	8,201	6,818	8,736	10,028	9,579
Mexico	407	402	468	526	611	703	875	1,252
Chile	1,036	1,128	899	1,379	1,319	1,929	2,633	2,817
Ecuador	115	174	222	298	434	617	644	--
Peru	7,530	4,145	3,448	4,344	2,537	3,369	3,682	2,709
Argentina	224	277	211	266	370	519	566	390
Brazil	602	726	753	653	748	803	843	850
Uruguay	17	16	26	34	48	74	108	130
Others	531	579	577	701	751	722	677	747

(Continued)

3

TABLE 1 (Continued)

	Average 1970-73	1974	1975	1976	1977	1978	1979	1980[b] Prelim.
				000 t				
Near East (Africa and Asia):	737	873	843	813	820	789	771	--
Asia:	14,225	16,688	17,260	17,790	19,025	18,891	18,492	18,493
Southern Asia:	2,908	3,418	3,440	3,377	3,585	3,425	3,487	3,361
India	1,801	2,255	2,266	2,174	2,312	2,306	2,343	2,200
Others	1,107	1,163	1,174	1,203	1,273	1,119	1,144	1,161
East and Southest Asia:	6,106	7,057	7,424	7,874	8,688	8,757	8,586	8,632
Indonesia	1,249	1,333	1,382	1,479	1,568	1,642	1,732	1,814
Korea, Rep. of	1,089	1,688	1,887	2,118	2,085	2,091	2,162	2,090
Malaysia	378	525	474	517	619	685	698	765
Philippines	1,167	1,371	1,443	1,393	1,508	1,495	1,476	1,507
Thailand	1,597	1,516	1,553	1,659	2,188	2,095	1,716	1,650
Others	626	624	685	708	720	749	802	806
Centrally Planned Economies:	5,211	6,213	6,396	6,539	6,752	6,709	6,419	6,500
China	3,482	4,134	4,247	4,320	4,463	4,394	4,054	4,135
Other Developing Countries	772	823	895	951	985	1,063	1,113	1,133

[a]Excluding all aquatic mammals and aquatic plants.

[b]Including estimates (1979 data repeated) for countries for which 1980 data are not yet available.

[c]Including Greece.

[d]Data available on fiscal year (July-June) basis only.

Source: Food and Agriculture Organization of the United Nations, Fishery Commodity Situation and Outlook, 1980-1981, Rome, May 1981.

4

the increase in landings by the USSR involved greater effort in areas already being exploited at or beyond sustained yield levels, particularly in the north Atlantic and in the northeast Pacific.

Landings of both the Soviet Union and Japan, the two dominant countries in high seas fishery operations, have declined during the last few years after long periods of continued increases. The drop in landings in 1980 was felt in both developed and developing country groups.

It is also clear that the stability of the 70s was achieved by substituting new species and/or new fishing areas for old as known and conventional populations were depleted. Thus, fishmeal operations in the northeast Atlantic have been maintained by moving successively from herring to mackerel, capelin and sprat. The catastrophic decline in north Atlantic herring catches were offset in large part by a massive increase in effort devoted to mackerel, but the latter stocks are now in a state of near collapse. Japanese and Russian fleets in the northeast Pacific, targeting initially on Pacific Ocean perch, have shifted to pollock, Pacific whiting, and other lower valued species, and showed marked declining tendencies in catches even before the American 200 mile Economic Control Zone was established in 1976.

In short, world landings are well below levels that might have prevailed had rational management of major stocks been initiated and aggressively enforced over the past two decades. As a rough estimate, world landings could easily stand at 85 - 90 million metric tons rather than 70, if such management measures had been instituted and observed (Robinson, 1980). Moreover, the addition would have come in the form of higher priced and more desirable market species-- obviously, the first to be depleted.

Future Expansion—Possibilities and Limitations

These are the principal facts that underlie the rather modest projections for expansion of world fisheries to the year 2000 now being released by FAO--probably the most authoritative single source. Robinson submits a sober estimate of a potential increase of 20-30 million metric tons over present levels, assuming that conventional species only are involved; i.e., those that are harvestable by existing types of gear and marketable in existing product forms. (See Table 2). Robinson points out, properly, that this forecast must be treated with considerable caution, since it assumes only about half of the estimated increase will come through increased fishing effort; the remainder can be expected only if improved management and rebuilding of previously depleted stocks is actually achieved.

This sobering view is in sharp contrast with forecasts based on the "potential of all stocks," primarily because it acknowledges the likelihood that price-cost relations will prevent exploitation of some species and the impossibility of expanding production of all interrelated species to maximum potential simultaneously.

TABLE 2

AQUATIC ORGANISMS--ACTUAL AND ESTIMATED PRODUCTION

	Production (Million Tons)				
	1963a	1975b	1980	1990	2000
World	47.7	72.5	75.3	84.7	92.5
Developing Countries:	22.8	34.1	37.3	45.6	51.9
Latin America	8.9	7.7	7.6	9.0	10.2
Africa	2.1	3.8	4.1	5.1	6.0
Near East	5.3	11.2	12.6	15.6	18.1
Asian Centrally Planned	5.9	10.3	11.5	13.8	15.3
Other Developing	0.1	0.3	0.5	0.7	0.7
Developed Countries:	24.9	38.4	38.0	39.1	40.6
North America	4.0	4.1	4.9	6.4	6.9
West. Europe	8.9	11.5	11.7	12.5	12.9
EEC	4.2	5.3	5.2	5.3	5.5
Other West. Europe	4.7	6.2	6.5	7.2	7.4
East. Europe and USSR	4.6	11.3	10.6	9.7	10.0
Oceania	0.1	0.2	0.3	0.4	0.6
Other Developed	7.2	11.3	10.6	10.1	10.2

a1963 = average 1961-65.

b1975 = average 1974-76.

Source: Robinson (1980).

Realizable catches will always fall short of levels that could be achieved if each stock could be managed selectively.

The regional composition of world fish landings also reveals some interesting trends in the last decade. Much of the post-war growth in marine fish landings of food fish came from Japan, the U.S.S.R. and other east bloc countries, and Spain. While the catches of the major developed countries have tapered off and started to decline, food fish landings in the developing world continued to increase and continue to be associated with increased per capita consumption in local markets. Preliminary FAO estimates for 1980, however, show a sharp drop in landings in both developed and developing nations. Only Chile and Uruguay showed significant increases. In some areas, the increase in catches in developing countries has been concentrated on the worldwide market for such high value species as shrimp, tuna, and rock lobster, all of which are valuable sources of foreign exchange.

Of the potential sources of growth in total world landings unselective increased fishing effort is one of the smallest. It is now abundantly clear that an overwhelming proportion of the world's economically viable fisheries lie within waters of the Continental shelf, and the few inshore populations that remain unexploited are economically unattractive. There are some possibilities remaining, of course. Increased quantities of cephalopods (squids, cuttlefish, octopus), smaller crabs, and many molluscs could be taken if markets can be broadened. The U.S., for example, makes virtually no use of its large squid resources, though they are widely consumed in southern Europe and Asia. A number of large pelagic populations are still underutilized, and an "internal margin" remains open in the form of higher-valued usage for many species. By and large, however, it seems impossible to achieve any large increase in total catches until and unless new fishing, processing and/or marketing techniques make it profitable to exploit presently unconventional species (e.g., mesopelagic stocks of Antarctic krill).

Increases at least as great could be realized by eliminating part of the waste that now occurs throughout the fish harvesting-marketing sequence. It is believed by FAO experts that at least 20 percent of the fish taken at sea end up as waste. Poor handling at sea and at primary landings, the lack of ice or other preservative methods, discarding of by-catches to save carrying capacity for more valuable species, and poor marketing practices all account for a portion of this waste.

Some loss is inevitable of course. There is no more reason to expect profitable use of every pound of fish caught than to expect profitable recovery of every barrel of oil or of every bushel of grain. But the losses in fisheries do seem greater than necessary.

Aquaculture

Aquaculture remains a latent giant. Potentially it seems capable of producing 15 - 25 million metric tons annually (both inland and marine), a figure which would represent a substantial gain over the 4-5 million tons of present estimated production. But an enormous amount of coordinated research must be undertaken before basic problems of feed, seed supply, disease control, and marketing can be resolved. Most enthusiasts for aquaculture have yet to be introduced to the concept of opportunity cost; and it is unfortunately true that in most developed countries the areas suitable for aquaculture are also highly desirable for other types of land-water usage. It should also be pointed out that aquaculture has rarely produced low-priced, high-volume protein supplies. Most of the successful aquaculture ventures throughout the world are producing high priced specialty items, primarily for the institutional and restaurant trades. Only in Asia and in a few places in Africa, where aquaculture has been successfully integrated with peasant agriculture, has the promise of very low priced protein been achieved.

Future Supply Prospects

Robinson's forecasts for future production are shown in Table 2. A number of interesting predictions stand out. First, landings in the developed countries are expected to show virtually no increase, although there may be major shifts in the relative shares of different developed countries as coastal country development programs within 200 mile limits are pushed more vigorously. Second, increases are expected, in some cases in rather significant quantities, in developing countries. The nearly universal extension of coastal country control over marine resources to 200 miles, coupled with the urgency of protein supply requirements in these areas, suggests that they may show substantial increases in output as a result of their ability to exclude or control the distant water fleets that have previously dominated fishing in most developing areas of the world. These are, of course, transfers of catch rather than increases in total output. It is sobering to note that Robinson's projection for 1980 (based on then current 1977 data) is about 4 million tons above actual 1980 landings.

World Trade in Fishery Products

Another aspect of the economic future of world fisheries is an anticipated increase in world trade in fishery products. In part this reflects the strong tendency to exclude or sharply reduce distant water operations by countries which remain major consumers of fish products. It also reflects the massive change in food processing technology in the frozen food industry that began in the 1960s, and the resulting increase in trade in processed and semi-processed frozen fish. Both trends have given new life to the joint venture concept, a technique which permits more rapid development of coastal country resources while allowing more orderly disinvestment in fishing and at-sea processing equipment by the distant water operators.

World Demand for Fish

In the face of this somewhat sober view of world supply prospects, demand for fishery products continues to increase, particularly in developing countries where income elasticities of demand for protein food are high. Even in the United States, where per capita consumption had been virtually stable for nearly 40 years, there has been a surprisingly large increase in the past 10 years, almost entirely confined to growth in consumption of packaged frozen fish, fish sticks and portions and canned tuna. Less dramatic but indicative increases in consumption of frozen packaged ground fish products are evident in virtually every country in Western Europe.

Without going into detail, it seems clear that world demand for fishery products can be expected to increase more rapidly than can be provided at current prices. In the less developed countries population growth, increases in per capita consumption with rising incomes, and better market organization will continue to increase the demand for seafoods. Even in the developed countries, where per capita consumption has been relatively stable, some increase in demand can be expected through population growth.

Several obvious but important conclusions follow from these general world trends. First, once the rapid run-up in real prices of fish that occurred in the mid- to late-1970s has been absorbed, further strengthening of real fish prices can be expected over the long run. Even if we are able to find products and markets for species presently unutilized, the elasticity of supply of total protein from the sea does not seem great enough to keep pace with increases in demand now anticipated. Second, a major part of the supply potential that does remain will come from rebuilding of presently depleted stocks. Coupled with the prospect of the rising real prices, this makes it all the more important that concepts of management be reexamined and that the reasons for failure to apply the knowledge gained over the last three or four decades be carefully evaluated.

U.S. Experience

Turning to the special circumstances of the United States, there have been significant changes in fishery production and demand during the past decade. After a long period of stability, landings jumped from 4.0 million pounds in 1975 to 6.3 million pounds in 1979. To a very considerable extent this increase stemmed from a shift in landings from foreign to American vessels as the full impact of the Magnuson Fisheries Conservation and Management Act of 1976 was felt. Displacement of foreign fishing occurred quite quickly in the New England and middle Atlantic states, and while similar displacement has been much slower in the more important northeast Pacific area, the quantities of fish taken there by American fishermen in joint venture operations has grown very rapidly in the past three years.

On the demand side, the driving force for this expansion in American fisheries and the more dramatic increase in imports has been the effect of the "frozen food revolution" of the 1960s on American eating habits. Frozen ground fish fillets, sticks, and portions are ideally suited for sale in packaged frozen form through retail outlets, and the burgeoning of this segment of industry brought a surge of increased demand in interior areas where supplies of fresh fish were notably deficient in quantity and variety. In addition, frozen portions, sticks and fillets are an ideal input for the fast food restaurants, which have achieved remarkable growth in the United States during the past 6-8 years. Tight control over size of portions and the ease of preparation make frozen ground fish products an ideal complement to meat and poultry products which were the initial basis for fast food operations.

Unfortunately, prospects for continued growth in the U.S. fishery are less bright. In virtually all coastal waters except Alaska landings are now largely resource-limited. Only minor foreign operations remain on the east and Gulf coasts, and these are centered on species of little interest to the American market.[1] There is an enormous potential for expansion of U.S. landings of Pacific whiting off the west coast and of pollock, yellowtail flounder, Atka mackerel, and cod in the Gulf of Alaska and the Bering Sea. However, detailed analyses, both by outside experts and by the industry itself, indicate that at present market prices it is simply impossible for American fishermen and American processors of these products to cover full opportunity costs and meet the competition of imported ground fish products. Until an increase in real fish prices of perhaps 20-25 percent occurs, it seems likely that any major expansion in American fishing activities will occur in joint venture arrangements rather than through a fully American harvesting-processing-marketing sequence.

Management Issues

In light of these meager long run supply prospects (and of the obvious importance which a good many nations attach to production of protein from the sea), it is astonishing that so little progress has been made in refining or applying the concepts of management developed over recent decades. There are few major fisheries in which even management for biological objectives has been effective, though many efforts have been made. And cases where economic and social as well as biological objectives have been made specific, with appropriate management measures tailored to meet those objectives, are almost nonexistent. Yet the literature in resource economics has produced a series of increasingly sophisticated discussions of the inadequacy of biologically oriented management programs and of both the need for and techniques for more efficient management geared to a simultaneous achievement of protection of stocks, minimization of cost, and equitable distribution of fishing benefits. (See, for example, Anderson, 1977; Clarke, 1976; Crutchfield, 1979; Scott, 1979).

A few examples will suffice. Despite the known sensitivity of clupeoid stocks to heavy fishing pressure, most herring stocks of the northeast Atlantic have been overfished to the point of complete collapse, and mackerel populations, to which the fleets shifted, seem to be approaching the same condition. Indeed, the inability of the EEC nations to establish a common fishery policy, despite the existence of an agreed program of management and enforcement, is evidence of the confusion that prevails in one of the most intensely studied fishing areas of the world. In the northeast Pacific the valuable King Crab fishery, spurred by the rapid increases in real prices for crab that occurred during the 1970s, has seen the familiar scenario unfold again: the rush to larger and larger vessels, with more power and more sophisticated equipment, even after it had become evident that full utilization of the resource had been achieved. We are now beginning to see the inevitable consequences: serious reductions in incomes to fishermen and vessel owners, defaults on loans and the frantic search for other deployment of the now tremendously redundant supply of fishing capacity. The tuna fishery of the eastern tropical Pacific continues to absorb larger numbers of huge oceanic purse seiners, despite growing evidence that yellowfin tuna in the area are already fully exploited, and that skipjack may be approaching that situation in some of the more heavily fished areas.

In short, we have yet to come to grips with the inevitable consequences of the common property problem. This is all the more frustrating in view of its thorough wringing-out in the economic literature of the past thirty years. From Scott Gordon's challenging 1954 article to the sophisticated discussions in the <u>Journal of the Fisheries Research Board of Canada</u> (1979) and the more recent reports of the Economic Council of Canada (1982), the single theme has been hammered home repeatedly--unless some way is found to convert fishing rights into some form of property right, competitive exploitation of living marine resources will inevitably degenerate into the economically wasteful and at times biologically destructive open fishing syndrome. The accessibility of major marine fish stocks to international exploitation simply exacerbates the situation. While the nearly universal adoption of 200 mile economic control zones over living resources has dramatically reduced the number of players, it is rarely sufficient to deal with the common property problem in its entirety.

Experience with Effort Control

Experience with limited entry programs has ranged from very good to ineffective. The British Columbia, Alaska, and western Australian experiences with limited entry programs with inadequate control over factor substitution illustrate the dangers of this approach (Fraser, 1979; Adasiak, 1979; Meany, 1979). What is needed is effective control over effort, where effort consists of optimal factor combinations in each fishing unit. It should be possible to control fishing power by limiting the number of fishing vessels but only if other parameters of fishing power are also controlled. Failure to do so results, inevitably, in some degree of factor distortion and excessive capital investment. On the other hand, freezing of technology designed to prevent such "upgrading" of fishing power would clearly stifle any incentive or opportunity for technological progress.

At the other extreme, the experience in the south Australian prawn fishery illustrates what can be accomplished if a limited entry program is initiated prior to or shortly after the fishery begins to develop. Only a small number of vessels were licensed to fish at the outset, and it was not considered necessary to limit the tendency to upgrade the fishing power of the individual unit as the profitability of the operation became well established. As a result, the state of south Australia has been able to hold the number of licensed units to 53, which are now catching approximately one-third the amount of prawns taken by more than 1400 boats in Queensland, where no attempt was made to limit entry until long after the massive expansion to be expected in a valuable fishery had taken place. (Natural productivity is roughly the same in both areas). Incidentally, it is recorded that a prawn license in south Australia or the Gulf of Carpenteria now sells for more than $250,000.

Because of the major difficulties encountered with the simpler limited entry programs, economists have become more and more interested in the possibility of establishing property rights in individual fish quotas which could be freely traded. The obvious advantages of a system of this type have been discussed thoroughly in the literature and need not be repeated here. Suffice it to say that the technique, because it is a true system of property rights, would permit the individual operator far more latitude than he would enjoy under any other system of management, and would produce the desired decrease in the total number of fishing units while compensating, through open market purchases, those who leave the fishery. Unfortunately, we have no experience from which to draw to indicate whether or not there are unforeseen difficulties with such programs (e.g., enforcement problems).

One of the more attractive features of the individual quota approach is its compatibility with multi-species fisheries and with fisheries in which the gear is deployed seasonally among different alternative occupations. Anyone connected with fisheries has long been aware of the serious divergence between theory, which runs largely in terms of single species models, and industry practice in which gear takes more than one species or can be deployed against more than one species as a regular practice. There are some notable exceptions (Cf. Anderson, 1975, 1980 and Huppert, 1979); but even these papers are based on very sketchy assumptions about the nature and degree of biological interactions among exploited stocks.

The Multi-Species Problem

Space does not permit a full exploration of the problems associated with multi-species fishing; these are covered in detail in Huppert's paper. The major difficulties, oddly enough, are not economic but biological. Despite long awareness of the problem, we simply have no adequate empirical knowledge of species interaction, of the nature of the response to selective fishing in multi-species environments, or of the time path of such changes. It has been painfully borne in on both industry and fishery managers that inter-species relationships are important and that protection of one stock may well lead to diminished availability of another (for example, if they stand in predator-prey relationship). But the ability to quantify in a way that would permit systematic management of inter-related stocks for any chosen objective set simply does not exist at the present time. Indeed, given the complex nature of inter-mingled fish stocks, and their inherent variability from natural causes, it may well be that this is simply not an attainable research goal. Rather, the multi-species problem may simply have to be addressed as an exercise in second (or third) best, with management directed at key species taken by such fisheries and the rest left to adjust as they will (or with control over total effort only without regard to individual species).[2]

Recent U.S. Experience in Management

In the U.S., despite sweeping organizational changes in fishery management brought about by the regionalization of fishery management under the MFCMA, the basic approach has not changed appreciably. Most of the eight regional councils have adopted a species-by-species approach in developing fishery management plans; and, with only a few exceptions, all have managed to avoid any open confrontation with the common property problem. The Act itself contains severely restrictive conditions on limited entry as a management tool and virtually rules out the use of taxes or fees for domestic fishermen to do more than recover direct administrative costs. However, there is increasing concern in the councils over the evident reaction of U.S. fishing capacity to reduction of foreign fishing in the American ECZ and the rapid increase in real prices that occurred during the late 1970s. Although it is difficult to obtain current data, it is estimated that the American fishing fleet has grown from about 13,600 to nearly 25,000 vessels since 1970. New vessel construction grew at an annual rate of about 7 percent from 1970 through 1977, and at a rate of almost 36 percent since 1977.

The reason for this phenomenon is clear: prices for fish increased much faster between 1970 and 1980 than the general price level or the prices of competing protein products. Since most U.S. fisheries which had been shared with foreign fishermen were quickly reserved under MFCMA for American fishermen to the full extent of their capacity to harvest, the attractive prices produced a veritable gold rush. Unfortunately, the increase in U.S. harvesting capacity has far outrun the increase in physical landings, and the familiar symptoms of excess capacity, declining earnings, and increased squabbling among various geographic areas and gear types have emerged. If the potential gains of the MFCMA to the American fishing industry, which are very real indeed, are to be realized, a vastly different concept of access to the resource and management of fishing effort must be forthcoming.

One of the more disturbing developments in fishery economics in recent years has been the increasing divergence between bioeconomic theory and the practice of fishery management. As economists became more familiar with the enormously complex environment of the ocean and the resulting variability of yield-effort functions, the complexity of bioeconomic models has increased exponentially. In a sense, the fishery economist is dealing simultaneously with two interacting dynamic systems, each driven by significantly different forces, but interrelated in ways that make them a single unit for modelling purposes. In the effort to make the models analytically more acceptable and satisfying, their complexity has grown by leaps and bounds.

By the same token, data requirements have soared far beyond the realm of practicality. A fishery manager, faced with the necessity of season by season adjustments, has neither the data nor the analytical ability to quantify even the simplest of the models which appear analytically correct from the standpoint of the bioeconomist. In effect, then, each has gone his own way: the economic theorist into more complex and more formal models, and the fishery manager back to his batch by batch prescriptions.

Clearly this will not do. Economics has a great deal to contribute to rational fishery management, but its prescriptions must be cast in a form that permits quantification in timely fashion. It also requires recognition of the enormous variability of parameters determining the availability and accessibility of fish year by year, and a set of clear answers to the question, "How little do we need to know in order to capture most of the benefits of management?"

The question of timeliness is particularly important in view of the appalling bureaucratic blanket that now stifles the operation of the regional councils. Even if management plans encounter no obstacles along the way, the time required by law and regulation, between initiation of the review process and implementation now runs over 300 days. In effect, it has become impossible to incorporate last year's data into this year's plan, even if it were assembled and analyzed instantaneously. Unless ways are found to permit flexible and rapid reaction to constantly changing needs, the management programs of the councils will simply break down. Efforts to streamline procedures are now taking form, and forthcoming amendments to the MFCMA may ease the problem.

Recreational Fishing

Finally the issue of allocation of marine fish between commercial and recreational users remains largely unresolved under the MFCMA regime. Although both a legal mandate and a mechanism to deal with the problem are found in the Act, implementation has been inadequite and, in most regions, biased in favor of commercial users. The conflicts, often bitter and harshly partisan, have not been ameliorated by transferring some state regulatory functions to the councils; they have simply been elevated to a new arena.

No single factor accounts for this unsatisfactory situation, though the most important is doubtless the continuing inability to find a common numeraire in which to measure the net contribution to the society of commercial and recreational use of marginal blocks of fish. Despite fairly clear definition of the nature of the measurement problems in evaluating angler days and translating those measures into values per fish, the techniques for simulating market values remain, in my opinion, too crude to be of much help in formulating allocation policies. (Indeed, the very term "allocation" is sufficient to raise hackles in both sport and commercial fishermen's groups).

A second major obstacle is the stubborn unwillingness of many marine anglers to accept the concept of user cost and the consequent mechanism of a salt water license and fee. Where that resistance has been overcome (for example, in Pacific Coast salmon fishing) the result has been, predictably, a notable increase in the accuracy of measures of the sport fishery's importance and in the strength of sport fishing representation in the allocation process.

Mineral Resources

The minerals discussed in this paper are found in one of three general provinces; the continental margins, the deep ocean basin, and in seawater. Figure 1 and Table 3 define the provinces and provide examples of minerals in each area.

In any discussion of ocean mineral development, it is essential to distinguish between reserves and resources, a distinction which is, in large measure, economic. Following conventional practice, mineral occurrences that are economically recoverable under current

14

TABLE 3

OCEAN MINERAL DEPOSITS

I. Continental Margins
    A. Aggregate and Placer Deposits
       1. Sand, gravel, and shell deposits.
       2. Placer concentrations
          a. Heavy Mineral Oxides--Tin, Zircon, Ilmenite
          b. Light Minerals--Diamond
          c. Native Metals--Platinum, Gold.
    B. Sub-Sea Floor Mineral Mining-Metal porphyry, Coal, Barite, Sulfur.
    C. Authigenic-Phosphorite.

II. Deep Sea
    A. Ferromanganese modules.
    B. Metalliferous sediments (Red Sea).
    C. Precipitation-Barite.

III. Extraction From Seawater
    A. Desalinization.
    B. Metals, Metal Salts and Non-Metals (Mg, MgO, NaCl, Br).
    C. Heavy Water (deuterium oxide).

---

market conditions are designated as reserves. Resources include reserves and shade into deposits with a grade or abundance too low, or recovery costs too high, to be produced at a profit under current conditions. Known resources include all identified sub-economic mineral deposits and reserves, and unknown resources are projections of deposits yet to be discovered.

The reserve-resource distinction is dynamic; changes in market conditions or technology may shift resources to the reserves category or reduce reserves to the resource classification. In addition, exploration will continue to affect the present pattern of reserve-resource distribution. In short, the reserve-resource distinction is far from clear, and all subdefinitions of reserves reflect probability-based judgment rather than hard fact. Nevertheless, the distinctions are useful in a preliminary discussion, if their subjective and changing nature is recognized.

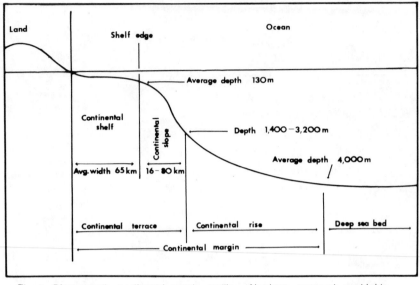

Fig. 1 Diagrammatic continental margin profile. Numbers represent worldwide averages.

Continental Margin Mineral Resources

The types of deposits discussed in this section are sea floor outcrops of minerals similar to onshore; placer concentrations of heavy and/or inert mineral sands; sub-sea floor soluble bedded deposits; and authigenic phosphorite deposits.

Tunnel Extraction

The sea floor mineral outcrops on the continental margins are frequently the extension of land expressions of minerals such as coal seams or metal porphyry ore deposits. This type of ocean mining can use conventional technology to access offshore minerals, through shafts and tunnels. Historically, this is well established. As recently as the mid-1970s more than 100 of these offshore mines were being worked. Minerals taken from these mines include coal, scheelite (calcium tungstate, $CaWO_4$) and tin.

World offshore coal production was 34 million metric tons annually in 1978. Coal is being extracted from offshore seams in Australia, Chile, Turkey, Taiwan, Japan, Great Britain and Canada, and Alaska may soon be in a position to consider exportation of offshore Cook Inlet basin coal. The United Kingdom's coal production from offshore workings amounts to 10 percent of its total production and workable offshore coal reserves in the U.K. are reported to be 550 million tons. Japan's offshore coal mines produce 9-10 million tons of coal annually.

Other minerals extracted by using shafts and tunnels to reach undersea ores include scheelite in Tasmania and tin in Cornwall, United Kingdom.

Sedimentary Deposit Solution Mining

Many minerals associated with sedimentary basin sequences may be identified and recovered by drill hole. These include salt, sulfur, potash, magnesium enriched brines, and evaporite minerals such as gypsum. Because of the association of these minerals with continental shelf and offshore basin sediments, they may be recovered as secondary production from petroleum operations. Minerals which are readily adaptable to borehole recovery include sulfur, alkali metal salts, and bromine and magnesium enriched brines.

Much of the sulfur currently recovered is from elemental deposits associated with evaporite sedimentary rock sequences. U.S. production from offshore sources (Gulf of Mexico) averaged 1.3 million tons from 1965-1977 (Drucker, 1981).

Magnesium and bromine can be produced from several sources and their separation from sea water will be discussed in a later section. Among the most common sources for both are highly concentrated brines from which these elements may be recovered. Although no offshore production figures exist for either commodity, their successful recovery from highly concentrated brines indicates the possibility of production from similar brines in offshore areas.

Deposits Which may be Recovered by Dredging

Placer Deposits

Continental margin deposits are often a result of winnowing and concentration of inert and heavy minerals. Placer deposits of this type provide several exploitable minerals, including sand and gravel, calcite and aragonite from shells and coral, gold, platinum group metals, tin minerals (cassiterite and stannite), diamonds, titanium minerals (ilmenite and rutile), and zircon.

Sand and gravel, an aggregate, is the most common continental margin deposit and currently accounts for the largest gross value of all commodities recovered from marine deposits. Offshore sand and gravel deposits in shallow water, with little or no overburden, near areas of demand, are obviously attractive. Proximity to the market area is very important with sand and gravel because of its low value per ton. Total U.S. sand and gravel production of 816 million short tons in 1980 was valued, at an average price of $2.81 per ton, at $2.3 billion (U.S. Bureau of Mines, 1980). The main marine sand and gravel producers in 1977 were the United Kingdom and Japan, with 14.8 and 41.3 million metric tons of production respectively. 19 percent of Japan's 1977 sand and gravel production was from marine sources. Denmark, the Netherlands, the United States, Sweden, Thailand, and Hong Kong also utilize offshore sand and gravel (Earney, 1980).

The primary source of tin metal is the mineral cassiterite (SnO_2). It occurs in ore grade concentrations in rock and in placer deposits above or near the source rock. Marine deposits of cassiterite are found both as solid ore in rock and as placer deposits. The lar-

gest concentration of this resource occurs in the southeast Asian
tin belt, stretching 2900 km from Thailand through Malaysia in to
Indonesia.

World tin production in 1980 was 250,000 metric tons. Offshore
tin production, primarily from southeast Asia, was about 13.7
million tons of ore in 1977, valued at $190 million (Earney, 1980).
Offshore operations in Thailand in 1980 accounted for about 2.0
percent of world tin mineral recovery. Indonesia operated 16
dredges during a similar period, producing about 5.3 percent of
world production. Indonesian offshore workings are located primarily near the famous "tin islands" of Bangka, Belitung, Sinkep,
and Bankinang.

Heavy mineral sand placer deposits of ilmenite, rutile, zircon,
and monazite are major sources of titanium, titanium dioxide, zir-
conium, and rare earth elements. These minerals are often found
together.

Offshore economic concentrations of these heavy mineral sands have
been identified in Australia, including one 1000 km concentration
between Newcastle and Frazer Island, but these deposits are not
yet being exploited due to the abundance and grade of ilmenite
beach sands. Similar deposits have also been identified but not
recovered along the Konkan Coast of India and Sri Lanka where
placer deposits lie 2-5 km offshore along a 200 km section of coast.

Phosphorite, a calcium phosphate mineral, is the primary source for
phosphorous in chemicals and fertilizer. Marine phosphorite occurs
in offshore banks as nodules, pellets, sands, and muds, generally
in water of less than 400 m. U.S. 1980 production, entirely from
land sources, was 54 million metric tons valued at $1.2 billion.
World phosphorite production in 1980 was 136 million metric tons.

Marine phosphorite deposits have been identified by Lockheed International Minerals Corporation off of southern California which
average 27 percent P_2O_5. Marine phosphorites have also been identified off the coasts of Baja California, Chile, Peru, South Africa,
New South Wales (Australia), and Southwest India. No marine phosphorite recovery is presently underway, however. Abundant land
phosphate rock usually of P_2O_5 concentrations averaging 31 percent
or more place most marine phosphorite occurrences, generally with
P_2O_5 concentration less than 27 percent, in the potential resource
category.

High gold prices have brought renewed interest in marine occurrences
of gold-bearing placer deposits. Gold placer deposits have been
identified in submerged river channels and gravel bars near the
Seward Peninsula in Alaska and in Southeastern Australia (offshore
of the famous Ballarat Region in Victoria, Australia). Submerged
beach deposits have also been identified in northern California and
southern Oregon, the source probably being the Klamath Mountains
(Cronan, 1980). Gold is not currently being extracted from marine
placer deposits, however.

Diamonds were recovered by the Marine Diamond Corporation from 1961 to 1971 in the Hottentot Bay area of South Africa. The operation yielded $1.7 million annually from placer gravels. Offshore mining ended in 1971 since the operation was no longer competitive with land based mining.

Authigenic barite occurs in concentrations up to 10 percent in deep ocean sediments at depths below 3500 m in the southeast Pacific, but is not presently economically recoverable. Barite is a prominent vein mineral and also occurs with carbonate rocks. It is in this latter association that barite is being mined from the marine environment. Marine production is estimated at 330,000-355,000 tons annually. This would be about 15 percent of the 1980 U.S. production and 4 percent of 1980 world production.

Deep Ocean Minerals

Two deep ocean resources will be discussed in this section. They are ferromanganese nodules and the minerals associated with thermal occurrences in ocean spreading centers.

Ferromanganese Nodules

The promise of an unexploited, economically attractive and technically feasible source of four important metals from deep sea manganese nodules has prompted the formation of several mining consortia, including some of the major mineral companies of the world (Table 4). Intense research and exploration by these consortia during the 1960s and 1970s expanded the working knowledge of deep ocean mining in two important areas: scientific and economic. Scientific understanding has broadened in the areas of ocean floor nodule distribution, factors influencing variations of metal concentrations within the manganese oxide lattice, and potential metal production quantities. Mining economic studies relate to projections of capital investment requirements to realize nodule recovery, minimum metal concentrations required for profitable recovery process best suited to the targeted end product. For a variety of reasons, however, no production scale operations have started as yet.

Ferromanganese nodules are concretions which form on and slightly below the surface of the ocean floor. The porous matrix of hydrous iron and manganese oxides accepts other metal oxides into the lattice, including cobalt, nickel, titanium, copper, and trace elements such as molybdenum, vanadium, and zinc. Individually their concentration within the manganese oxide matrix varies directly with their respective seawater and sediment concentrations. Additionally, cobalt displays an inverse quantitative relationship with depth. Nickel, copper, and cobalt, although minor constituents of nodules by volume, are the focus of the nodule recovery effort.

Nodules vary in abundance on the ocean floor and are found in abundance in areas shielded from terrigenous sediments. (See Figure 2). The concentrations of different metal constituents are also highly

TABLE 4

MAJOR CONSORTIA THAT ARE, OR HAVE RECENTLY BEEN
ACTIVELY WORKING ON MANGANESE NODULE
MINING PROGRAMS

- Ocean Mining Associates (OMA)
  - United States Steel Corporation
  - Sun Company, and
  - Union Miniere (Belgium).
- Ocean Management Incorporated (OMI)
  - International Nickel Company,
  - Sedco, Inc.,
  - AMR Group (Metallgesellschaft; Preussag and Salzgitter) (Germany), and
  - Deep Ocean Mining Company (DOMCO); a consortium within the Consortium comprised of 23 Japanese companies headed by Sumitomo, Nippon Mining, Dowa Mining and others.
- Ocean Minerals Company (OMCO)
  - Lockheed Missile and Space Corporation,
  - Billiton International Metals (Royal Dutch Shell, the Hague).
  - Amoco Minerals Division of Standard Oil of Indiana, and
  - Bos Kalis Westminister Group, the Netherlands.
- Kennecott Consortium
  - Kennecott Copper Corporation
  - Rio Tinto Zinc
  - Mitsubishi Corporation
  - Consolidated Gold Fields, Ltd.
  - Noranda Mines and
  - BP Minerals.
- Afernod
  - Centre National Pour l'Exploitation des Oceans (CNEXO)
  - Commissariat l'Energie Atomique (CEA)
  - Society Metallurgique Pour Le Nickel (SMN)
  - France Dunkerque (Empain Schneider Group)
  - Bureau Recherches Geologique et Minieres (BRGM).

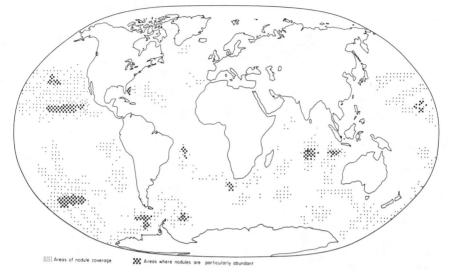

Figure 2.   Distribution of manganese nodules in the World Ocean
(after Rawson and Ryan 1978, and other sources).

variable. To be attractive to a first generation recovery effort,
sea floor nodule deposits must be sufficiently abundant and must
have minor constituent concentrations on the order of Ni 1-2 percent, Cu 1-2 percent, and Co 0.1-0.5 percent. This relationship
between grade and abundance is important in the estimation of recoverable manganese nodule resources and of the abundance required
for a first generation mine. The average nodule abundance required
to support a first generation mine has been estimated at 10 kg/m^2
with a minimum of 5 kg/m^2 (Archer, 1979). The average and minimum
cut-off concentrations of Ni + Cu are 2.27 percent and 1.18 percent
respectively. Using these criteria, prime areas are 3.4 million
km^2 of northeastern equatorial Pacific between the Clarion and
Clipperton fracture zones; and 1 million km^2 in the South Pacific
(Cronan, 1980). Small areas in the Indian and Atlantic Oceans
have marginally attractive manganese nodule deposits.

Economic evaluation of manganese nodule recovery potential requires:
(a)   identification of the value of metals that can be extracted
from manganese nodules;   (b)   comparison of nodule to land operations yielding similar metals;   (c)   market behavior for projected
quantities of specific metal commodities recoverable from nodules,
including current demand, price and price elasticity of specific
metals; and   (d)   projections of long term market growth for individual commodities. In particular, the output of a minimum efficient scale of nodule operation, relative to the market in which
it will be sold, is critical.

The value and weight distribution of the metals contained in a
"typical" good nodule ore are summarized in Table 5.

TABLE 5.   Metal Value Per _Dry_ Short Ton of Ore

	Grade	Amount	Price/Lb	Value
Mn	30%	600 Lb	$0.175	105
Ni	1.3%	26 Lb	$2.10	55
Cu	1.1%	22 Lb	$0.80	17
Co	0.2%	4 Lb	$3.00	12
				$189[1]

SOURCE: Agarwal et al., (1979).

[1]Using 20 June 1981 Nickel commodity prices. Ni in this example is worth $91 and ore value to $225.

Manganese stands out as a large contributor to ore value. Manganese market entry would be difficult, however, because demand is keyed to steel production; and lower cost, higher grade (50 percent) land manganese ores are available. The probable Pacific Ocean site of first generation nodule mining would also require increased transportation costs to major U.S. steel producers on the East Coast. Japan and China might be alternative markets for nodule manganese.

Nickel, the second largest contributor to ore value, is a superior recovery target. Nickel demand has been growing at an annual rate of 6-7 percent. Nickel laterites are the primary new land source of nickel, so a nodule mining venture targeted to nickel must be competitive with laterite operations.

Projected revenues from cobalt and copper are about one-half that of nickel but are attractive coproduction commodities. Most world cobalt is recovered as secondary production from copper mining. Cobalt from nodule sources would be a substantial addition to world production. The strategic value of cobalt and nickel is also a factor in their recovery in light of the political instability in the world's primary cobalt producers (Zaire and Zambia).

The target metal is also a factor in the choice of the metallurgical processing (metal extraction) method. Four processes proposed for nodule refining are:

1)   Solution reduction-ammoniacal leach.
2)   High temperature reduction and ammoniacal leach.
3)   High pressure sulfuric acid leach.
4)   Low pressure hydrochloric acid reduction leach.

There is no concensus among the various consortia on the most acceptable process. The metals slated for recovery determine in part, which process is likely to be chosen.

Considered as nickel ore, manganese nodules compare favorably to land nickel laterite operations. Return from the other metals recovered through coproduction improve the nodule-laterite comparison. Nodule abundance and grade requirements will be reduced as recovery and processing technology is refined.

Red Sea Metal Rich Sediments

The Red Sea is a young ocean basin, with an active spreading center along its axis. Eighteen metal-rich deposits have been identified in Red Sea Deeps. In the Atlantis II Deep, where metalliferous sediment formation is still taking place, metal rich deposits have been formed of sufficient grade and quantity to be economically attractive. The heavy metal-rich sediments and brines appear in layered deposits of several types, including clays, hydrous oxides, sulfides, and carbonates. Economically, the most attractive of these sediments are the sulfide layers which contain iron, copper, zinc, cadmium, lead, and silver. These sediments are of hydrothermal origin, as are the dense brines (56°C) which effectively seal the sediment deposits from further oxidation.

Conservative quantitative estimates of the 60 km^2 Atlantis II Deep, the one deposit presently regarded as economically recoverable, indicate 10^6 metric tons of zinc, 10^6 metric tons of copper, and 5,000 tons of silver in the sulfide layers of the deposit. Tentative values of $2.3 billion to $3.5 billion have been assigned to this deposit (Mustaffi, 1978). This promise has been sufficient to prompt Sudan and Saudi Arabia to conclude an agreement creating the Saudi-Sudan Joint Red Sea Commission to resolve overlapping resource claims and encourage recovery of the metal-rich deposits. The Commission has authorized the West German mining firm Preussag AG to survey the various deposits and develop technology to facilitate their recovery. Oil refining by-product high sulfur petroleum fuel is a plentiful low cost fuel source for any smelting process conducted in the Red Sea area. The mining pilot phase is scheduled for completion in late 1981 and precommercial activity is expected to continue until 1988.

Metal rich deposits of hydrothermal origin have also been identified at ocean spreading ridges. They range from MnO_2 crusts to metal sulfide deposits surrounding active low and high temperature vents respectively. Mounds of oxidized hydrothermal sediments have also been identified at the site of dead hydrothermal vents. Hydrothermal activity has been detected at the 21° Northeast Pacific Rise (EPR), Galapagos Ridge and TAG area (26°N) of the Mid-Atlantic Ridge. The thermal and mineral occurrences at ocean ridges are of considerable scientific interest, and have begun to attract investor interest in the United States in recent months.

Minerals Dissolved in Sea Water

Most naturally occurring elements or compounds containing these elements are found dissolved in the oceans. Only a few, however, occur in recoverable quantities. These include magnesium, magnesium salts, bromine, fresh water, heavy water, and common salt (MaCl).

The ocean is the world's largest source of heavy water (deuterium oxide) which is used as a moderator in heavy water fission reactors and is an important constituent fuel in nuclear fusion research. It is estimated that there are 25 trillion tons of heavy water in the ocean. U.S. production of heavy water is entirely from well water. Internationally, Canada, Norway, India and Argentina are operating heavy water production facilities from sea water sources.

Bromine is used in the form of ethylene bromide, a gasoline addition. Other uses include fire retardants, anti-bacterial agents, and in agriculture. Sea water is an almost unlimited source of bromine with an estimated 10^{14} tons of bromine at a concentration of 65 ppm. Higher concentrations are available in subsurface brines and saline lakes (e.g., Dead Sea, Great Salt Lake). U.S. production of bromine from sea water was stopped in 1969 as subsurface brines in Arkansas and Michigan were more attractive economically. Because of elemental bromine's physical characteristics (toxicity and corrosiveness) and low value per weight, it is not an attractive export commodity. Bromine is still produced from seawater in England and Japan.

Magnesium metal is most valued for its use in metal alloys which are light but strong. Demand for magnesium therefore is tied closely to the demand for titanium and aluminum and fluctuates with demands from the aircraft and aerospace industry.

Magnesium is present in seawater in vast quantities at an average concentration of .13 percent by weight. Competing land sources include well and lake brines and rocks: magnesite, dolomite, dunite, brucite and periclase. Production from seawater has declined due to competition from lower cost lake and well brines and rock sources of magnesium minerals. In 1977 one U.S. company (Dow Chemical in Freeport, Texas) and one Japanese company (Ube Kyosan) were producing magnesium metal by initially recovering magnesium chloride from seawater.

Magnesium compounds are produced from seawater by eight U.S. companies located in California, Delaware, Florida, Mississippi, New Jersey, and Texas. Internationally, four Japanese companies and two Italian companies produce magnesium compounds from seawater. Smaller producers are also located in Canada, Ireland, Israel, Mexico, and Norway.

U.S. 1979 production of magnesium and magnesium compounds was estimated at 163,000 tons and 980,000 tons respectively, valued at $500 million (U.S. Bureau of Mines, 1980). The U.S. remains a net exporter of magnesium metal. Depletion of land sources and increasing development costs may again shift production back to the abundant although lower concentration seawater source.

Common salt (NaCl) is produced from the entrapment and evaporation of seawater. When most of the water was evaporated, the residual brines or bitterns are drained off. Salt produced from seawater averages about 13 percent of total U.S. production. Because of its enormous supply potential, it sets an effective ceiling on prices from other sources.

Desalination of seawater provides a small but increasingly significant part of the world's fresh water supplies, and is assuming major importance in arid areas such as the Middle East (e.g., Kuwait, Saudi Arabia, and Israel) and parts of South America (e.g., Venezuela and Mexico.

Space limitations preclude detailed discussion of the various lines of development, but they can be summarized briefly. Reverse osmosis techniques have proved to be highly useful for relatively small installations because of their divisibility into "constant cost modular units." Larger units employ multistage flast distillations, vapor compression or multiple effect techniques, with various heat sources. The most interesting may well be the combination of water and electricity production, with otherwise waste heat used to distill seawater or other brines.

Summary

The oceans are posing less of a barrier to mineral exploration and recovery as time goes on and technological and scientific knowledge build up. Some hard minerals identified on the Continental Shelf are presently being recovered. Tin, barite, sand and gravel, and phosphorite deposits are examples of recovery operations in progress. Seawater continues to be an important source of a few dissolved minerals. The deep ocean, with its enormous deposits of manganese nodules, beckons the major industrialized nations, who have developed the technology to recover these deposits.

Recovery of these deposits would be conducted by private consortia and would occur in international waters, traditionally regarded as the property of no nation. There is little international support or precedent for claims to exclusive use of sections of the ocean floor or for protection of national consortia by naval forces. There is, then, no assurance that claim jumping on a grand scale could not occur. However, the $.5 billion capital investment requirement for a nodule recovery effort would restrict participation. It is precisely this lack of assurance as to the legal regime for deep sea mining that is at issue in the United National Conference on the Law of the Sea (UNCLOS). The problem of an adequate, internationally recognized legal framework is still unresolved. Its resolution will directly effect any future plans to recover other deep ocean mineral resources, such as ocean spreading center resources and perhaps even thermal energy ventures.

Although less widely publicized, the competition of land-based sources is probably a more important reason for the comparatively slow economic response to technically feasible and identified opportunities to mine at sea. In their comprehensive survey of future mineral supply, demand, and prices, Fischman et al., (1980) regard most of the major minerals discussed above as available in adequate quantities with only modest increases in real prices expected over

the next decade or two. If marine mineral exploitation is waiting
in the wings because cheaper sources are available, so be it: mankind is that much better off.

Thus, there seems little reason for new and vigorous public action
to accelerate the pace of marine mineral development on purely
economic grounds. Given reasonable resolution of the legal tenure
problems in deep waters and of environmental concerns in near-shore
areas, the market would appear to provide an adequate time table
for development.

The case for intervention would therefore seem to rest largely on
security and political grounds. But for most metals stockpiling is
an easy alternative to "forced draft" expansion of marine mining as
a response to interruptions of trade; and the structural differences
between oil and mineral markets suggest that the threat of OPEC-like
cartel tactics is remote.

There remain a number of serious questions of economic impact that
can only be answered as production gets underway. What would be
the effects on world prices of a rightward shift in the world supply
function as a result of reduced cost of marine production? What
changes in metallurgical use might then result from changes in the
relative prices of alloys? What change in national income and
balance of payments positions of major land-based producers would
follow these shifts in price and utilization? What would be the
relative effect on marine vs. land-based producers of continued increases in energy costs? Could OTEC be harnessed to sea-based processing units to offset heavy costs of transporting nodules (with
little or no back-haul other than wastes from the reduction plant)?

Clearly there is a rich menu of economic research ahead if and when
technological progress and resolution of the tenure issue make them
relevant.

Energy from the Sea

The dream of harnessing the enormous latent energy in the world's
oceans is a very old one, but in some areas it is edging slowly toward reality. Research and development have concentrated in five
areas: ocean currents, ocean waves, tides, temperature differentials, and salinity differentials. While research in all of these
areas is going forward in many countries, with the United States,
France, the U.K., the Netherlands and Japan as leaders, it is still
at a relatively low level as compared to nuclear energy, solar
energy, and other alternatives to hydrocarbons.

In the United States, as in most other countries concerned with
ocean energy research, greatest interest is now centered on ocean
thermal energy conversion (OTEC). Basically the system consists of
a set of alternative techniques for extracting heat from temperature
differences between surface water and cold deep water pumped up to
a tethered platform from depths ranging from 700-1000 meters.
These heat sources vaporize and condense ammonia in a closed power

system which runs a turbine generator. This closed cycle style of operation is considered "conventional" for OTEC and has been carried forward much farther than alternative open and grazing systems. In this section attention is focused on OTEC and its possibilities pretty much to the exclusion of alternatives for reasons outlined below.

Tidal Sources

Energy from tidal movement has been developed in technically feasible form in several areas, most notably in the famous Rance Project in France and in new projects in St. Malo and Korea. As with every other althernative source, interest in tidal energy has received new impetus as a result of the soaring prices of hydrocarbons. One outcome of that renewed interest is resolution of the problem of maintaining continuity of generation even through periods of slack tides; indeed, all of the technical feasibility issues with respect to tidal energy seem capable of resolution at today's level of knowledge.

Unfortunately, this does not resolve the economic problems. Tidal power might well be described as a kind of energy equivalent of the SST--technically feasible but an economic monstrosity. In addition, the areas most suitable for large-scale generation of energy from tidal movements often involve opportunity costs of horrendous proportions. Both market and non-marketed services would be disrupted significantly by any large-scale development. It is difficult to see how an environmentally satisfactory project could be developed in the United States, for example, with present attitudes. Since the very high cost of tidal power and the environmental and other economic disruption issues loom so large, no further discussion seems warranted.

Wave Action

The possibility of developing useful energy from wave action and ocean currents is still under study, and a variety of pilot schemes have been developed to demonstrate technical feasibility. Although this work continues, notably in the U.K. and Japan, the projected economic costs are so high that it is receiving relatively low priority in most countries. At the moment, wave generation is limited to buoys (5-60 watts output) and barge-mounted plants producing 1-2 mw. In the U.K. some twenty different fixed array designs are being studied, but the lowest target cost for any of them falls in the range 11 to 34¢/kwh--far more than any of the important alternatives. The same is true of the even more remote possibility of using salinity differences to generate useful power.

OTEC[3]

We return, then, to OTEC as the most logical source of ocean power on which to center attention. Its advantages are very attractive indeed. It operates at low temperature; involves no discharges of carbon dioxide or solid waste materials; requires little valuable

coastal or urban land; and is the only solar option which can provide a stable base load twenty-four hours a day. The United States
has considered OTEC promising enough to provide governmental support (under PL96-310) to fund research, development, and demonstration of the technical and economic feasibility of OTEC plants. The
specific objectives are to accelerate OTEC development to provide
a demonstration plant by 1986, and a larger commercially scaled demonstration plant by 1989; and to raise the level of technology to
the point where it is cost competitive by the mid-90s. The program
is intended to stimulate private participation and requires cost
sharing with private industry. As in most programs of this type,
preference is given to domestic firms.

The concept, at least, has already been demonstrated in hard fact.
The world's first OTEC plant began testing off Hawaii in 1979,
and has demonstrated its ability to produce net energy. Japanese
plans for an experimental operation at Truk are well advanced;
Guam plans a 48 megawatt plant to be constructed between 1982 and
1986, financed entirely through the public sector; France is in the
initial stages of developing an OTEC plant for Tahiti; and a Dutch
firm will install a 10 mw plant in the Caribbean.

Problem Areas

So much for the optimistic side. As always, there are thorns on
the rose. First, the areas of the world where OTEC plants are feasible are circumscribed by the requirement that thermal differences
of 20 degrees C. be available between the surface and depths of
approximately 1000 meters. This requirement restricts OTEC to areas
in the tropics. From the standpoint of the United States, this
largely limits the OTEC concept to the extreme southeastern tip of
the continental mainland and the island territories of the Caribbean and the Pacific.

These are, of course, far from trivial. An OTEC plant system off
Florida could serve much of the Southeastern U.S. Both Hawaii and
Puerto Rico have heavy concentrations of population and industry
that are energy-demanding, and both are growing rapidly. They
are, like most island areas of the world, completely dependent on
imported oil at the present time. On a world basis, there are
large numbers of tropical coastal and island areas (on one estimate, about fifty) for which OTEC may represent a highly desirable
stable base load source of energy, free of international market
and political complications.

Even in cases where local demands are short of the output of a
minimally scaled OTEC plant, the second generation of research and
development may permit production of ammonia or hydrogen as a
transportable fuel to be used in adjacent areas. It is also possible that OTEC plants could be linked with at-sea processing of
ocean minerals, at least to a first stage.

A second reason for the limited acceptance of the OTEC concept to
date is the general distrust of claims of technological capability

and cost projections of its more enthusiastic proponents. With respect to the latter, OTEC projections by the U.S. Department of
Energy contemplate costs in the vicinity of 60-90 mils per kilowatt
hour. These are, however, exclusive of all governmental costs for
research and development; and starting at this point in time,
society has a reasonable right to expect that these costs be included in any comparison of long run supply costs with other energy
sources.

The matter of technical limitations is more serious. Although proponents speak casually of technical feasibility as already established, at production levels (i.e., plants with 400-500 megawatts
capacity) there are still enormous problems to be resolved in the
engineering area. For example, the water flow required for a 400
megawatt plant (less than half the size of a standard nuclear
plant) would be equal to that of the Mississippi River. The technology required to produce cold water pipes to handle flows of this
magnitude, the demanding requirements for materials and operating
standards for heat exchangers, the tremendous size and capability
of the pumps required, and the necessary measures to deal with bio-
fouling of various parts of the operation are yet to be resolved in
a final operating sense. The critical nature of these problems is
emphasized by the low efficiency of a generating system operating
at such low temperature differences (2-3 percent).

There are also severe technical problems to be overcome in designing cables to transmit power from OTEC plants to shore. Voltages
anticipated for OTEC riser cables range from 350 to 500 kilovolts
DC, with currents from 1000 to 1500 amperes. These cables must be
capable of long life and high reliability under extreme mechanical
cycling conditions. It is estimated that 120,000,000 bending or
twisting cycles will be experienced during a thirty year cable life.

None of this should be interpreted as implying that technical obstacles are completely intractable. The comments above simply emphasize the fact that a great deal of work remains to be done before OTEC could be regarded as a firm technology, and recent experience with nuclear power makes both engineers and economists
justifiably skeptical about cost and reliability estimates at this
stage of the game. With interest rates expected to continue at
levels well above those experienced in the past, public utilities
are understandably shy about incurring very heavy front-end costs,
particularly after their experience with nuclear plants.

Finally, there are environmental questions to be resolved. The
impacts of OTEC plants on marine biota are yet to be determined.
There is at least a possibility of some damage to populations that
spawn in the open sea, or which are highly sensitive to temperature
changes in surface water that can be expected to occur in the vicinity of OTEC arrays. On the other hand, a single OTEC plant would
be the equivalent of a substantial upwelling, and could be expected
to provide nutrient enrichment over a fairly wide area. There has
been a good deal of theoretical discussion about the possibility of
some type of aquaculture in the vicinity of the plants to take

advantage of that characteristic. While it seems unlikely that fishery impacts would swing the balance either toward or away from economic feasibility, they must certainly be dealt with, if for no other reason than the emotional strength with which these matters are approached. One could almost guarantee that any decline in fish production from any cause whatsoever will be attributed to an OTEC plant located within 500 miles.

Conclusion

It is simply too early in the development process to make any kind of economic assessment of the potential role of OTEC plants in the national and international energy picture. For what they are worth, cost estimates for very small plants seem very high, even at the experimental level. For example, the Department of Energy's 40 megawatt pilot plant is estimated to cost approximately $280,000,000 (at 1980 prices) with possible variations of 40 percent upward and 20 percent downward. A 10 megawatt Japanese pilot plant is estimated to cost about $100,000,000. What this means in terms of a full 400-500 megawatt plant is simply impossible to determine at the moment. The history of technology transfer from government to private industry and from pilot plant to operating levels is not one that would generate optimism.

On balance there would seem to be good reasons to continue government-sponsored research and development work at a level which would permit evaluation of OTEC's capabilities within a period of four to five years. It now seems generally accepted that there will be no single solution to the world's energy problems, and even though this particular increment might not seem large in either U.S. or world terms, it would still represent a useful addition to the energy arsenal, with minimal environmental and political difficulties, if it can be brought to a level of cost effectiveness.

Offshore Oil and Gas

The offshore petroleum industry is so large, so kaleidoscopic in structure, and is changing so rapidly that it is almost impossible to capture it in a summary review.

Tables 6, 7, and 8 tell something of the story. In 1980, 37 countries were producing oil and/or gas from the marine environment, and exploration is going off the coasts of many others. Every continent has seen some offshore activity, though the major producing areas continue to be: North America (Gulf of Mexico, California, Alaska); North Sea; Southeast Asia (Indonesia, Malaysia, the Philippines); Mid-East (Suez-Red Sea Basin, Arabian Sea, Persian Gulf); West Africa; and South America (Venezuela, Colombia, Brazil).

As indicated in Table 6 offshore sources continue to provide an increasing share of total world crude production, reaching 22.9 percent in 1980. Despite the formidable obstacles imposed by harsh offshore environments, the combined effects of OPEC prices, the relative ease of exploration at sea rather than on shore, and a

TABLE 6

OFFSHORE DAILY AVERAGE CRUDE PRODUCTION
(Thousands of bbl)

Country	1980	1979	1978	1977	1976
Saudi Arabia	2,958.00	2,828.00	2,621.40π	1,621.40π	1,694.80π
U.K.	1,650.00	1,571.40	1,070.00	760.00	446.00
Abu Dhabi	1,322.01	596.83	590.66	627.00	560.00
Venezuela	1,095.58	1,050.00	1,083.50	1,249.80π	1,677.22π
U.S.	1,038.09	1,066.00	1,123.50	1,237.80•	1,064.00•
Norway	628.81	407.34	356.46	279.72	242.61
Nigeria	579.05	543.52	384.37	536.40π	525.05
Indonesia	533.05	374.66	545.24	590.97	425.97
Mexico	500.23	430.00	40.20	48.39	45.39
Divided Zone	403.00	395.20	240.00π	165.60	247.10
Egypt	390.31	430.00	396.00	399.00	231.12
Dubal	344.95	362.73	362.00	317.04π	308.34
Australia	323.21	401.00	414.75	430.55	348.00
Malaysia	280.32	271.03	225.00	178.10π	151.40
Qatar	247.55	275.73	260.02	244.34	--
U.S.S.R.	200.00	190.00•‡	200.00π	205.00•	220.00•
Brunel	192.24	189.61	191.00	223.00	170.17
Gabon	177.90	196.00	138.00	183.20	165.92
Trinidad/ Tobago	166.51	167.44	175.55	189.31	180.07
Iran	150.00	200.00‡	654.50π	507.40π	426.54
India	142.14	81.36	61.74	80.00π	15.00
Cabinda	96.96	160.00	94.62	130.50π	33.61π
Brazil	73.00	72.00	38.94	28.83	35.42
Tunisia	43.57	48.50	45.23	45.53π	37.00
Spain	31.25	22.18	20.00	23.00	33.33
Peru	29.86	29.14	28.92	28.60π	31.75
Congo	27.00	52.00	52.44π	25.00π	38.03
Zaire	21.51	20.84	18.96	23.38π	19.96
Sharjah	10.00	12.08	25.44	32.58π	37.00
Denmark	6.63	12.00	8.50	10.20	8.00
Italy	6.27	4.84	4.31	12.01π	10.10
Ivory Coast	5.80	--	--	--	--
Philippines	4.00	26.00	--	--	--
New Zealand	3.16	--	--	--	--
China	2.00	2.00	2.00	--	--
Ghana	2.00	2.00	5.00	--	--
Japan	1.53	0.50	2.50	3.10	3.00
TOTALS	13,687.49	12,491.93‡	11,480.75	11,436.75	9,431.91
WORLD TOTAL	59,812.00	62,768.00	60,337.00	56,567.00	57,210.00
% OFFSHORE	22.88	20.15	19.02	20.20	16.50

π = Estimate.
• = Crude and condensate.
‡ = Revised figures.
Source: Offshore, June 20, 1981.

31

TABLE 7

WORLDWIDE OFFSHORE PRODUCTION
(By Field)

Country, Field	No. of Wells	First 6 Mo. Avg. b/d 1980	Discovery Date
ABU DHABI			
Arzanah	8	22,000	1973
Abu Al Bukhoosh	20	75,000	1969
Mubarras	31	22,000	1971
El Bundug		--	1965
Umm Shaif	--	250,000	1958
Upper Zakum	--	48,000	1964
Lower Zakum	--	200,000	1964
ANGOLA/CABINDA			
Erva	1	547	1969
Kamba'a	1	1,606	1971
Kungulo	9	7,817	1975
Limba	10	19,376	1969
Livuite	1	633	1979
Malorgo N.	57	27,591	1966
Malorgo S.	30	9,948	1966
Malorgo W.	41	27,922	1969
Cunta'a	1	1,519	1978
AUSTRALIA			
Barascuta	2	1,966	1968
Cob'a	1	1,502	1972
Halibat	19	65,784	1967
Kingfish	42	147,471	1967
Mackerel	15	101,522	1969
Tuna			
BRAZIL			
D. Joao Mar	404	8,177	1947
Dourado	4	327	1970
Guaricema	24	6,648	1968
Ubarana	21	8,762	1973
Agulha	7	5,397	1975
Enchova	4	12,781	1976
Cacao	3	2,862	1978
Garoupa	3	6,120	1974
Namorado	4	11,510	1975
Camurim	21	3,019	1971
Curima	3	1,088	1978
Faz Cedro	16	1,491	1972

(Continued)

TABLE 7 (Continued)

Country, Field	No. of Wells	First 6 Mo. Avg. b/d 1980	Discovery Date
BRUNEI			
Ampa S.W.	178	61,917	1963
Champion	150	81,431	1970
Fairley	39	19,733	1969
Fairley-Baram	5	3,055	1963
Magpie	9	21,177	1975
CAMEROON			
Betika	12	6,460	1972
Ekoundou S.	13	11,570	1975
Kole	14	11,340	1974
Kombo Centre	16	26,400	1976
CHILE			
Ostion OS-1	--	--	1977
Posesion PO-2	--	--	1977
Spiteful SP-1	31	17,429	1978
Spiteful SP-2	--	--	1978
CONGO			
Emeraude	112	27,000	1969
DENMARK			
Dan	19	6,630	1971
DIVIDED ZONE			
Khafji	121	296,000	1971
Hout	26	7,000	1969
DUBAI			
Fateh	46	151,712	1966
S.W. Fateh	34	182,165	1970
Falah	7	9,479	1972
Rashid	3	1,589	1973
EGYPT			
El Morgan	--	--	1965
GS-195	4	29,712	1978
GS-382	3	8,964	1977
July	24	47,967	1973
Ramadan	14	100,738	1974
SG-300	2	6,260	1976
Shoab Ali	12	18,047	1978
Belayim Marine	29	64,000	1961

(Continued)

TABLE 7 (Continued)

Country, Field	No. of Wells	First 6 Mo. Avg. b/d 1980	Discovery Date
GABON			
Anguille··	--	12,130	1962
Anguille NE··	--	5,357	1969
Anguille NNE··	--	875	1971
Batanga··	--	216	1960
Barbier··	--	15,337	1974
Breme··	--	12,771	1976
Clairette··	--	480	1957
Doree··	--	614	1974
Girelle··	--	5,914	1975
Gonelle··	--	5,090	1976
Grondin··	--	28,051	1973
Mandaros··	--	15,139	1974
Olende··	--	1,104	1976
P.G.S. Marine··	--	1,964	1978
Port Gentil Ocean··	--	1,653	1964
Tchenque Ocean··	--	410	1963
Torpille··	--	8,331	1971
Lucina-Marine	9	8,405	1971
INDIA			
Bombay High	--	--	1974
INDONESIA			
Ardjuna	123	119,130	1969
Arimbi	11	7,096	1972
Bekapai	31	36,685	1972
Handil	74	163,621	1974
Attaka	63	95,070	1970
Melahin	6	1,583	1972
Keardingan	8	931	1972
Sepiraggan	12	9,525	1973
Yabin	14	1,918	1976
Uding	7	9,825	1974
Cinfa	--	--	1970
Gita	--	--	1972
Killy	--	--	1973
Nora	114	96,237	1973
Rama	--	--	1974
Selatan	--	--	1971
Zeida	--	--	1971

(Continued)

TABLE 7 (Continued)

Country, Field	No. of Wells	First 6 Mo. Avg. b/d 1980	Discovery Date
IRAN			
Bahregansar	--	--	1960
Hendjan	--	--	1968
Nowruz	--	--	1966
Rakhsh	--	--	1969
Rostam	--	--	1966
Ardeshir	--	--	1969
Cyrus	--	--	1962
Darius	--	--	1961
Fereidoon	--	--	1966
Sassan	--	--	1965
ITALY			
Gela	79	10,022	1956
Santa Maria "A" Mare	7	5,110	1974
JAPAN			
Aga-Oki	24	1,439	1972
MALAYSIA			
Bekok	--	--	1976
Pulai	56	110,000	1973
Tapis	--	--	1975
Tembungo	--	--	1971
Bakau	3	1,387	1971
Baram	33	8,173	1963
Baronia	40	33,741	1967
Betty	9	20,339	1967
Fairley-Baram	2	1,446	1963
West Lutong	25	10,206	1966
Temana	10	5,465	1972
Takau	32	17,148	1966
Samarang	60	68,365	1972
South Funous	4	4,050	1974
MEXICO			
Arenque	14	9,198	1970
Isla de Lobos	3	709	1963
Marsopa	11	3,026	1974
Atun	33	3,825	1966
Bagre	29	8,982	1973
Cantarell	26	474,492	1976

(Continued)

TABLE 7 (Continued)

Country, Field	No. of Wells	First 6 Mo. Avg. b/d 1980	Discovery Date
NEW ZEALAND			
Kapuni	11	3,441	1959
Maui	7	2,836	1969
NIGERIA			
Delta	27	35,474	1965
Delta South	27	42,187	1965
Isan	11	5,136	1970
Malu	15	15,483	1969
Mefa	5	3,985	1965
Meji	21	33,431	1965
Meren	50	77,780	1965
Okan	62	72,489	1964
Parabe/Eko	25	14,647	1968
W. Isan	9	14,474	1971
Adua	9	15,594	1967
Asabo	11	15,980	1956
Ekpe	14	23,047	1966
Ekpe-ww	12	14,934	1977
Eku	6	4,424	1966
Enang	23	32,942	1968
Etim	8	22,492	1968
Idoho	5	3,084	1966
Inim	10	21,924	1966
Mfem	3	6,195	1967
Ubit	43	32,070	1968
Unam	4	8,154	1968
Utue	7	10,794	1966
Pennington	10	7,358	1965
Middleton	6	3,199	1972
North Apoi	16	41,773	1973
NORWAY			
Ekofisk	36	218,807	1969
West Ekofisk	10	32,846	1970
Cod	6	71,571	1968
Tor	10	75,722	1970
Albuskjell	12	30,588	1972
Edda	6	26,876	1972
Eldfisk	18	118,166	1970
Statfjord	4	54,238	1974
PERU			
Humboldt	345	22,086	1960
Litoral	113	6,727	1955
Providencia	51	1,021	1967
Other	5	27	--

(Continued)

TABLE 7 (Continued)

Country, Field	No. of Wells	First 6 Mo. Avg. b/d 1980	Discovery Date
PHILIPPINES			
South Nido	5	13,800	1977
QATAR			
Bul Hanine	12	147,019	1970
Idd El Shargi	15	19,162	1960
Maydan-Mahzam	17	81,364	1963
SAUDI ARABIA			
Abu Safah	18	136,000	1963
Berri	70	531,000	1964
Manifa	6	44,000	1957
Marjan	15	59,000	1967
Qatif	30	115,000	1945
Safaniyah	245	1,512,000	1951
Zuluf	37	561,000	1965
SHARJAH			
Mubarek	4	10,000	1972
SPAIN			
Amposta Marino North	6	650	1970
Casablanca	2	11,950	1975
Castelion B	1	7,600	1972
Dorado	3	2,797	1975
TRINIDAD			
Teak	45	45,359	1972
Samaan	38	35,159	1972
Poui	30	40,623	1974
Soldado	250	40,394	1955
Galeota	30	3,966	1972
Brighton	66	1,005	1908
TUNISIA			
Ashtart	14	43,570	--
UNITED KINGDOM			
Montrose	16	26,370	1969
Thistle	24	106,077	1973
Forties	50	523,000	1970
Ninian	25	207,700	1974
Statfjord	4	10,262	1974
Argyll	5	16,623	1971
Beryl	22	108,900	1972
Claymore	20	84,359	1974

(Continued)

TABLE 7 (Continued)

Country, Field	No. of Wells	First 6 Mo. Avg. b/d 1980	Discovery Date
UNITED KINGDOM (Cont'd)			
Piper	31	222,385	1973
Auk	9	13,117	1970
Brent	18	137,608	1971
Cormorant South	4	19,586	1972
Dunlin A	7	82,317	1973
Heather	9	12,488	1973
UNITED STATES			
Granite Point	30	4,378	1965
McArthur River	71	20,958	1965
Middle Ground Shoal	40	4,931	1963
Prudhoe Bay	233	597,452	1968
Dos Cuadias	147	8,044	1969
Huntington Beach	981	10,368	1920
Wilmington	2,153	41,316	1932
Bay Marchand 2	148	14,444	1949
Grand Isle 16	57	2,225	1948
South Pass 24	431	7,050	1950
South Pass 27	235	2,928	1954
Eugene Island 330	187	16,171	1971
Grand Isle 43	220	7,006	1956
Main Pass 41	111	4,290	1957
Main Pass 306	98	3,073	1969
Mississippi Canyon 194	11	5,023	--
Ship Shoal 204	58	3,581	1968
Ship Shoal 207	61	3,318	1967
Ship Shoal 208	93	4,165	1962
South Pass 61	123	10,409	1968
South Pass 62	81	4,892	1965
South Pass 65	56	3,526	1969
South Timbalier 21	91	5,146	1965
South Timbalier 135	59	2,123	1956
West Delta 30	176	8,560	1949
West Delta 73	85	3,257	1962
West Delta 79	80	6,360	--
VENEZUELA			
Bachaquero	1,664	311,020	1930
Cabimas	618	47,638	1917
Lagunillas	3,285	511,116	1926
Tia Juana	1,991	225,810	1928
ZAIRE			
GCO	7	1,605	1970
Mibale	5	17,843	1973
Mwambe	2	2,062	1979

.. = 220 wells for all fields.   Source: <u>Offshore</u>, June 20, 1981.

TABLE 8

OFFSHORE GAS PRODUCTION
(MMcfd)

Country	1980	1979	1978	1977	1976
U.S.	14,703.27	12,937.30	13,983.84	9,804.60	11,864.46
U.K.	3,610.00	3,981.48	3,925.92	3,880.00	13,912.10§
Norway	2,426.00	2,252.79	1,375.00	269.00	560.00‡
Abu Dhabi	1,434.00	627.00	629.00	615.00	510.00
U.S.S.R.	1,225.00	1,161.00	1,064.00	996.00	897.00
Netherlands	1,170.00	1,062.33	530.00•	530.00	298.40
Brunei	984.80	1,030.00	988.00	--	--
Nigeria	500.00	500.00	220.00•	218.80π	500.00‡
Indonesia	440.00	439.28	561.00	621.90	345.66
Trinidad/ Tobago	420.00	404.40	428.50	344.30	311.20
Australia	388.00	504.00	847.00	651.00	293.00
Ireland	125.00	125.00	1.79	--	--
Brazil	100.00	91.38	65.92	25.00•	26.00•
New Zealand	84.04	25.18	--	--	--
Colombia	64.72	33.00	--	--	--
Egypt	57.85	65.00	72.00	--	--
Japan	47.70	35.00	60.00	--	--
Mexico	25.00•	22.80	107.90	--	--
Italy	22.00	23.00	38.00	--	--
Ghana	8.00	--	--	--	--
India	2.67	48.52	3.44	--	--
Gabon	0.00	0.00	.60	--	--
Spain	0.00	0.00	850.07	--	--
Saudi Arabia	0.00••	300.00•	300.00•	300.00•	200.00
TOTALS	27,838.05	25,668.46	26,051.98	18,285.60	29,732.82

• = Estimate.
‡ = Estimate based on oil/gas.
π = Nigerian Gulf Oil Co. only.
§ = Decrease caused by difference in reporting procedure.
•• = All gas flared.
Source: Offshore, June 20, 1981.

phenomenal pace of technological research, development, and application have kept the industry in high gear.

The industry continues to set new technical records: offshore producing wells are now found in water depths in excess of 1000 feet; wells have been drilled at sea to depths of over 20,000 feet; pipelines have been laid at depths of over 2000 feet; and a sub-sea completion has been accomplished in 600 feet of water. Work is being pressed on multiple versions of floating production systems, and serious consideration is being given to a floating airfield to service North Sea operations.

In terms of production the Middle East continues to dominate, with Saudi Arabia first and Abu Dhabi third in total offshore output. The North Sea follows, with the U.K. second and Norway sixth. Venezuela is in fourth place, while the U.S. has slipped to fifth. As indicated in Table 8, however, the U.S. continues to dominate offshore gas production.

In terms of current activity, the Beaufort Sea, Southeast Asia, Newfoundland, and South America are all promising areas for new development. In terms of potentially productive geological formations, it has been estimated that the Beaufort Sea may have 50 to 90 promising areas, some of which could be as large or larger than Prudhoe Bay. Despite disappointing results off the middle Atlantic states, major finds are anticipated off New England and New Foundland. In industry circles there is intense interest in the Chinese coast. The People's Republic of China, apparently concerned by a persistent drop in land-based production, is now seeking arrangements with foreign companies to explore its coastal areas, ranging from the Gulf of Bohai to the South China Sea. The immensity of the areas involved and at least moderate prospects for success have generated a substantial amount of industry competition for participation rights.

There is obviously a sharp disparity between the distribution, known and potential, of offshore hydrocarbons and the distribution of the capital and technical capacity to explore, develop, and produce oil and gas from marine sources. The stakes have become so high, in terms of the impact of oil and gas in GNP and balance of payments positions, that many strange bedfellows have emerged in the form of contractual relations, equity joint ventures, etc. in addition to greatly modified terms for concessionnaires. In addition, the cluster of specialized manufacturing and service industries that support offshore petroleum operations have assumed international proportions.

From the standpoint of development, then, the industry and the market appear to be perfectly capable of providing means and incentive respectively. The question of legal tenure has been largely resolved by the extension of coastal state jurisdiction to (and beyond) the portions of the continental margins of interest for hydrocarbon production. From the standpoint of the U.S. the issues that remain unresolved relate primarily to externalities: the adequacy of

procedures for leasing OCS tracts; the social and economic impact
of OCS exploitation on shoreside communities; the impact of the
whole range of offshore operations, from exploration to transport,
on the marine environment; and the appropriate pace of OCS development.

Since these issues are discussed in Dr. Tussing's paper and in the
workshop summary, they are not treated in detail here. Suffice it
to say that all are vitally important, since they comprise, jointly,
the framework within which we seek to identify and account properly
for the host of external costs (and some external benefits) associated with offshore oil and gas production. In so doing they also
impose substantial constraints on the level, location, rate of expansion and costs of those activities.

In some respects, all of the externalities referred to above are researchable; but quantification at a level of accuracy sufficient to
support important policy decisions that must be made is another
matter. Research into the biological impact of oil in the marine
environment, though extensive and of highly professional quality,
has barely scratched the surface of the uncertainty that exists. A
recent effort to quantify the economic costs of the Amoco Cadiz
spill, though analytically sound, could assign reasonably hard
numbers to no more than a fraction of the identified social costs.
While such studies will serve as an antidote to some of the wilder
claims of damages, they are likely to fall far short of providing a
basis for legal action or for planning alternative abatement or pre-
vention measures. The failure lies not in the absence of economic
techniques for evaluating social costs, but rather in the tremendous
complexity of the biological systems affected and the multiplicity
of impact possibilities.

Much more attention needs to be paid to the socio-economic impact of
offshore oil-related activities on coastal communities. The normal
sequence of exploration-development-production guarantees a highly
peaked level of induced economic activity and population in these
communities and an equally disturbing but inevitable degree of
uncertainty about the duration of each phase. Experience in the
Scottish Highlands and Islands, Alaska, and elsewhere suggests that
the mixture of benefits and costs to coastal communities is complex
but capable of amelioration with proper forecasting and planning.

The appropriate pace of OCS oil and gas development raises a host
of issues that relate to forecasting of energy supply and demand
from all sources. It does seem appropriate, even in a review paper,
to draw attention to some of the less defensible arguments. For
example, the assumption that industry would, free of governmental
interference, discount future net benefits at a rate that would
guarantee optimal timing is totally unfounded. The balance of payments argument for accelerated OCS production is hardly more sensi-
ble, viewed over a proper time horizon and against the background of
total resource supplies from domestic and imported sources. In
short, there is, as yet, no clearly defined approach to definitions
of the public interest in alternative rates of development of offshore hydrocarbons.

Notes

1. The Japanese longline and seine fisheries for tuna are an exception. Both the directed fishery for tuna and the by-catch of swordfish and gillfish are of considerable concern to U.S. recreational fishermen.

2. Modified versions of this concept are found in groundfish management plans of the New England, Pacific and North Pacific Management Councils.

3. Information in this section is based on briefing materials presented to the Ocean Policy Committee of the National Academy of Sciences, October, 1981.

References

Adasiak, A. (1979). "Alaska's Limited Entry Program: Another View," Journal of the Fisheries Research Board of Canada 36: 770-82.

Anderson, S.G. (1977). The Economics of Fisheries Management, Johns Hopkins University Press (Baltimore).

____ (1975). "Analysis of Open Access Commercial Exploitation and Maximum Economic Yield in Biologically and Technologically Interdependent Fisheries," Journal of the Fisheries Research Board of Canada 32: 1825-42.

Archer, A.A. (1979). "Progress and Prospects of Marine Mining," Mining Engineering 25, No. 12: 31-32.

Clark, C.W. (1976). Mathematical Bioeconomics: The Optimal Management of Renewable Resources, Wiley-Interscience (New York).

Cronan, D.S. (1980). Underwater Minerals, Academic Press (New York).

Crutchfield, J.A. (1979). "Economic and Social Implications of the Main Policy Alternatives for Controlling Fishing Effort," Journal of the Fisheries Research Board of Canada 36: 742-52.

Drucker, M. (1981). NOAA, Office of Ocean Minerals and Energy, personal communication, June 10, 12.

Earney, F.C.F. (1980). Petroleum and Hard Minerals from the Sea, V.H. Winston and Sons (London).

Economic Council of Canada (1981). The Public Regulation of Commercial Fisheries in Canada, Technical Reports 15-19, Ottawa, (October).

Fischman, et al. (1980). World Mineral Trends and U.S. Supply Problems, Resources for the Future, Inc. Research Paper R-20, Johns Hopkins Press (Baltimore).

Fraser, G.A. (1979). "Limited Entry: Experience of the British Columbia Salmon Fishery," Journal of the Fisheries Research Board of Canada 36: 754-63.

Huppert, D.D. (1979). "Implications of Multipurpose Fleets and Mixed Stocks for Control Policy," Journal of the Fisheries Research Board of Canada 36: 845-54.

Meany, T.F. (1979). "Limited Entry in the Western Australian Rock Lobster and Prawn Fisheries: An Economic Evaluation," Journal of the Fisheries Research Board of Canada 36: 789-98.

Mustaffi, Z., H. Amman (1978). "Ocean Mining and Protection of the Marine Environment," Proceedings, 10th Offshore Technology Conference, OTC 3188: 1199-1212.

Robinson, M.A. (1980). "World Fisheries to 2000--Supply, Demand and Management," Marine Resources, Vol. 4, No. 1, January: 19-32.

Scott, A.D. (1979). "Development of Economic Theory on Fisheries Regulation," Journal of the Fisheries Research Board of Canada 36: 725-41.

U.S. Bureau of Mines (1980). Mineral Facts and Problems, Bulletin 611.

Living Marine Resources

Dan Huppert

I. Introduction

The living, renewable resources of the sea provide diverse and valuable raw products for human consumption, recreation, animal feed and industrial use. Resources of historical importance to the United States are mainly fish, shellfish and marine mammals. Marine plants are exploited extensively in the Orient, but U.S. production has never been very significant.[1] Commercial fishing, which is historically the most important use of living marine resources in the United States, produced an average annual ex vessel value of roughly $2 billion in recent years (Table 1). The wholesale value of fishery products is a bit more than twice this amount. Recreational activity associated with marine fish and shellfish has great economic value, too, but is more difficult to assess quantitatively. (See G. Brown's contributions to the workshop proceedings for an extensive discussion of valuation problems). A recent study of the economic impacts of marine recreation (see Table 2) estimates that total sales of equipment and services in the United States directly associated with marine recreational fishing were about $1.8 billion in 1975. Management of these marine fisheries is one area of broad responsibility in NOAA, thus making biological and economic research in fisheries an area of current, active interest.[2]

Marine mammal harvests in the United States are limited to the Pribilof Islands fur seal hunt which is operated under an international convention with Japan, Canada and the USSR. During the 1975-1979 period the average annual harvest amounted to 32 thousand seal skins which brought an average annual value of $1.16 million to the U.S. Treasury.[3] While some additional commercial usage is made of marine mammals for research and entertainment, the historically important domestic whaling industry is extinct, and few other commercial uses are permitted under the Marine Mammal Protection Act. Thus this paper is concerned primarily with the economics of marine fisheries, and the research necessary to support public management responsibilities and provide policy guidance on fisheries-related issues.

TABLE 1. United States Fisheries: Quantity and Ex vessel Value of Landings of Major Species Groups, 1975-79 Averages and 1980 Domestic and Foreign Catch

Species Group	1975-79 Landings (Metric Tons)	Average Value[1] ($1000)	1980 Landings (m.t.)	1980 Value ($1000)	1980 Foreign Catch in U.S. Zone (m.t.)
Salmon	162,123	205,127	278,423	352,277	--
Tuna	181,007	232,901	181,181	233,125	--
Shrimp	179,865	470,058	154,090	402,697	--
Groundfish[2]	240,633	157,040	320,606	209,232	1,477,302
Molluscs[3]	92,438	272,840	94,877	280,039	50,636
Crustaceans[4]	212,974	310,051	274,457	399,558	7,288
Pelagic Fish					
a. Anchovy & Menhaden	1,071,427	109,525	1,180,981	120,724	--
b. Other[5]	371,141	263,662	455,761	239,550	95,550
TOTAL	2,140,467	2,021,204	2,689,776	2,237,202	1,631,021

[1]Based upon the 1980 ex vessel prices.

[2]Includes cod, cusk, flounders, haddock, hake, halibut, ocean perch, pollack, rockfishes and others.

[3]Principal species are clams, oysters, scallops and squid.

[4]Includes crabs, lobsters but not shrimp, which are reported separately.

[5]Other pelagic finfish includes a wide variety of fishes, the most important of which are herring and mackerel.

SOURCES: National Marine Fisheries Service, Fisheries of the United States, 1975 through 1980 Issues.

Ideally, a program of economic research would address widely-accepted resource management objectives and other public policy goals. Because ocean policy is formed in a decentralized, multi-layered system, however, we are often faced with a set of conflicting and/ or inexplicit policy guides. Existing guidelines for living resources promulgated by the Congress, NOAA, state agencies and regional fishery management councils seek to (1) encourage the development of U.S. commercial fisheries, (2) manage marine fisheries to achieve "optimum" yields from fish stocks, (3) enhance marine recreational fishing opportunities, and (4) preserve fishery habitat and protect marine mammals and endangered species.

TABLE 2.   Direct Economic Impacts Associated With Marine Recreational Fishing

	Millions of Dollars			Employment (Person-Years)
	Retail Sales	Value-Added	Wages & Salaries	
Fishing Tackle	136	93	36.2	5,260
Boats, Motors & Trailers	271	126	58.0	7,440
Marinas	240	96	64.0	6,500
Commercial Sport-Fishing Vessels	122	73	35.4	4,900
Boat Fuel	86	29	7.3	1,270
Food, Lodging & Travel	543	191	98.4	19,140
Other	442	90	43.0	6,070
TOTAL	1,840	698	343.1	50,580

SOURCE: Centaur Management Consultants, Inc., 1977. Economic Activity Associated with Marine Recreational Fishing. Final Report to National Marine Fisheries Service, NOAA.

There are substantial resource allocation and production decisions linked to the achievement of these objectives. With its emphasis on "efficient" use of resources, traditional economic analysis can provide some guidance here. Economics research is also important to the design of tariff schedules and other policies affecting international trade. Finally, where objectives conflict and when unavoidable income redistributions accompany ocean resource policies, economic studies can assist decision makers by identifying the probable scope of such redistributions and by estimating the size and type of compensatory policies needed.

In the next section of the paper I address some problems encountered by economists attempting to apply existing economic theory to fisheries. While several good, extended treatises have recently appeared on the economics of fisheries (e.g., Anderson, 1977; Bell, 1978; Clark, 1976; Crutchfield and Pontecorvo, 1969; Hannesson, 1979; or Scott, 1979), a number of theoretical issues remain to be adequately addressed. Among these are the treatment of multiple purpose fishing vessels, multi-species resource systems, and uncertainty in environmental and market conditions. Research needs for further development of domestic management procedures are discussed in section three. Property rights, institutions and administrative costs are central concepts needed to focus applied theory and empirical research on the costs and benefit of various regulatory arrangements. Section four is devoted to a discussion of international trade and foreign fisheries. The main research topics include the analysis of domestic protection through tariff policy and the optimum pricing and allocation of fishing by foreign fleets in the United States' Fishery Conservation Zone (FCZ). In the fifth section I explore some ways that economic research can assist decision-makers dealing with resource conflicts and direct allocation or income distributional problems. Because the near-shore marine environment is intensively exploited and because much of the living marine resource base is "common property," conflict and allocation issues are frequently at the forefront of policy decisions. In my concluding section I provide a summary statement of the economic research needs that are pertinent to NOAA's responsibility for living marine resources.

II. Theory of Fisheries Management

The established economic theory of fisheries as represented by Clark (1976), Anderson (1977) or Hannesson (1978) examines the fundamental economic issues in a renewable resource management under severely simplified assumptions and produces conclusions of great generality. In this respect fisheries theory is like most economic theory. For pedagogical purposes generality and abstraction are most welcome, since an uncluttered theory brings out potential issues in sharp relief. But for the specific, applied analysis required for NOAA's mission, the empirical content of theory must be improved and ecological and structural complexities must be met head-on. Thus I suggest that further theoretical development is warranted in the areas where current theory is most abstract. Work is needed to specify underlying bio-physical relationships, assumptions about industry structure and market power and the uncertainty arising from both nature and the market.

It is unlikely that major conclusions of the existing theory will be altered significantly by further development along these lines. Atomistic competition will undoubtedly violate production efficiency criteria even when fish are harvested from complex ecosystems; and direct control of harvesting technology will still be inferior to fiscal controls or property rights that marshall the support of fishermen's self-interest. I am not sufficiently familiar with the theory under uncertainty to guess whether the sweeping generalities of deterministic theory will fail to be as sweeping under conditions of stochastic biological relationships and markets. The reward for theoretical work will be in the elimination of some striking contrasts between theoretical assumptions and perceptions of reality. This will help in communicating economists' conclusions to non-economists and in interpreting empirical observations of the fishing industry. Particular attention should be paid to the impact of industry structure on the need for, and optimal configuration of economic controls. Likewise, one effect of fishermen's uncertainty regarding prices and fish stock abundance may be to alter essential characteristics of the firm and industry. Without a reasonable theoretical framework as a guide, observed industry structure and conduct can easily be misinterpreted.

Turning first to the underlying biophysical relationships, the peda-
gogically convenient "surplus production" models,[4] like the Schaefer
model, are often unacceptable from an ecological standpoint. This
is true when characteristics of a single species fail to meet the
assumptions of the model (e.g., when long lags occur between spawning and recruitment or when stocks adjust slowly to changes in fishing pressure), and when interactions between species in the "food
web" are essential to the dynamics of the exploited stock(s). Several authors have examined more complicated single-species models
such as the age-structured models (also called dynamic pool models)
made popular by Beverton and Holt (1957), and others have introduced some simple predator-prey models of two-species systems (e.g.,
Anderson, 1977; Clark, 1976). Strand and Hueth (1977) developed
a multispecies age-structured model with lagged recruitment, but I
am unaware of the theoretical results of this effort.

Most fish species are in fact embedded in much more complex systems.
May et al. (1979) for example, describe the southern ocean ecosystem in which baleen whales, crabeater seals and cephalopods compete
for krill, while male sperm whales extensively exploit the cephalopods. Thus there are three "top level" predators, an intermediate
group, and a pure prey species. Given that each species has a unique rate of adjustment to changes in food supply and predation,
alterations in whaling activities must set into motion some exceed-
ingly convoluted sequences of equilibrating adjustments in the
system (if, indeed, an equilibrium exists). Optimal economic management of such a system will undoubtedly require some sophisticated
control policies. One suspects that most marine ecosystems contain
this level of complexity.

More closely associated with the economist's interest is the theory
of the firm and industry. Very few published investigations have
focused on the consequences of alternative specifications of the
firm's cost and production functions or of industry structure.
Briefly, the simplest models of fishing (e.g., H.S. Gordon, 1954)
assume that catch rate per firm is proportional to the fish stock
density. Thus the average cost of harvests (which equals marginal
cost) is inversely related to fish stock density. Under these
conditions the activity of a firm can be captured in what A. Scott
has called an "omnibus variable," fishing effort. Recognizing
that fishermen do exhibit short-run maximizing behavior, A. Scott
(1955), V. Smith (1968) and others have adopted the more neoclassical assumptions in the theory of the firm which yield short-run
adjustments to input and output prices. Since firms have upward
sloping marginal cost curves, intra-marginal rents can be earned,
at least in the short-run. As Weitzman (1974) has noted, if the
supply curve of variable inputs to the harvesting sector is upward
sloping, intramarginal rents are available in the long run as well.
In contrast to the "one firm equals one unit of fishing effort"
model, the neoclassical concept of the firm yields some important
conclusions regarding the possibility of achieving an economically
efficient production program through the use of direct limitations
on some fishery inputs (e.g., Fraser, 1979).

Anderson (1976) has sought to integrate the neoclassical theory of the firm with the effort-based catch model. A key feature of Anderson's model is the expression of average and marginal cost curves as functions of fishing effort rather than as functions of output. Industry-wide short-run marginal cost of effort is the sum of the firms' marginal cost curves, and, assuming free entry of identical firms, the long-run marginal cost for the industry is horizontal (and, of course, equals the minimum average cost of the typical firm). Industry equilibrium is depicted as the intersection of the long-run marginal cost curve with the industry average revenue-per-effort curve. The average revenue-per-unit-effort diminishes linearly with increasing effort, because catch per effort from the fish stock falls linearly with aggregate effort. This behavior of the long-run average revenue curve is consistent with the "traditional fisheries model" (see Fullenbaum, et al., 1971), while the firm's U-shaped average cost of effort curves are ostensibly consistent with the neoclassical theory of the firm. While this is the best attempt yet to integrate fish stock dynamics into the theory of firm and industry, I see at least two directions for further work.

First, the question of how changes in the fish stock affect the revenue and cost curves deserves more attention. Anderson (1976) follows the traditional assumption that equilibrium catch per effort is inversely related to total effort, but several authors have suggested that this relationship depends upon fish schooling behavior, density gradients and fishing technology (e.g., Huppert, 1975; MacCall, 1976; Clark, 1980). Of more general importance, however, is the question of whether the industry's average revenue per effort curve can be constructed independently of the firm's cost curves. For this to be possible, the firm's production function must exhibit a certain form of separability.[5] The traditional model assumptions (that catch equals effort times biomass times catchability coefficient) and both the Cobb-Douglas and CES production functions have the necessary separability. But other plausible functions do not. It occurs to me that the theoretical foundations of fishery economics would benefit from a thorough examination of plausible production functions, the resulting cost functions, and the ultimate implications for various kinds of control policies.

The effects of industry structure upon private production from natural resources have been derived for the polar cases of monopoly and atomistic competition. As in the case of mineral deposits, a monopolist producer of a renewable resource may choose to produce at a lower rate (and sell at a higher price) or at a higher rate (and sell at a lower price) than a competitively organized industry, depending primarily upon the shape of the demand curve for the industry's output.[6] A sole owner of the resource without market power, however, acts like neither a monopolist nor a competitive industry. Since the sole owner sells at a fixed market price, but properly values the resource, his private optimum equals the social optimum. This was, of course, stated by A. Scott in 1955. Recently, Clark and Munro (1979) examined the consequences

of monopsony in the processing sector. They found that a monopsonist purchasing from a competitive harvesting sector will restrain
the fishery due to the apparent excessive harvesting costs incurred
and will maintain the fish stock at a greater than socially optimal
level. If the monopsonist integrates into the harvesting sector
while remaining a competitor in the product market, and, in so doing, eliminates the excessive costs that occur with competitive
fishing, we are back to the sole owner, socially optimal, result.
Give the integrated processor/harvestor some market power, and,
again, the results are ambiguous as in the monopoly case.

Clark and Munro suggest, and I agree, that a promising direction
for further research would be an examination of the kinds of bi-
lateral agreements that might occur when fishermen organize to
counter the market power of monopsonist buyers/processors. This
case seems to be descriptive of that found in many west coast
waterfront markets. It might be important to know whether the
"fishermen's" organization is a labor-dominated group (e.g., union)
or a capitalist-dominated group (fishing vessel owners association).
The labor-dominated cooperative, for example, might opt for higher
employment than would a vessel owners' cooperative. The implications of this, and other possible variations, for optimal regulation of the fishery would have immediate practical consequences.

Finally, on the question of risk and uncertainty, I am reluctant to
anticipate how the theory might develop. In a fairly simple and
intuitive framework, however, I have shown that the private benefits from operating a multi-purpose fleet occur with either uncertainty regarding which fisheries will be profitable or seasonal
variability in fishing costs (Huppert, 1979). Also, interpretation of the fleet size requires that the probability distribution
of future optimum harvest rates be considered. "Excessive" numbers
of vessels, as revealed by crowding or excess operating time in a
given year, does not necessarily indicate over-capitalization.
The optimum inventory of vessels to maintain must be greater than
the minimum number needed to take the average catch. Other implications of uncertainty for the optimum harvest rates or the optimum capital stock may be useful to the practicing fishery economist. J. Wilson (1980) draws upon both the industry structural
features and market price uncertainty to "explain" the existence
of quasi-contractual reciprocal agreements between fishermen and
buyers in the New England fresh fish market. Although the narrative
interpretation given by Wilson is specific to New England, similar studies elsewhere could provide potentially fruitful suggestions leading to a more general concept of waterfront markets.

Although theoretical development cannot be NOAA's highest priority
for economic research, I hope the foregoing suggestions demonstrate
the importance of maintaining a cadre of theoretical economists in
the universities and research centers. The work of theorists keeps
practitioners on their toes, and assures that the practice of
economics adapts to new methods of analysis and new interpretations
of data.

III. Economic Research for Domestic Fishery Management

Recent developments in United States fishery management institutions have expanded the formal requirements for application of economic analysis to fishery management issues. The Magnuson Fisheries Conservation and Management Act is the most obvious change, of course, but the administrative requirements applying to all federal regulations are equally demanding. These requirements call for cost-benefit studies of all prospective regulations, and encourage the development of regulations that are less burdensome to small enterprises. This trend in national policy coincides with the emergence of a growing interest in "limited access" or "limited entry" procedures in marine fisheries. Two major conferences have been held in North America to consider economic rationalization generally and limited entry specifically.[7] The reports from these conferences have focused attention on a series of practical management problems, some of which were mentioned in the section of this paper on theoretical research. I will discuss these issues in two parts, one addressing the problem of defining and computing the quantitative characteristics of an optimally managed fishery, and the second exploring the institutional arrangements that could lead to the realization of a given fish production program, optimal or not.

Research efforts to determine economically optimal programs of fishery production can be organized around bio-economic models. That is, economic values and costs are functionally related to the major determinants of biological change such that the economic problem presented contains, inherently, the fishery conservation problem. Such models typically contain one or more variables that can be treated as control variables, In full dynamic garb, the optimizing problem is to find a time path of the control variable such that the net discounted value of the fishery is maximized. Regardless of what mathematical optimization methods might be used, applied economic research must find tractable, yet realistic, specifications of the cost functions and gross value functions, and tie these to biological relationships. Some early economic applications to the fisheries attempted to quantify the static Schaefer-type models (e.g., Bell, 1972; O'Rourke, 1971) and were limited to finding optimum levels of fishing effort or rate of harvest. Other studies (e.g., Gates and Norton, 1974) have specified dynamic pool models which permit the investigation of mesh size or fish size regulation. And some very recent publications show how to incorporate risk (e.g., Smith, 1980; Dudley and Waugh, 1980) and even how to design a harvest strategy incorporating adaptive control for learning about the equilibrium yield (e.g., Walters and Hilborn, 1976). Each of these studies seems to overlook or assume away some important feature of the fishery being studied. Like the simplified theory, therefore, the simple empirical models provide useful insights into the resource management problems, but a richer, more realistic empirical representation of fisheries is needed for management purposes.

Applied research efforts for fisheries management should emphasize two main areas. First, as a counterpart to the theoretical research suggested earlier, there must be empirical investigations of production and cost functions for single and multi-species harvesters. Specifically, multiple input production technologies should receive substantial attention due to the importance of input substitution induced by regulations on fishing gear and fishing seasons. Targeting among mixed species stocks and shifting among alternative fishing activities by multi-purpose vessels may be investigated using production models developed for multi-product firms and discrete choice models developed by McFadden (1974) and others. Moreover, the cost functions for fishing in various kinds of fisheries should be developed with up-to-date econometric techniques in order to specify the bioeconomic models for management.

Second, a substantial effort needs to be directed toward the careful description of market organization and industry structure for major fisheries subject to federal management regulations, and a companion effort should involve econometric examination of fishery product markets. This effort will assist in interpreting existing industry practices and in quantifying the economic benefits of regulation. With the results of these studies in hand, the economic aspects of optimum yields will be sufficiently well specified to allow explicit use of economic reasoning in the derivation of optimum yields and regulatory measures. Of equal importance, however, is the search for institutions and mechanisms for inducing the fishery to follow the ideal production program.

A useful conceptual framework for this purpose was suggested by A. Scott (1979) and further developed by P. Pearse (1980). Drawing upon the economics of property rights literature (e.g., Demsetz, 1967; Cheung, 1970; and Dales, 1968), Pearse notes that the range of alternative institutional arrangements for fisheries management can be presented as a continuum of options with varying degrees of exclusivity in property rights. Common property is depicted as the extreme of non-exclusive property rights. At this extreme there is essentially no property defined with respect to the resource in the sea. At the other extreme would be "sole ownership," or exclusive private rights in which owners could exclude others from resource use, could engage in transactions in property rights, and could exercise a wide degree of latitude in using the fish to which they hold property rights. Between the two extremes would lie conditional property rights, such as those represented by license limitation programs, and individual fisherman quotas or quantitative rights to harvests.

Any property right convention within the feasible range will entail some level of organizational costs. These costs include "transactions costs" borne by the private businessmen (fishermen), which are made up of costs incurred in negotiating among firms, in "distinguishing, protecting, managing, and harvesting" the resources to which the firms have rights, and in complying with regulatory authorities. Administrative costs borne by the public management agency include costs incurred in gathering information, making internal decisions, and regulating fishermen's activities. The total organizational costs, made up of transactions and administrative costs, should be kept to a minimum by judicious choice of property rights arrangements.

To be of practical use, this conceptual framework must enable the analyst to determine how costs change as management institutions are changed along the property rights spectrum. Pearse suggests that transactions costs are very low in a common property fishery because the fishermen have very little to negotiate about or organize outside the individual enterprise. As property rights move toward more exclusive private rights, fishermen have more latitude to organize and trade among themselves and have more responsibility for managing and protecting the stock to which they have rights. Thus, as a general rule, one expects that transactions costs rise with increasing exclusivity of fishing rights. To hold truly exclusive rights to fish, the owner must be able to identify his fish (by tagging or enclosure) and protect them from unauthorized capture. Private property rights do not naturally evolve for fish stocks, according to this interpretation, precisely because there is no reasonably inexpensive way for them to be enforced and exchanged. This conclusion depends upon specific circumstances and one would not expect it to hold for relatively sedentary and divisible resources like oyster-beds, coral and abalone. For the more migratory, fugitive stocks of fish, however, it is reasonable to assume that transactions costs are too high for the economic use of exclusive rights by large numbers of competitive fishermen.

Public administrative costs are probably highest in the common property regime because all decisions pertaining to resource use must be made by the public agency. Also, in the absence of effective individual incentives to assure fishermen's compliance with harvest rules, the monitoring and enforcing of regulations is likely to be a significant burden. At the other extreme, with exclusive property rights to the resource, the government has only the usual responsibilities associated with providing legal support for private contracts, protecting individuals from criminal action, and regulating other aspects of fisheries that may impinge upon public resources or social policy (e.g., air and water pollution requirements, safety rules, etc.). Thus exclusive rights imply low administrative costs but high transactions costs, while common property implies high administrative and low transactions costs.

Given this framework, the best institutional regime for fisheries management is the one that minimizes the total organizational cost while achieving the level of harvest or other measure of optimum yield derived from the bio-economic model. The economic research agenda should include an effort to describe and quantify the "transactions" and "administrative" costs likely to occur under different regulatory structures. A great deal of thought has been given the cost implications of regulatory institutions, both by Pearse and, within a different conceptual framework, by economists studying the regulation of air and water quality. A general conclusion from Pearse (1980) is that a system of "stinted exploitation rights," i.e., the provision of transferable and divisible rights to take fish, would substantially reduce administration

53

costs of the regulatory authority (p. 200). The authority would need to assess the potential yield from the resource, prescribe the total catch, and enforce the rules of fishing. But because the authority need not become involved in the technology or economics of fishing, Pearse concludes that administrative costs would be lower than under a common property system. Fishing enterprises would incur greater transactions costs while at the same time finding economic incentives to reduce the costs of taking the prescribed amount of fish. That is, with marketable harvest rights, fishermen will undoubtedly find opportunities for profitable exchange, hence incurring transactions costs; but in each such transaction there is a presumption that a net gain is made. And since the individual fishing enterprise can acquire an enforceable, quantitative right, it can devote entrepreneurial effort to cost minimization that would otherwise go to offset the efforts of other fishermen to catch more fish.

These arguments have a familiar ring to the environmental economist. Marketable permits for pollution of water and air have been a standard proposal for years, and the efficiency of invoking private incentives for cost minimization has been quantitatively estimated in several instances.[8] But it may be too facile to assume that administration of a quantitative rights system would be less costly than administration of, say, an aggregate quota with gear limitations and season closure. Depending upon the number and geographic dispersion of outlets for whole, fresh fish and the number and identifiability of fishing enterprises, the enforcement of a quantitative rights scheme might be either simple or unwieldy. Especially with fully marketable permits, the enforcement authority must keep close tabs upon both the ownership of catch rights and the actual landings. Thus it seems to me that no general statement can hold regarding the least costly form of fishery regulation.

Research on this subject will suffer from a lack of precedents and case histories, and will, therefore, require that results of investigations in environmental regulations be mined for useful analogies. Much field research is also prescribed, since little documentation is currently available on enforcement and management costs in fisheries. The probable administrative costs may be balanced by the presumed, substantial cost savings by the fishing firms. Based upon the production and cost studies recommended above, the research here should be very straightforward. Although this is a relatively unexplored field for the fisheries economist, development of cost-benefit studies to evaluate alternative regulatory regimes should be a high priority item for an agency, like NOAA, with extensive regulatory responsibilities.

IV. Research on International Economics

Two important topics related to the United States' international economic policy are (1) the effects of U.S. trade and commercial policies (tariff and non-tariff barriers to trade, domestic subsidies to import-competing sectors) on the domestic fishery and support sectors, and (2) development of optimal foreign fishing fees and foreign catch allocation mechanisms. Both of these

subjects have attracted occasional serious research efforts, but
the urgency of policy decisions often makes impossible the mounting
of extensive studies. International trade patterns are clearly affected by a mix of ad-valorem tariffs, import prohibitions and domestic regulations on marine products. These are presumably meant
to protect and enhance domestic fisheries or to retaliate for similar actions by trading partners. The main point of the first topic
listed above is to determine the degree to which various sectors of
the domestic industry are protected by trade restrictions. The
second topic, foreign fishing fees and catch allocations, involves
the trade-off between different means of extracting economic benefits from the resources of the Fishery Conservation Zone. One
source of economic gain is the direct monetary rewards obtainable
from acting as a resource owner with market power; i.e., obtaining
a maximum payment from foreign fishing nations for the harvest of
U.S. fish. A second source of gain is the advantage given to
domestic fisheries through bargaining for trade concessions and reducing foreign competition. I outline the conceptual issues and
suggested directions for research below.

Some domestic trade restrictions affect all U.S. fisheries. These
include the prohibition on use of foreign-built vessels for landing
fish in domestic ports, and tariffs on certain electronic equipment
and artificial fiber netting. Current import duties on man-made
netting, for example, are equivalent to about 42 percent ad-valorem.
On the other hand, the domestic fisheries share a number of government assistance programs, including the federal loan guarantee program and the establishment of tax-free capital construction funds.
Besides these general provisions there are special trade restrictions such as the 35 percent ad-valorem tariff on canned tuna in
oil, and a 12 percent tariff on fish sticks and portions. Most un-
processed or very slightly processed fishery products, such as
frozen whole tuna and frozen groundfish blocks, enter the United
States free of tariff or under very low tariff rates. The ultimate
effect of this combination of trade restrictions and domestic assistance programs is not immediately clear. When the trade and
tariffs are found on raw products, intermediate products, and final
products, all within one sector, the impacts may be assessed using
the concept of "effective rate of protection" developed by B.
Belassa (1965) and W.M. Corden (1966).[7] The rate of effective protection for any given industry sector is essentially the percentage
increase of that sector's value-added due to the tariff structure.

Knowing the effective rates of protection will not only assist in
evaluating the effects of trade policy on fisheries, but will also
establish the degree to which one sector of the industry may be
aided at the expense of another sector. For example, the tariff
on canned tuna in conjunction with the free entry of raw, frozen
tuna is an unambiguous advantage for domestic tuna canners. The
tuna harvesters, however, seem to be disadvantaged by the tariffs
and prohibitions on inputs to harvesting (tariffs on some electronic gear, for example) in combination with the free entry of frozen
tuna. But the financial assistance programs may result in an overall beneficial protective effect of federal policy on domestic

fishermen. For NOAA to provide ready advice to Congress and Executive agencies on the probable impact, quantified if possible, of U.S. trade policy, the economic research could center on the effective protection rates as well as international comparisons of comparative advantage, trade barriers and industry subsidies, and the effects of these upon international markets and trade flows in affected commodities.

A second topic related to the U.S. international economic relations is the policy on foreign fishing fees and catch allowances. Under the Fishery Conservation and Management Act (FCMA) the Secretary of Commerce, in consultation with the Secretary of State, is responsible for determining what quantities of fish are available for harvest in excess of the domestic industry needs. Foreign nations are permitted to take these foreign allocations with specific stipulations as to species, location and season. Because the U.S. controls the foreign harvest and is able to levy fees on the foreign fishing enterprises, an interesting economic question concerns the appropriate level of fees. As a sole owner, in effect, of the fishery resource, the U.S. could seek to maximize the revenue collected. Alternate economic benefits can be extracted by ex changing catch allocations for trade concessions, marketing assistance, or technical assistance in harvesting and processing--the so-called "fish and chips" policy.

During its first 5 years, U.S. foreign fishing policy has undergone several changes. In 1977 and 1978 the fee schedule included annual permit fees on fishing, processing and other support vessels, and "poundage fees" on harvests equal to 3.5 percent of the ex-vessel value. Additionally, foreign vessel operators were required to recompense the U.S. government for the costs of placing U.S. observers aboard the foreign vessels. Foreign catch allocations were about 1.7 million tons per year in 1977 and 1978, and the total fees collected amounted to $10 million (Table 3). In 1979 and 1980 a 20 percent surcharge was added to the poundage fee in order to capitalize the Fishing Vessel and Gear Damage Compensation Fund under the Fishermen's Protective Act, as amended. Finally, the American Fisheries Promotion Act of December 1980 established a cost recovery objective for the foreign fee schedule. To recover the full costs of administration, enforcement and research attributable to the operation of foreign fisheries in the U.S. zone, the poundage fees are to be double the 1979 level in 1981 and will be further increased in 1982. Assuming that the foreign share of the total costs of operating the fishery management system in the Fishery Conservation Zone equals the foreign share of the catch times the total cost, the total fee collection must be on the order of $50 to $60 million.

Besides collecting more in fishing fees, the United States is now attempting to use domestic fishery development objectives as a basis for allocating catch quotas among foreign fishing nations. Since 1979, when this "fish and chips" policy was officially announced, we have sought to trade access to fish stocks in the Fishery Conservation Zone for trade concessions, agreements to

TABLE 3.   Fees Collected From Foreign Fishing Vessel Owners

| | Million Dollars | | | | |
	1977	1978	1979	1980	1981
Vessel Permit Fees	0.89	0.74	0.92	0.79	.20[3]
Poundage Fees	7.14	8.76	11.03	12.0[1]	24.0[3]
Surcharge	--	--	1.95	3.5	--
Observer Fees	0.80	0.67	2.41	2.4[2]	2.4[2]
TOTAL	8.83	10.17	16.31	18.7	26.6

SOURCE: [1]Preliminary estimate.

[2]Unknown, but probably approximately equal to 1979 figure.

[3]Projected.

purchase U.S. fishery products, and agreements resulting in the transfer of technical or marketing knowhow to U.S. fisheries. For example, in 1980 Japan agreed to modify her import quota system to allow increased sales of nontraditional U.S. products to that country. Since Japan is the leading importer of U.S. fishery products, a reduction in Japanese trade barriers could provide substantially expanded export opportunities. In contrast to assessment of foreign fishing fees, evaluation of trades for various quantitative and non-quantitative commercial policy instruments requires analysis of much more than market demand and supply relations.

Economic analysis necessary to set fees properly, in the absence of the "fish and chips" policy, would focus on the standard problem of a profit-or-rent-maximizing resource owner with market power. Although there are many species and stocks available for allocation, the central issues in setting fees are the aggregate level of collections and the indirect effects upon U.S. fishing costs. Both of these aspects are readily analyzed with standard economic theories. As a first approximation we can assume that the domestic cost of enforcing and monitoring foreign fishing rules is unrelated to the level of fees, so that the problem is to determine for each important species what level of fee yields the most revenue and the greatest cost savings to U.S. fishermen. Cost savings would occur where direct interference with gear is reduced and where reduced foreign fishing would cause fish stock density increases sufficient to raise domestic catch rates. The main areas for economic research are estimation of market demand curves for U.S. fish, foreign supply functions of substitute fish products, and the domestic production and cost consequences of varying levels of foreign fishing in the U.S. Zone.

With the "fish and chips" policy, rent-maximization is not the goal. Where the "chips" traded for access to U.S. fish stocks are equivalent to tariff reductions, the economic evaluations needed will require the same kind of commodity market analysis as required for foreign trade policy research. Assuming that the main thrust of the policy is to increase domestic fisheries at the expense of foreign fisheries, U.S.-produced fish should begin to substitute for foreign-caught fish in both domestic and foreign markets. Where tariff levels were previously prohibitive, however, a reduced tariff level may or may not result in expanded sales of U.S. goods in the foreign market. Even when reduced trade barriers do increase U.S. exports, the magnitude of the effect, and therefore the value of the trade concessions, will depend upon the shape of the foreign demand schedule and the elasticity of the supply curve of the foreign country's home industry. Thus to provide quantitative economic evaluations of various trade concessions during a bargaining session will require an immense amount of preparation.

An even more difficult task will be the calculation of relative values to the U.S. of fishery development-oriented technical assistance. As any economic development specialist knows, capital goods and production methods are often profitable only with input prices similar to those in the originating country. Thus techniques adapted to different labor conditions and energy prices may fail miserably when shifted to a new environment. To evaluate an exchange of foreign fish catch for information regarding fishing and processing methods therefore requires not only that the potential demand for a U.S. fishery product be estimated, but also that profitability of new technology for U.S. enterprises be assessed. Although the required research is of a well-understood, applied sort, NOAA's economic research establishment would have to be expanded substantially if it were to provide the kind of quantitative evaluations needed prior to foreign fishery negotiations.

V. Resource Conflicts and Income Distribution[10]

It is widely recognized that public decision-making is largely directed toward income distribution rather than economic efficiency. Due to the common property status of most marine resources, income distribution (or allocation of available resources among competing users) is an especially prevalent concern. Classic resource use conflicts involve (1) recreational versus commercial fishermen claims to fish stocks, (2) industrial and residential development in coastal wetlands versus preservation of natural ecological systems, and (3) OCS petroleum drilling versus shoreline habitat protection. To these we might add the maze of conflicts between watershed activities and salmon propagation. Many additional sources of conflict are manifested in the environmental management area covered by C. Russell's paper. In all of these instances, public decision-makers focus on distribution, as well as the aggregate size, of benefits.

One approach to the recreational versus commercial fishing issue, noted by both G. Brown and J. Crutchfield in their companion papers, is to calculate economic values for each fishing activity. The economic calculus would suggest that an optimum allocation between competing groups occurs where marginal values to the two groups are equalized. While such valuation exercises might influence public decisions, I am not optimistic about the economists' ability to calculate reliable recreational values for a wide range of activities at reasonable cost. Nor do I believe that recreational value estimates provide a comprehensive basis for allocations.

We need to recognize at least two additional issues. In many instances there is a substantial difference between the income class of recreational anglers and that of the consumers of commercially-caught fish. I suspect that the allocation of marlin to recreational use in California directs benefits toward higher income classes. At the other extreme, anglers catching bottomfish off shoreline structures are likely to be from lower income classes than are the patrons of seafood restaurants which use much of the commercially caught fish. Thus, allocation of species or segments of the fishery yield to one group or the other can easily involve redistributions of benefits among income classes. It occurs to me that a very useful function for the economist is to provide quantitative information about these redistributions.

Similarly, the management of commercial fisheries by season and area closures or by gear restrictions has potentially important distributional effects. These effects are not limited to redistribution among income classes but include significant changes in geographic distribution of economic activity (which might be reflected in regional income impacts) and alterations in product quality and storage costs. In highly regulated fisheries, like the Pacific salmon fisheries, potential changes in economic gains to special groups have a powerful (possibly controlling) influence on resource policy. Because this is so important, economists should provide reliable projections of distributional effects. Also, once an explicit allocation objective is chosen, economic research can seek the least-cost means of implementation.

VI. Conclusions

Because fisheries dominate the economic output of marine living resources, I have emphasized the economic research issues pertinent to domestic management and international economics of the fishing industry. That is, research needs are spawned by the need to develop commercial policy and fishery management methods. Since theoretical aspects of fisheries economics are the foundation for most good empirical applications, it is essential that we continue to study the theory of fisheries economics and improve its applicability and empirical content over time. I want clearly to discourage the separation of theoretical and empirical work. As noted by Boulding (1975), the learning process depends "on the creation of certain shocks or inconsistencies, what Leon Festinger has called 'cognitive dissonances,' which force a reorganization of the structure" of images. To the extent that economists' recommendations are drawn from the image of the world provided by economic theory, learning implies revision of theory. And the major source of "cognitive dissonances" to stimulate this seems to be the frequent confrontations between theoretical simplifications and the perceptions developed through empirical testing and policy application. The particular areas in which I perceive "cognitive dissonances" are implicit in my discussion of theoretical research needs. I suggested that this research emphasize the development of tractable models with complex multi-species resources; investigate production and cost functions for multiproduct, multi-input fishing firms; and study optimal adaptive strategies with uncertain biological and economic conditions.

Research in support of domestic fishery management should focus on applied industry organization and econometric analysis for use in bioeconomic models, as well as a study of benefits and costs of alternative management institutions. Selection of management criteria, such as optimum yields, is the main task of the bioeconomic models, whereas selection of efficient control mechanisms is sought through examination of organizational costs for different institutional (or property rights) alternatives.

In the area of international economics I emphasized the analysis of trade policy for fishery products and the assessment of U.S. foreign fishing policy. Both of these areas of application draw upon estimates of market demand and supply relationships, and both also require that benefits from alternative policies be comparably estimated. Trade restrictions benefit some sectors of the economy at the expense of other sectors, and with tariffs on intermediate and final products the benefits of protection are unevenly distributed vertically within a sector like the commercial fishing industry. The purpose for a study of "effective rates of protection" is to quantify some of these benefits and costs. Similarly, foreign fishing in the FCZ may be managed for generalized benefits through payments to the Treasury or to benefit the domestic fishery through trade concessions and "development assistance." Both the Magnuson Fisheries Conservation and Management Act and the American Fisheries Promotion Act favor the specific use of fisheries policy to benefit U.S. fisheries. The economic research proposed above can help to identify efficient ways of achieving this goal as well as expose the costs of choosing not to exploit alternative policies.

Finally, the economic distribution of benefits implied by resource policies is of critical importance to decision-makers. Research aimed at quantifying the distribution of benefits among income classes, geographic divisions and user groups is needed. Productive research in the four basic directions I have outlined here should lead to better economic advice on policy issues and, ultimately, to more economic benefits from living marine resources.

The broader theoretical research and widespread data-gathering programs must be the responsibility of established and continuing research programs in the various agencies. Some special studies that might be undertaken by NOAA's Office of Resources Coordination and Assessment are suggested below.

Summary of Research Topics

1) Develop commodity market models for the frozen groundfish fillet and shrimp trade in the United States, and

use the models to evaluate a variety of policy issues regarding tax and subsidy incentives and tariff structures. Evaluate the trade-off between protection of domestic fishing industry sectors and economic benefits to domestic consumers.

2) Develop international market models for the kinds of fresh and frozen food fish taken in the foreign fishery in U.S. waters. Utilize the estimated demand and supply relationships to assess the impacts of foreign fishing fees on the foreign industry and on subsequent levels of seafood supply to the U.S. market.

3) Determine the specific economic consequences to the commercial fishing industry of "conflicts" with petroleum exploration and development. Conflicts include fouling of trawl gear on subsurface and bottom structures and debris, reduction of obstacle-free trawling grounds, and local disruption of fishing due to oil spillage. Case studies would focus on New England bottom trawling, Gulf Coast shrimping and Alaska shellfish fisheries.

4) Delineate the variety and magnitude of distributional effects of the management provisions applied to the Pacific salmon fisheries off of Washington, Oregon and California. This would be a very broad study encompassing (1) the impacts of traditional gear, season and size restrictions on geographic distribution of fishing effort and income, (2) the effect of existing 70/30 split of ocean salmon catch between commercial and recreational fisheries, and (3) a detailed breakdown of the redistributions of income among fishing gear groups caused by past and present management procedures.

5) Using agency records, investigate the full administrative costs of information-gathering, scientific research, rule-making, and enforcement efforts devoted to managing an important marine fish population. Several candidate fisheries are the tropical tuna fishery, the New England groundfish and lobster fisheries, the Bristol Bay sockeye salmon, and the California anchovy. The objective would be to document the public costs of various administrative activities so that alternative management institutions could be better evaluated.

6) Examine the costs to commercial fishing interests of prohibiting commercial fishing on nearshore banks and kelp beds in southern California. This would involve an allocation of nearshore fishing locations to recreational use. The main economic issue would be the consequent increase in fishing costs and/or decrease in local commercial fishery production. The procedures developed would also be applicable to recreational fishing preserves in the Gulf of Mexico.

Research topics raised during discussion include:

1. Assess the feasibility of fish farming, including the potential substitution of "private" fish for "public" fish. Study the regulation difficulties (if they exist) created by such an enterprise.

2. Determine the elasticity of substitution between types of effort and types of gear in single and multiple species fisheries. The estimates are necessary for evaluating regulations suggested in the text.

3. Determine in a multispecies context the effect of regulation of access to one species on exploitation of other fisheries and the development of multispecies fishing capacity over time.

4. How do regulating bodies (councils) choose regulations? Develop a theory of regulator behavior, including choice of regulations, development of constituencies.

5. What are feasible regulation policies to adopt when there is uncertainty in the physical and economic variables?

Notes

1. The most current study of U.S. seaweed usage appears to be Silverthorne and Sorenson (1971). They estimate that the annual harvest is worth slightly more than $1 million.

2. The Magnuson Fisheries Conservation and Management Act established Federal fishery management authority in the FCZ which extends 200 nautical miles to sea while leaving the States with primary management authority for fisheries in the 3-mile territorial sea. In 1980, 30 percent of commercial harvests (40 percent of ex vessel value) occurred in the FCZ, 62 percent (47 percent by value) occurred in the territorial sea, and the remainder was taken in international waters or in the 200-mile zones of other nations.

3. From the Department of Commerce (1980), pp. 20-45.

4. In "surplus growth" models the rate of growth in the fish stock is assumed to be a function only of the stock size, and the potential annual growth equals the equilibrium annual fishery yield.

5. A production function is "separable" if the inputs can be grouped so that the marginal rate of substitution (MRS) between inputs within a group is independent of the quantities of inputs outside the group. Anderson's theory of the fishing firm seems to assume that substitutions among purchased inputs are unaffected by the fish stock density.

6. See Dasgupta and Heal (1979) for a thorough summary of exhaustible resource theory.

7.   See Pearse (1979) and Ginter (1980).

8.   For an extended discussion of the advantages and disadvan-
      tages of marketable permits and modified fiscal incentives
      for air and water pollution control see Tietenberg (1980),
      Blackman and Baumol (1980), or Rose-Ackerman (1977).

9.   As an illustrative example suppose industry i uses a_{ji} dol-
      lars worth of input j per dollar of output (i.e., a_{ji} is the
      (i,j)th element in an input-output table). Further suppose
      that the nominal, ad-valorem tariff rate on imported pro-
      ducts competing with industry i is t_i, while t_j represents
      the corresponding rates on imported inputs. Now the "effec-
      tive rate of protection" for industry i is

$$\frac{t_i - \sum_j a_{ji} t_j}{1 - \sum_j a_{ji}}$$

      Since the a_{ji} are computed from dollar values, $(1 - \sum_j a_{ji})$
      is the value added for industry i.

10.   Added in response to comments by L. Anderson and others.

References

Anderson, L.G. (1976). "The Relationship Between Firm and Fishery
    in Common Property Fisheries," Land Econ. 52(2): 179-191.

_____ (1977). The Economics of Fisheries Management, Johns
    Hopkins University Press, Baltimore.

_____ forthcoming. Fisheries Utilization in Developing Countries:
    A Manual for Management and Development, Food and Agricultur-
    al Organization, Rome.

Balassa, B. (1965). "Tariff Protection in Industrial Countries:
    An Evaluation," J. Polit. Econ. 73: 573-94.

Bell, F.W. (1972). "Technological Externalities and Common-Pro-
    perty Resources: An Empirical Study of the U.S. Northern
    Lobster Fishery," J. Polit. Econ. 80: 148-158.

_____ (1978). Food From the Sea: The Economics and Politics of
    Ocean Fisheries, Westview Press, Boulder, Colorado.

Beverton, R.J.H. and S.J. Holt (1957). "On the Dynamics of Exploit-
    ed Fish Populations," Fishery Investigations, Series II,
    Vol. 19. Her Majesty's Stationery Office, London.

Blackman, S.A.B. and W.J. Baumol (1980). "Modified Fiscal Incen-
    tives in Environmental Policy," Land Econ. 56(4): 417-431.

Cheung, S.N.S. (1970). "The Structure of a Contract and the Theory
    of a Non-Exclusive Resource," J. Law Econ. 13 (April): 49-70.

Clark, C.W. (1976). Mathematical Bioeconomics, John Wiley and Sons, New York.

_____ (1980). "Towards a Predictive Model for the Economic Regulation of Commercial Fisheries," Canadian J. Fish. Aquatic Sci. 37: 1111-1129.

Clark, C.W. and G.R. Munro (1980). "Fisheries and the Processing Sector: Some Implications for Management Policy," Bell J. Econ. 11(2): 603-616.

Corden, W.M. (1966). "The Structure of a Tariff System and the Effective Protective Rate," J. Polit. Econ. 74: 221-237.

Crutchfield, J.A. and G. Pontecorvo (1969). The Pacific Salmon Fisheries: A Study of Irrational Conservation, Johns Hopkins Press, Baltimore, Maryland.

Dales, J.H. (1968). Pollution, Property and Prices: An Essay in Policy Making and Economics, Univ. of Toronto Press, Toronto.

Dasgupta, P.S. and G.M. Heal (1979). Economic Theory and Exhaustible Resources, Cambridge University Press, Great Britain.

Demsetz, H. (1967). "Toward a Theory of Property Rights," Amer. Econ. Rev. 57 (May): 347-59.

Department of Commerce (1980). "Final Environmental Impact Statement on the Interim Convention on Conservation of North Pacific Fur Seals," National Marine Fisheries Service, Washington, D.C.

Dudley, N. and G. Waugh (1980). "Exploitation of a Single-Cohort Fishery Under Risk: A Simulation-Optimization Approach," J. Environ. Econ. Manage. 7: 234-255.

Fraser, G.A. (1979). "Limited Entry: Experience of the British Columbia Salmon Fishery," J. Fish. Res. Board Can. 36: 754-763.

Fullenbaum, R.F., E.W. Carlson, and F.W. Bell (1971). "Economics of Production from Natural Resources: Comment," Amer. Econ. Rev. 61 (June): 483-87.

Gordon, H.S. (1954). "The Economic Theory of a Common Property Resource," J. of Pol. Econ. 62 (April): 134-142.

Hannesson, R. (1978). Economics of Fisheries: An Introduction, Universitetsforlaget, Bergen, Norway.

Huppert, D.D. (1975). Economics of a Multi-Species Fishery, Ph.D. dissertation, University of Washington.

_____ (1979). "Implications of Multipurpose Fleets and Mixed Stocks for Control Policies," J. Fish. Res. Board Can. 36: 845-854.

MacCall, A.D. (1976). "Density-Dependence of Catachability Co-efficient in the California Pacific Sardine (Sardinops sagax caerulea) Purse Seine Fishery," CalCOFI Rep. XVIII: 136-148.

May, R.M., J.R. Beddington, C.W. Clark, S.J. Holt and R.M. Laws (1979). "Management of Multispecies Fisheries," Science 205 (20 July): 267-277.

McFadden, D. (1974). "Conditional Logit Analysis of Qualitative Choice Behavior," in P. Zarembka, Frontiers in Econometrics, Academic Press, New York.

National Marine Fisheries Service (1975-1980). Fisheries of the United States, Current Fisheries Statistics Series, Washington, D.C.

Niskanen, W.A., Jr. (1971). Bureaucracy and Representative Government, Aldine-Atherton, Chicago.

O'Rourke, D. (1971). "Economic Potential of the California Trawl Fishery," Amer. J. Agricul. Econ. 53(4): 583-592.

Pearse, P.H. (1980). "Property Rights and the Regulation of Commercial Fisheries," J. Bus. Admin. 11: 185-209.

_____ (ed., 1979). "Symposium on Policies for Economic Rationalization of Commercial Fisheries," in J. of the Fisheries Research Board of Canada, Issue 7, Vol. 36 (July 1979).

Peltzman, S. (1976). "Toward a More General Theory of Regulation," J. of Law and Econ. 19(2): 221-240.

Posner, R.A. (1974). "Theories of Economic Regulation," The Bell J. of Econ. 5(2): 335-358.

Rettig, B. and J. Ginter (1980). Limited Entry as a Fishery Management Tool, University of Washington Press, Seattle.

Rose-Ackerman, S. (1977). "Market Models for Water Pollution Control: Their Strengths and Weaknesses," Public Policy 25(3): 383-396.

Scott, A.D. (1955). "The Fishery: The Objectives of Sole Ownership," J. Polit. Econ. LXIII(2): 116-124.

_____ (1979). "Development of Economic Theory on Fisheries Regulation," J. Fish. Res. Board Can. 36: 725-741.

Silverthorne, W. and P.E. Sorenson (1971). "Marine Algae as an Economic Resource," Marine Technology Society Preprints for 7th Annual Conference: 523-531.

Smith, J.B. (1980). "Replenishable Resource Management Under Uncertainty: A Reexamination of the U.S. Northern Fishery," J. Environ. Econ. Manage. 7: 209-219.

Stigler, G.J. (1971). "The Theory of Economic Regulation," The Bell J. of Econ. 2(1): 3-21.

_____ (1974). "Free Riders and Collective Action: An Appendix to Theories of Economic Regulation," The Bell J. of Econ. 5(2): 359-365.

Strand, I.E. and D.L. Hueth (1977). "A Management Model for a Multi-Species Fishery," Chap. 18 in L.G. Anderson, Economic Impacts of Extended Fisheries Jurisdiction, Ann Arbor Science Press.

Tietenberg, T.H. (1980). "Transferable Discharge Permits and the Control of Stationary Source Air Pollution: A Survey and Synthesis," Land Econ. 56(4): 391-416.

Walters, C.J. and R. Hilborn (1976). "Adaptive Control of Fishing Systems," J. Fish. Res. Board Can. 33: 145-159.

Weitzman, M.L. (1974). "Free Access Vs. Private Ownership as Alternative Systems for Managing Common Property," J. Econ. Theory 8: 225-234.

Wilson, J.A. (1980). "Adaptation to Uncertainty and Small Numbers Exchange: The New England Fresh Fish Market," Bell J. Econ. 11(2): 491-504.

Living Marine Resources

Lee G. Anderson

Dan Huppert has presented an excellent discussion of the economic research needs for living marine resources and I agree with practically everything he says. In the interest of space-saving I will not summarize his main points or quibble about small differences of opinion. Rather I will focus on what I think is an important area which he did not address.

James Crutchfield makes two very important points in his overview paper. First, he says that total landings could be increased by about 21 to 28 percent if proper management regimes were instituted. Since these increases would be in higher valued species the increase in the value of output could well be much more than this. He then goes on to say, however, that fisheries management in the U.S. has been essentially a failure. In his view, the basic problem of open-access has not been suitably solved and, given the existing regime, it is not likely to be solved in the foreseeable future.

If management can indeed provide such significant gains and yet has failed to do so, I think that research on why we get the types of regulation we do is in order. Anthony Scott (1979) has made a similar suggestion in indicating that we really do not have a coherent body of theory on fisheries regulation. Note that Huppert's suggestions deal primarily with the classical economics of resource management and commercial policy. This has been the essence of fisheries economics since the work of Gordon (1954). If the points raised by Crutchfield are true, we need to start looking at a wider range of issues. With this in mind I would like to propose the following framework for viewing research into fisheries management.

This framework can be described with reference to Figure 1. On the vertical margin of the box are two theories of regulation, the public interest theory and the economic theory. According to public interest theory, the traditional role of regulation in economic analysis is to eliminate unfortunate allocative consequences of different types of market failure. Practitioners of this theory, either explicitly or implicitly, assume that maximizing efficiency is the government's goal, and they try to help achieve it by deriving

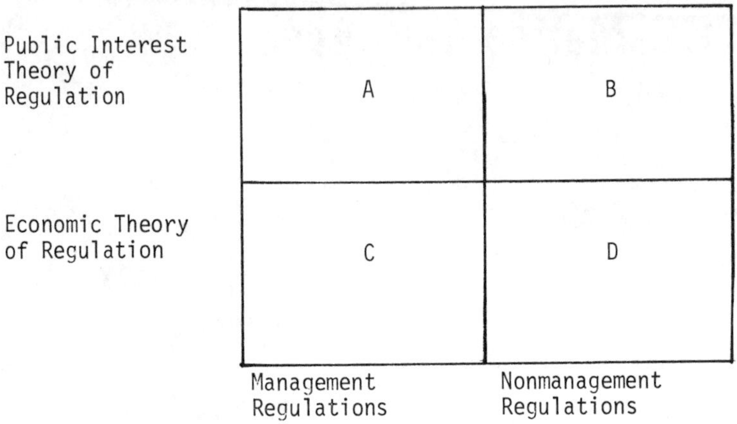

	Management Regulations	Nonmanagement Regulations
Public Interest Theory of Regulation	A	B
Economic Theory of Regulation	C	D

FIGURE 1

---

regulation policies that, if implemented, would correct for the relevant market failure.

The economic theory of regulation, on the other hand, views government as the supplier of regulation and individuals, firms, or groups of either, as demanders of regulation. According to this theory, the types of regulation which actually occur are the result of interactions between demanders and suppliers of regulations, where both operate so as to maximize their individual utilities rather than some notion of social utility. For a further description of the economic theory of regulation see Stigler (1971, 1974),* and Peltzman (1976).

On the horizontal axis of Figure 1 are two types of fisheries regulation. Management regulations are defined as those regulations which attempt to correct for the potential biological and economic ill effects of open access utilization of fisheries. Nonmanagement regulations refer any other type of government intervention in the fishery industry such as import controls, construction subsidies, industry development grants, quality control regulations, worker safety rules, etc.

I contend that the traditional approach to fisheries regulation has focused, to a very large degree, only on that part of the box represented by A. That is, it has been a study of management regulations using the public interest theory of regulation. I would suggest that analysis of areas B, C, and D so as to develop a general model of fisheries regulation which will cover a broader range of government interventions would provide many benefits. Such a theory should attempt to explain what types of regulation can be expected

---

* For references, see bibliography following Huppert paper.

to follow from certain types of government and industry structures, as well as what types of regulations would, in theory, achieve economic efficiency.

The expansion to area B, use of public interest theory on nonmanagement regulation will cover almost virgin territory. More work is needed in this area to specify more clearly when management and nonmanagement regulations are interdependent and the exact nature of the interdependency. It is also necessary to describe optimal regulations in the presence of the interdependencies. This type of work has direct policy relevance, because for the most part, the departments responsible for management and nonmanagement operations in the councils and the National Marine Fisheries Service operate independently of each other. The results here could describe where closer cooperation is necessary, and what forms that cooperation should take. The type of research proposed by Huppert under the title of international economics falls in this category. Fisheries development is another nonmanagement activity that should be studied as well. Development and management often work in opposition to each other with one trying to expand the fishery and the other trying to reduce redundant effort. While development activity can sometimes be justified, we need to develop better methods of coordinating it with present or future management.

With respect to areas C and D, it would be fair to say that with the exception of the brief discussion by Scott cited above, there has never been an application of the economic theory of regulation to either type of fisheries regulation. It is thus hard to specify the direction in which such work should go. However, the following elementary attempts can provide an idea of what will have to be considered when a formal theory is developed.

Figure 2a contains the average and marginal revenue curves and the marginal cost curve which are standard to the traditional fisheries economics model. Effort is assumed to be produced with constant costs, and so average cost (AC_E) equals marginal cost (MC_E). See Anderson (1977) for an extended treatment of this model. The open access equilibrium will occur at effort level E_1 where AR_E equals AC_E. However, optimal utilization will occur at E_2 where MR_E equals MC_E. The net marginal benefits of a regulation policy which reduces effort can be measured by the difference between MC_E and MR_E at a particular level of effort. For example at E_1 the marginal benefit of effort reduction is G. The marginal gain gradually diminishes to zero as effort is reduced from E_1 to E_2.

This marginal benefit relationship is plotted in Figure 2b as the curve labeled MB. Note however that the horizontal axis here is different; it measures the amount of reduction in effort, where the starting point for measuring is E_1, the open access level. As indicated, the point where the MB curve crosses the horizontal axis is equivalent to the point E_2 in Figure 2a. Let the curve labeled MC_{reg} plot the marginal cost of regulation as a function of the amount of effort reduction. It is then obvious that from a true social cost point of view, the optimal level of effort reduction is

Figure 2

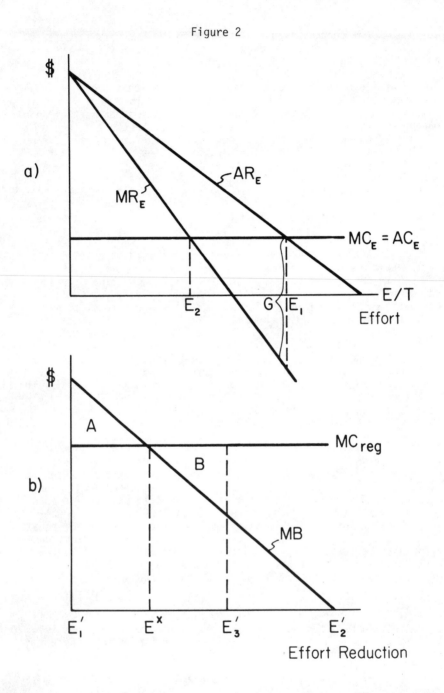

E^*, where the marginal benefits of regulation equal the marginal cost. Therefore the true optimal level of effort is E_2-E^*, not E_2, as indicated by strict adherence to the traditional model.

Taking the costs of government regulation into account will be one of the gains from this expanded theory. Another more important goal, however, will be to incorporate the behavior of the regulatory agencies. This can be done in terms of this diagram by using the results of Niskanen (1971). He postulates that bureaucrats try to maximize their budget (because this leads to higher salaries, more prestige, etc.), and are sometimes able to do so because they are the only ones with enough information on the nature of the benefits and costs of their operations. Applying this analysis here leads to the result that effort may be reduced as far as E_3^c. The agency will try to expand their budget, which in terms of this analysis means that they will try to extend effort reduction. They have to get approval of their action from the legislature and according to Niskanen, this approval is not likely to be forthcoming unless the net benefit of regulation is at least non-negative. Note that at E_3^c the loss from effort reduction beyond E^*, as indicated by area B, is just equal to the gains of going from no regulation to E^*, area A. Therefore the net gains from regulation at this point are zero. To the extent that this analysis is correct, one would expect that bureaucrats would act so that the fishery would operate at level of effort equivalent to E_3^c units of reduction.

According to this model, there are at least three points of interest: the open access equilibrium, the government regulation equilibrium, and the socially optimal level of effort. In this case there is no reason to believe that any two of these will occur at the same level of effort.

As another example of what the new regulation theory should consider see Figure 3. Figure 3a contains the standard static analysis of fisheries exploitation given a downward sloping demand curve. (The analysis in Figure 2 assumed that price was constant). The open access equilibrium level of output will occur at Q_1, where average cost is equal to price. Ignoring for the moment regulation costs, the socially optimal level of output will occur at Q^*, where price equals marginal cost. Maximum monopoly profits will be achieved if the fishery is operated at Q_m. Following Peltzman (1976) this information can be used to investigate the behavior of a regulator who is trying to maximize his utility in a Stiglerian regulation model. Assume that the regulator has two constituencies, consumers of fish and producers of fish. At least some producers will be pleased if profits to the fishery are increased (those that are allowed to continue fishing), while all consumers will be pleased if more output is placed on the market, especially since this will also result in a price decrease. The regulator will therefore try to choose that combination of output and profit that will maximize his utility. There is, of course, a trade off between profit and output as drawn in Figure 3b. It is the locus of possible combinations of output and profit from which the regulator can choose and it follows directly from the way the curves are drawn in Figure 3a.

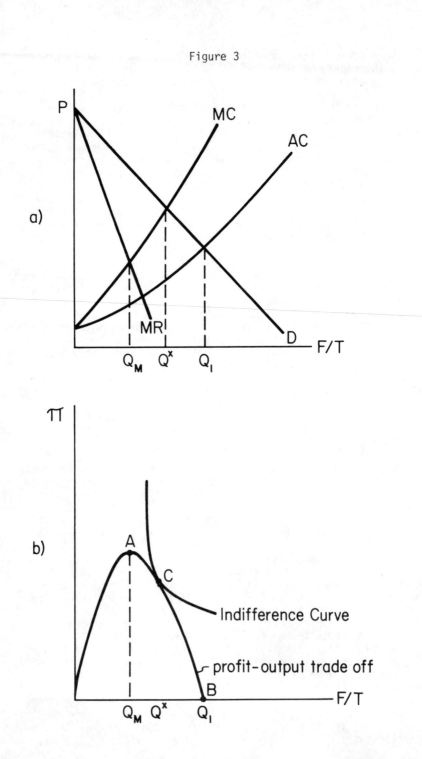

Figure 3

(The curves are drawn assuming that the government does not change the shape or position of the demand or cost curves). The relevant portion is between point A, which corresponds to the maximum profit point, and point B which corresponds to the open access or zero profit point. In other words the range AB on the profit output trade-off curve represents a movement from point Q_m to point Q_1 in Figure 3a. The regulator's utility function can be represented by a series of indifference curves in profit and output space. The shape and position of the curves will depend upon the bargaining power of each of the two groups and the degree to which each of them can provide votes or other things of value.

It can be seen that the regulator will maximize his utility at point C and hence this will tend to be the government regulation equilibrium point. By the nature of the curves, the government control equilibrium must be between the open access and the monopoly profit position, and it may correspond to the optimum point.

In order to be useful, the models will have to be made operational. The indifference curves in the above analysis may well have to be simplified to rules and regulations of operation of the various agencies, taking whatever operational freedom into account by empirical studies dealing with voting patterns of councils and consistent decision patterns of other fisheries agencies.

In summary, while there will more than likely be positive returns to undertaking the research suggested by Dr. Huppert, gains should also be possible from expanding the focus of research according to the above discussion. Even the most public spirited bureaucrat can not make appropriate decisions without a sufficient amount of accurate information. By studying the decision making process, however, it may be possible to suggest institutional structures and organizational rules such that the probability of using that information to its best advantage is increased.

Deep Ocean Mineral Resources

James Sebenius

I. Introduction

The dark depths of the deep seabed may someday yield up a treasure trove of minerals. Before that occurs on a large scale, however, economic researchers will certainly find many aspects of these resources worth careful study. This paper details my view of the most needed and promising such areas to be examined over the next decade.

My suggestions are colored by a very particular perspective about which the reader should be forewarned. I shall deal exclusively with the currently prominent, but by no means the only, deep ocean mineral resource, namely so-called manganese nodules.[1] Experience working for the National Oceanic and Atmospheric Administration, on the Law of the Sea Delegation, for a seabed mining modeling group at MIT, and as an economist in a public policy school has fixed my attention on the kind of information and analysis that would have been or promise to be useful in guiding policy formulation and implementation. While strictly theoretical issues constantly intrigue me, here I shall concentrate more on what seems to be more immediately usable knowledge.

Such policy is continuing and will continue to be made on several, related fronts. Recent U.S. legislation allows seabed miners to proceed with their plans and to commence commercial nodule production in 1988. In the interim, various regulatory tasks must be carried out domestically. The legislation, however, envisions a seabed regime composed of many "like-minded" states which would pass compatible seabed mining laws. So far the Federal Republic of Germany has gone forward in enacting legislation, and other states such as the United Kingdom, Italy, and France may not be far behind. A variety of questions need to be answered, such as how a "reciprocating states" scheme gets underway, if in fact it does so.

In the news, of course, is the system of nodule exploitation being negotiated at the United Nations Law of the Sea (LOS) Conference, about whose very existence the new Administration recently expressed grave reservations. Whether the Conference succeeds or fails, however, it has framed many policy questions that cry out for good economic analysis. When the nodules were unanimously agreed in 1970 to be "the common heritage of mankind," few could have foreseen the range of resource issues that would come up in attempting to give this grand concept some operational meaning. Whether the negotiations ultimately produce a regime, however, they will surely influence future consideration of other, ostensibly "common" or, more accurately, "international" resources, such as the moon, the airwaves, or Antartica.

The LOS Conference will continue its deliberations, possibly pushed in new directions by the Reagan Administration. If it concludes successfully, the signed treaty itself will bequeath a series of tough questions to a "preparatory commission," whose regulation-writing (and often, inventing) will need to be done before the U.S. Senate takes up ratification.

In short, there are multiple, hungry consumers--the U.S. government implementing unilateral legislation, its possible foreign compatriots, and a potential Preparatory Commission--awaiting good analysis. Along with academics and other naturally curious parties, these groups comprise the audience for any work that might be stimulated or influenced by the ideas in this paper.

Any resource discovered by an oceanographic expedition a century ago, designated by the whole of the United Nations as mankind's "common heritage," searched for by Howard Hughes' and the CIA's Glomar Explorer, and subjected to full-scale U.S. Congressional action naturally has stimulated a flood of physical, chemical, engineering, economic, legal, political, and other research. As a result, my effort to describe the gaps can in no way constitute a literature review. I shall cite some important studies, which themselves often contain impressive bibliographies, but generally I shall assume that potential researchers and their sponsors themselves would ferret out the relevant, earlier work.

In Section II, I start with a sort of baseline case, the underlying economic analysis that should be done on several aspects of seabed mining as it might develop in the absence of significant domestic or international regulation. Section III sets forth the work that could coherently define the United States' economic interests in this resource and various national policies that might be undertaken to realize those interests. In Section IV, the resources are examined from an international perspective. I try to lay out some of the more interesting economic issues raised by the LOS negotiations, a few alternatives to these emerging policies, and some of their ramifications for other arguably similar resources. Throughout the discussion, I shall try to relate the indicated studies to each other so that a sense of priorities may emerge.

II. Basic Economic Questions

Economic Analysis of the Resource Base

Many researchers have tried to estimate the quantity of minable manganese nodules. Usually, this is expressed in terms of the number of "minesites," or 40,000 to 60,000 square kilometer areas thought necessary to support seabed mining operations over their 20 to 30 year economic lives. Various authors have pegged the number of prime sites from three to four hundred.[2] Such estimation is a tricky thing: It depends not only on the quantity, but on the quality, and grade of nodules, as well as on the bottom topography. Samples are expensive to take, are subject to measurement errors, and, in any case, are sparse relative to the area involved. The geologists and oceanographers who have made these estimates have often done very good work but their results need to be explicated more carefully in terms of the requirements and projected capabilities (mainly, recovery efficiency) of mining operations.[3]

The results, which should be expressed probabilistically and as a function of recovery efficiency, are extremely important for giving an idea of how significant the resource may be, the potential evolution of the industry, the impact of internationally proposed production controls, any financial regime, and the character of regulations that may be imposed on the industry.

Engineering and Cost Modeling of Seabed Mining Operations

There have been numerous public attempts to analyze the engineering characteristics and costs of seabed mining operations. Most have been superficial or derivative; a few have been detailed and serious studies.[4] Such work is especially important for constructing cost functions and for situating seabed mining on the long run supply curves of the various metals. It is also useful for determining the relative sensitivity of project economics to constituent factors, which may have significant swings, such as energy prices or shipping costs. Needless to say, these efforts should be encouraged and strengthened.

The chief problem with such work so far is that it is generally deterministic and static, which greatly reduces its usefulness and applicability, especially given policy-making horizons. Granted, it is hard enough to make point estimates of costs where technological and economic uncertainty is the signal characteristic of the subject under study. This is precisely the reason, however, that more appropriate techniques (such as Monte Carlo methods) should be judiciously employed. The results would be vastly more informative than point estimates, even when the effects of varying component factors by 10 to 25 percent are examined in the accompanying sensitivity analyses.

The analyses to date, moreover, are mostly snapshots of expected first-generation mining technology and costs. (Most of these

76

studies make revenue assumptions as well, but with far less analysis than the cost side receives.) While particular values do come out of such work, similar effort should go toward identifying how different elements of the mining system are likely to change over time. For example, what parts of the system will be subject to "learning" or "experience" curve effects? Where is technology likely to change the fastest? Will factor prices alter? While this work would necessarily be more qualitative than current modeling efforts, it will give a much better sense of future trends.

Market Assessment

The future markets for copper, cobalt, nickel, and manganese are obvious focal points for economic investigation of nodule mining. Much work has been and is being done in this area, but complementary research would be useful as well, for example:

> Careful characterization of trends in the economic environment of ocean mining. Some analysts, principally from industry, have looked at broad trends that will affect the economic elements of ocean mining.[5] These trends include, for example, changes in the gross value of nodule contents, changes in metal use, changes in the characteristics of new terrestrial mines (for example, infrastructure costs and types of orebodies), and changes in bulk transportation costs. While these and many more such factors are implicit in almost all economic analyses of ocean mining, rarely are they systematically considered and evaluated.

> Econometric investigation. Ideally, of course, such work would be fully incorporated into formal models of metal markets. A number of such models have been constructed and modified.[6] The principal difficulty with these otherwise creditable attempts has come on the supply side. The painstaking work required to estimate the long run marginal cost of new supplies has not been satisfactorily carried out. Most studies, for example, take the amount of seabed production as exogenous and then investigate its effect on prices, export earnings, and the like. This is largely caused by the lack of good data (as would be generated under II (Engineering and Cost Modeling) above). Much needs to be done in this area.

I need not stress the widespread and fundamental importance of certain results of such studies. Figures should be constantly examined and updated as the models evolve. Included among these numbers are projections of metal prices and quantities, trade patterns, and, particularly, the general effects on the economics and foreign exchange earnings of land-based producers of the minerals to come from the sea. I cannot overemphasize the importance of being able to disaggregate the various measurements by country. Distributional effects are central.

77

Industrial Organization and Market Failure

The possibility of a seabed mining industry offers a unique opportunity to apply the tools of industrial organization prospectively.
(Of course, it is quite artificial to separate such analysis from
the formal modeling just endorsed. All the good current efforts
explicitly include the gross characteristics of market structure--
whether competitive in the case of copper, oligopolistic for nickel,
or monopolistic for cobalt--in their models.) There are a number of
dimensions along which the industry's possible evolution could profitably be analyzed. Candidates for examination include scale
economies, the degree of vertical integration, coverage of marketing channels, the site-specificity of the technology (here, the
number of sites again becomes important), corporate forms and character of early entrants, and possible entry barriers whether for
absolute cost reasons, technical or patent hurdles, or others. It
would be quite valuable to have thoughtful, prospective analyses of
industry structure, conduct, and performance, the latter obviously
in terms of allocative, technical, and dynamic efficiency.

Hand-in-hand with these questions are the issues of possible market
failure. Beyond small numbers and barriers to entry, there are a
series of questions about ocean mining that have received only
rudimentary treatment. For example, given the apparent resource
characteristics and the shape of the early industry, is the depletion rate likely to be optimal? Will there be a "common pool"
problem? Are externalities involved in information and production
troublesome? How about pollution and interference with other ocean
uses? Is claim-jumping likely in the absence of regulation? How
does the unavoidable joint production of the minerals affect the
analysis, if at all?[7]

These questions have been addressed, but, typically not in a very
sophisticated framework. For example, the small number of early
players and the multiple sources of uncertainty are frequently
neglected analytic factors that should surely impinge upon conclusions. Another challenge to analysts of possible market failure is
that of devising means of measuring and quantifying the extent of
any divergence from optimality. If there are problems with the unfettered development of this industry, how precisely could and
should domestic or international regulators respond? What is virtually certain is that environmental, health, safety, and financial
regulation will be present. But the levels and criteria for setting these levels remain unanalyzed from an economic point of view.

III. United States National Interest in Seabed Mining

General Economic Effects

No area of ocean resource study needs cogently developed analytic
frameworks and numerical estimates more than does the topic of
U.S. economic interest in the deep seabed. It is not that researchers and policy advocates have ignored the question of interest.[8]
But when the subject arises in a typical policy discussion, someone

mumbles something about lower prices, the notion of cartels is trotted out, and very soon the topic becomes strategic minerals and a "resource war." I will first briefly set out the obvious candidate measures of national interest and then discuss some of the reasons why their explicit analysis would be useful.

The effect of changes in prices and quantities is best captured as change in consumer surplus and producer surplus (profits). There are, of course, many pitfalls in such applied welfare economics exercises, but, for this study, a firm conceptual apparatus and order of magnitude estimates are all that are required. Using common welfare measures, is a freely developed ocean mining industry conceivably "worth" $10 million, $100 million, $1 billion, or $10 billion? (Of course, such estimates can be derived in a straight-forward manner from the market analyses discussed in the last section.)

A number of other indicators of national interest need to be studied and embedded in a comparable framework. These include changes in employment, balance of payments, and Federal and State tax revenues. (Much less quantifiable, and probably of much more long-term significance, would be analysis of ocean technological development and spinoff for other, non-nodule resources).[9]

Strategic Value

A great deal of useful analytic and empirical work needs to be done on the "strategic" value of seabed minerals. It is obvious that the existence of a strong domestic (or friendly) seabed mining industry could produce changes in the probability of successful cartelization of these minerals and of outright supply disruption. Should either of these events occur, their effects would be mitigated by alternate seabed sources of the relevant metals.

The magnitudes of such national ("political") security benefits can be determined, or at least bounded, by insurance-like analysis. Required are analyses of the (necessarily subjective) probabilities of cartelization or disruption and of their duration, as well as of their economic consequences for prices and quantities. Along with analysis of the appropriate attitude toward risk, whether Arrow-Lind public risk neutrality or the infinite risk aversion of a responsible government bureau, the security value of a nodule industry can be calculated, at least parametrically with respect to the above factors.

Such work, of course, has taken place in a variety of other contexts. Optimal stockpiling analysis uses the same factors and has been a frequent topic of study, especially in energy-related work. The appropriate "premium" for imported oil has a direct analytical analog in the now-important minerals that would come from the sea.[10]

(While I have cast this section explicitly in terms of U.S. interests, many of these effects generalize readily to other countries or to the rest of the world. For example, changes in overall consumer and producer surplus have bearing on worldwide economic efficiency while changes in probability and severity of mineral supply manipulation would mostly be relevant to industrialized consumer-importers.)

Policy Responses

There are several reasons for my emphasis on careful assessments of economic interest. To the extent that the Law of the Sea negotiations continue seriously, there is the implicit question of trade-offs between navigational interests and seabed mining interests. Some measures of national worth could at least help to inform such tradeoff discussions.

Achieving certain anticipated benefits of a seabed mining industry may require more government action than a green light to would-be miners. For example, suppose that the national security benefits of a more certain mineral supply were determined to be fairly large. If mining were privately profitable, such a value would be realized automatically as the industry developed. But if enough mining would not likely occur, whether for simple market reasons or due to onerous international treaty conditions, the government might wish to investigate a variety of policies to assure the security benefits.

It might consider changes in the size of national stockpiles or, perhaps, look into private stockpiling, possibly induced by tax law changes. Price supports for seabed or terrestrial mines could be considered. A variety of direct and indirect subsidies might be appropriate, whether in traditional areas such as research and development or in capital and operating cost assistance as in the maritime industry. The government might consider measures as mild as tax policy or risk insurance, as well as more drastic departures from usual practice such as setting up direct federal mining operations. Whether by any of these or other options, the point is easily stated: once the benefits of seabed mineral development are more precisely specified, much greater confidence can be placed in tradeoff decisions. At the same time, the effects of a variety of alternatives can be examined for relative desirability.

One rather more mundane aspect of better specification of the national interest lies in the evaluation of various tax and regulatory measures. In designing regulations to prevent pollution or to achieve a more nearly optimal depletion rate, the effects on various indicators of value can be more explicitly taken into account. When setting tax policies with respect to depletion allowances, investment tax credits, depreciation, and so forth, it is quite useful to gauge the effects on private attractiveness of seabed mining. An obvious place to begin such analysis is with the recently passed U.S. legislation that allows miners to proceed under domestic auspices. (An important set of considerations, especially to the extent that the security benefits of a domestic seabed industry are important, is the effects of different countries' tax policies on mining operations' location decisions.)[11] The hoped for reciprocating states regime would presumably have provisions that were close to those of U.S. law.

IV. An International Ocean Resources Regime And Its Implications

The task of giving specific meaning to the idea that ocean resources are the "common heritage of mankind" has occupied Law of the Sea Conference negotiations since 1974. By the time that the new American Administration decided to undertake a comprehensive review of the Conference in March 1981, a blueprint was in place for an international regime of nodule exploitation.

This blueprint is of special interest since, unlike most pronouncements relating to the "New International Economic Order," it is very specific and detailed. It sets out terms for who can mine the seabed and under what conditions. A regulatory body is described along with the charter of a new international economic entity that itself would mine on behalf of the world community. This proposed creation, resulting from thousands of delegate-years of effort, offers any number of tempting subjects for applied economic analysis. I have somewhat arbitrarily suggested three broad areas in which careful thought should produce useful results.

Equity Rationales for the "Common Heritage" Idea

A variety of political and economic trends were involved in the common heritage declaration and its evolution in the Law of the Sea Conference. There was the idea that first-come--first-served was an inadequate ethical basis for deep ocean resource exploitation. There was a cluster of emerging ideas on the strongly-felt injustice of the existing international economic system that found expression in the widespread desire for a "New International Economic Order." Among many Third World countries, the idea of "Permanent Sovereignty Over Natural Resources," which had animated many a renegotiation of domestic mineral concession arrangements, naturally extended to international stewardship of ocean resources that were located outside of any country's national jurisdiction.[12] A generalized Third World desire was manifest for control over markets (expressed most forcefully in the case of OPEC) and international organizations, as well as over natural resource developments. Many industrialized nations, to greater or lesser degrees, accepted or at least acquiesced in these sentiments. The suggestive power of the resulting concepts has been immense with respect to ocean resources.

The "common heritage" idea has been applied to or suggested for various other resources. These include the moon, asteroids, space in general, the electromagnetic spectrum, available geosynchronous satellite orbits, Antartica, and other ocean resources.

In general, however, there is not a well-articulated view of the intended meaning of such a phase although it is frequently interpreted to mean "public good" or global "commons." It involves an amalgam of several concepts. Allocation of property rights is, of course, central to the "common heritage" notion. Ensuring widespread participation in the development or exploitation of a candidate resource is often implied as is sharing in financial benefits derived therefrom.

A very useful exercise would be an investigation of several alternative conceptions of "equity" with respect to resources that may come to be regarded, in some way, as international or "common."

The development of analytic means for applying equity criteria would be a major step forward. The accustomed tools of the economist in these matters--techniques for efficiency analysis--useful as they may be, could be very profitably augmented by better-defined equity concepts for such resources.

Particulars of the Proposed Seabed Regime

At the outset of the LOS negotiations, the developed countries that aspired to seabed mining typically wanted an international body to act as a claims registry, more or less passively facilitating the orderly development of mining. Some revenue from operations might be shared in deference to the common heritage principle. Most developing countries, by contrast, wanted an international organization to be the sole exploiter of deep seabed nodules. With these positions in opposition to each other, negotiations soon deadlocked. In 1976, Henry Kissinger threw his weight behind a sort of "split-the-difference" compromise that has come to be called the "parallel" system. On one "side" of the system, private miners or state companies could mine, while on the other "side," an international entity--appropriately to be called the "Enterprise"--would mine directly on behalf of mankind.

In order for this compromise to have meaning it was necessary that the Enterprise have access to minesites, finances, and technology. Much negotiating effort was spent on these issues as well as on measures to protect current, land-based producers of the metals that were expected to come from the seabed.

Each of the proposed elements of the parallel system deserves careful economic analysis. In each case, there are many alternatives that were not adopted. I shall discuss briefly what seem to be the most important such questions.

Participation: The Enterprise

The proposed Enterprise represents a new economic form. It is not a one-person Smithian firm, a partnership, a private domestic firm, a state-owned enterprise, or a transnational corporation (no hierarchy intended). The Enterprise would be chartered by an international treaty, would be responsible to an international Authority (equipped with an Assembly and Council), and would attempt to earn mining revenues either for distribution to the world community or, by the Authority's choice, for reinvestment in further Enterprise operations. The form and charge themselves are worth some analysis.

To get underway, the Enterprise would receive half the estimated $1 billion required for its initial operation in the form of long-term, interest-free "loans," supplied by treaty signatories in accordance with UN assessments. The balance of its needs would be met by loans guaranteed by the states that are party to the treaty. Some good economic analysis needs to be done on the best way to allocate this money (drawing upon and further developing the tools of international public finance or international investment evaluation). The Enterprise could choose to carry out the first operation entirely on its own, it might engage only in mining, it might invest in other consortia, or set up a variety of joint venture arrangements, some of which undoubtedly await invention.

When a company makes application to mine on the "private" side of the parallel system, it must submit two prospected sites. The Authority chooses one of the sites, "banks" it for later Enterprise use, and the company mines the other. The possible gaming involved in this system is worth a bit of analysis.

As a result of developing country fears that the requisite technology would be unavailable to the Enterprise, the treaty makes mining technology transfer or "fair and reasonable commercial terms and conditions" mandatory as a matter of last resort. Before this remedy is sought, however, other means must be tried. There is room for careful study, inspired by work on technology transfer in developing countries, of the best ways of accomplishing the desired end.

The Enterprise is granted a variety of other privileges ranging from tax advantages to training programs. Coupled with liberal early financing, technology transfer, and banked sites, these characteristics could make the potential Enterprise a formidable economic force in the seabed. At a minimum, such an entity deserves thorough scholarly analysis both from a seabed point of view and as a model (positive or negative) for other international resource development.[13]

Sharing Financial Benefits: International Obligations of
Private Miners

The current LOS text embodies a complex financial formula (fee, royalty, profit-share) that has payments progressive with the real present value of the mining operation. The system is quite sophisticated from a risk sharing point of view. As modeling of the economics of a single operation evolves, the workings of this financial scheme should be investigated with an eye to the resulting rate of return to the miner and the magnitude of payments to the seabed Authority.

There are, of course, numerous alternatives to prior specification of the financial terms of seabed contracts. Separate negotiations could be undertaken with each new entrant. The Authority might auction sites, with the competing firms bidding bonuses, royalty or profit sharing rates, or even equity shares. Since these auctions would likely have only a small number of participants and other complicating factors such as uncertainty, some real care should be taken in their design.

A great deal of work has been done on the effects of different tax instruments on a firm's entry, timing, ore-grade and technology choices, output, pricing, and shutdown decisions. Especially where considerable uncertainty and risk aversion are present, the tax system can have a significant impact on these decisions. Some of this previous work should be applied more explicitly to the seabed case, as should knowledge about the administration of tax systems to multinational, vertically-integrated enterprises.

Protection of Land-Based Producers

A powerful group, spearheaded by Canada, was able to get a production limitation written into the draft treaty. For a period of twenty years, seabed production is supposed to be restricted to filling 60 percent of the growth increment in the world nickel market. Other metals are not explicitly mentioned.

This means of protecting land-based producers deserves thorough analysis on its own terms. How well does it protect those producers? Is the constraint likely to be binding? How many sites will be allowed? What is the welfare cost? (These questions all have straightforward answers to the extent that the analysis of Section II is completed.) What are the effects on industry structure?

There are some more basic economic issues as well. A variety of alternatives exist to the "preventive" approach embodied in the draft LOS text. For example, international commodity agreements, buffer stocks, or other commodity stabilization approaches are possible. A major class of responses would be compensatory rather than preventive. Compensation might go to those countries, which on the basis of equity criteria, were thought to need it the most (such as Zaire, whose cobalt earnings would be expected to plummet). Compensation might come directly from the financial payments of firms on the private side of the system or from expansion of existing mechanisms such as the International Monetary Fund's Compensatory Financing facility.

Overall Effect of the Proposed
International Regime for Nodules

There are a host of other aspects of the proposed Authority and Enterprise from the decision making and dispute resolution procedures to other types of regulation that I did not mention above (such as work requirements, reporting and auditing duties, national "antimonopoly" provisions, and methods of applicant selection). While analysis of the components is essential, an overall effort should be made to evaluate the workings of the proposed system taken as a whole.

If the scheme were adopted, what would be the results? Would either or both sides of the parallel system be likely to proceed at all? If so, how rapidly? How much would the banking system, financial arrangements, technology transfer provisions, and general dealings with an international regulatory body affect the rate and level of investment and technological development on the private side?

Would the two sides of the system quickly come to some sort of agreement to erect high barriers for potential new entrants? Would a seabed cartel be effectively stimulated? The list of such questions is obvious and almost endless. What is clear is the need for the careful application of economic analysis. In particular, the methods that have been used to understand domestic regulatory activities should be transferable, at least in part, to this proposed international creation. Beyond this analysis lies the question of alternative international regimes. Considering both efficiency and equity criteria, what systems would be preferable to the one that evolved from six years of diplomatic wrangling?

I have mentioned several other resources that are potential candidates for internationalization. Whatever one's reaction to those possibilities, it is clear that they supply much of the motivation for such detailed economic examination of the seabed case. Perhaps one of the most interesting studies that could be performed would contrast the relevant economic characteristics of these other resources with those of the deep seabed. Implications for preferred development regimes could then be set forth. If "Economic Lessons from Proposed Seabed Exploitation" were readily at hand for discussion of the next ostensibly common resource, the decades' research should be considered a rousing success.

Summary of Research Topics

Basic Economic Questions

1) Perform an economic analysis of the extent and significance of seabed nodules as a resource. Express this estimate as a probability distribution of the number of available minesites. Specify the dependence of this figure upon recovery efficiency, composite nodule value, and other relevant parameters. Discuss the relationship of this estimate to policy issues such as the importance of the resource, the potential evolution of the industry, and the affects of international production controls.

2) Update and advance existing modeling work on engineering and financial aspects of mining. As a high priority, make such models explicitly reflect the substantial underlying uncertainties of mining by the use of Monte Carlo methods. Discuss important long run considerations that will affect the engineering and cost aspects.

3) Update and advance existing analyses of the markets for copper, cobalt, nickel, and manganese. Evaluate significant trends in these markets. Pay particular attention to the long run marginal cost functions.

4) Integrate existing work under topics 2 and 3. Allow the amount of seabed production to be endogenously determined within the model.

5) Investigate market failures that could be encountered in unfettered development of the seabed mining industry.

National Interests in Seabed Mining

1) Based on the analysis of topics 1 through 4 above, develop estimates of the discounted value of changes in consumer and producer surplus that would result from the development of a seabed mining industry. Develop estimates of other indicators of national interest such as changes in employment, balance of payments, trade flows, and tax revenues.

2) Develop a clear economic conception of the strategic value of seabed resources. Estimate their magnitudes. Analyze a variety of possible alternative government responses--stockpiles, tax law changes, risk insurance, direct federal mining, and so forth--that might be appropriate if strategic benefits were significant and would not be realized by private actions.

3) Examine the potential of a developed seabed mining industry to stimulate a variety of other marine industries.

An International Ocean Regime

1) Develop alternate economic conceptions of the equity rationale that is implicit in the designation of seabed resources as the "common heritage of mankind."

2) Analyze the proposed international "Enterprise" as a new form of organization. Relate the analysis to the existing work on international organizations and state-owned enterprises.

3) Analyze the technology transfer provisions of the proposed treaty. Relate the analysis to what is known about technology transfer to developing countries by other means such as joint ventures.

Research topics raised during discussion include:

1. Develop an interactive computer model for studying strategic and economic impacts of mining issues. The framework should allow for changing weights on goals and for varying constraints. Dimensions of the model include: economic gains to the U.S., Third World countries, and others; environmental problems with disposal; and the effect of Law of the Sea (LOS) clauses and alternative stipulations on the pace and profit of development and its distributive effects.

Of particular interest are the likely benefits of exotic technology transfer to Third World nations and the impact alternative transfer requirements have on the economic attributes of the "exporting" agents.

2. Determine the expected international distribution of income likely to result from the following types of treaty agreements and stipulations:

   - Like-minded nations (first come first served);

   - Common heritage (parallel system, joint ventures);

   - Preventive protection of land based miners (stipulation of maximum percent of world supply);

   - Compensation of land based miners.

3. Analyze past attempts at international transfer of advanced technology. Evaluate them for successful techniques and inhibiting factors (e.g., legal situation, incentives, contract specifications). A possible industry for study would be nuclear energy. Develop a set of criteria for "successful transfer."

4. Determine the effect of continued uncertainty about LOS on sea mining development, present investment in new land mines.

5. Determine the projected costs to present mining (sand, etc.) operations if the Law of the Sea applies.

Notes

1. Other promising minerals are discussed in McKelvey (1980).

2. For the low estimate see Bastien-Thiry, Lenoble, and Rogel (1977): 86, 171; the high number is referred to in Johnson and Logue (1976).

3. A good example of the approach that should be extended is in Pasho and McIntosh (1976); the best summary and comparison of existing work is in Frazer (1980); also Pasho (1979).

4. The best such studies are Little, Inc. (1977), recently summarized and updated in Enzer (1980) and Nyhart, Antrim, Capstaff, Kohler, and Leshaw (1978), soon to be completely revised.

5. See, for example, Welling (1976). These factors are also considered at length in Antrim, Spencer, and Woodhead (1980).

6. Adams has done a number of good econometric studies over several years under UNCTAD auspices. Some of the recent results are summarized and discussed in his "The Law of the Sea Treaty and the Regulation of Nodule Exploitation" (1980); Interim results of important joint work undertaken by MIT and Charles River Associates are discussed in Reddy and Clark (1980) and in Burrows (1980).

7.   See Sweeney, Tollison, and Willet (1974).

8.   Charles River Associates, in particular, has been making extremely useful analyses and estimates. See Burrows and Reddy and Clark.

9.   Conrad Welling, in particular, stresses the national importance of this long-term aspect.

10. See Hogan (1980).

11. This point was raised by Dan Nyhart.

12. G.A. Res., 1803, U.N. GAOR, Supp. (No. 17), 15 U.N. Doc. A/5217 (1962).

13. Douglas McCleod, in his 1980 MIT masters thesis (Sloan School), made a good start on a number of these questions.

References

Adams, F.G. (1980). "The Law of the Sea Treaty and the Regulation of Nodule Exploitation," Journal of Policy Modeling 2(1): 19-33.

Antrim, L., P. Spencer, W. Woodhead (1980). Copper, Cobalt, Nickel, and Manganese, Office of Ocean, Resources, and Scientific Policy Coordination, United States Department of Commerce, Washington, D.C.

Bastien-Thiry, M., O.P. Lenoble and P. Roge. (1977). "French Exploration Seeks to Define Mineable Nodule Tonnages on Pacific Floor," Engineering/Mining Journal 178: 86, 171.

Burrows, J. (1980). "The Net Value of Manganese Nodules to U.S. Interests, with Special Reference to Market Effects and National Security," in J. Kildow, Deepsea Mining (Cambridge, Ma.).

Eckert, R. (1979). The Enclosure of Ocean Resources (Stanford).

Enzer, H. (1980). "Economic Assessment of Ocean Mining," paper presented at the Joint Meeting of the Institute of Mining and Metallurgy, The Society of Mining and Engineers of the AIME and the Metallurgical Society of the AIME, London.

Frazer, J. (1980). "Resources in Seafloor Manganese Nodules," in J. Kildow, ed., Deepsea Mining (Cambridge, Ma): 41-83.

Hogan, W. (1980). "Import Management and Oil Emergencies," Energy and Environmental Policy Center Discussion Paper E-08-80, Kennedy School of Government, Harvard University, September.

Johnson, D.B. and D.F. Logue (1976). "U.S. Economic Interests in Law of the Sea Issues," in R. Amacher and R.J. Sweeney, eds., The Law of the Sea: U.S. Interest and Alternatives (Washington, D.C.): 37-76.

Kildow, J. (1980). Deepsea Mining (Cambridge, Ma.).

Little, A.D., Inc. (1977). "Technological and Economic Assessment of Manganese Nodule Mining and Processing," prepared for the Department of the Interior (Stock No. 024-000-00842-B), Superintendent of Documents, Washington, D.C.

McKelvey, V.E. (1980). "Seabed Minerals and the Law of the Sea," Science, 209 (25 July): 464-472.

Nyhart, J.D., L. Antrim, A. Capstaff, A. Kohler, and D. Leshaw (1978). "A Cost Model of Deep Ocean Mining and Associated Regulatory Issues," Massachusetts Institute of Technology Sea Grant Program, MIT SG-78-4.

Pasho, D.W. (1979). "Determining Deep Seabed Minesite Area Re-quirements--A Discussion," in United Nations Ocean Economics and Technology Office, ed., Manganese Nodules: Dimensions and Prospectives (Dordrecht): 83-112.

Pasho, D.W. and J.A. McIntosh (1976). "Recoverable Nickel and Copper from Manganese Nodules in the Northeast Equatorial Pacific--Preliminary Results," Canadian Institute of Mining and Metallurgy Bulletin 69: 15.

Reddy, B.J. and J.P. Clark (1980). "Effects of Deepsea Mining on International Markets for Copper, Nickel, Cobalt, and Manganese," in J. Kildow, Deepsea Mining (Cambridge, Ma.).

Sweeney, R.J., R.D. Tollison and T.J. Willet (1974). "Market Failure, the Common Pool Problem, and Ocean Resource Exploi-tation," Journal of Law and Economics (April).

United Nations General Assembly Resolution 1803, United Nations General Assembly Official Records, Supp. (No. 17), 15 U.N. Doc. A/5217 (1962).

Welling, C. (1976). "Ocean Mining System," Mining Cong. J. (Sept.).

Discussion
Deep Ocean Mining Resources

Conrad G. Welling

I. Introduction

The extensive exploration of the continents has been under way for
many centuries. However, in this century, particularly the latter
half, exploration activity has expanded at a rapid rate. The development of indirect measurement techniques, based upon magnetic,
electric, sound, chemical, radiation and electromagnetic measurements has played a very important part in this rapid expansion by
greatly aiding the explorer. Regardless of advances in exploration
technology and techniques, however, one of the principal driving
forces for exploration activity is the ability economically to mine
the ore once found, and second, but not least, the ability to market the minerals once processed. This is no less true for marine
minerals.

The physical characteristics of seawater--its near opacity to electromagnetic waves, its high dynamic drag and its great depths--have
been and will continue to be a great challenge to efficient marine
exploration. Hopefully, continued technological developments of
the eighties will make it possible in the 90s to design and build
marine exploration equipment with greatly improved efficiencies.

Only manganese nodules have been discovered in sufficiently extensive deposits and with sufficiently high grade, to attract the
mineral industry. None of the other discoveries of non-fuel marine
minerals have produced the necessary incentive, except in a minor
way.

For example, the largest ocean mining activity of non-fuel minerals
involves the aggregate of sand, gravel and shells. These and other
placer deposits, such as cassiterite (tin) and Ilmenite (titanium),
are all located on the shallow waters of the Continental Shelf and
are extracted by use of conventional dredge operations. In comparison to land mining, however, these activities cannot be considered large. There have been no discoveries on the Continental
Shelves other than the previously mentioned activities that could

lead to the development of large scale mining. The main deterrent has been the lack of efficient exploration tools and the resulting high exploration cost.

II. Exploration

Figure 1 illustrates the various techniques being used today by the manganese nodule exploration activities (Gronon, 1980). The dredge bucket (A) is used principally to obtain a large sample of nodules, approximately 500 kilograms per haul. The most used device (B) is the bounce sampler. This device allows hundreds of samples to be taken over a wide area during a cruise. It recovers nodules from a two-tenth square meter area of the sea floor. The box corer (C) takes an undisturbed section of the seafloor nodules and sediment to a depth of approximately one-third meter. The deep tow device (D) is towed a few meters above the seafloor and can be equipped with combinations of cameras, television, side scan sonar and precision depth sonar. This device is valuable for its ability to give continuous seafloor microtopography and nodule information. Its disadvantage is the low tow speed of approximately one knot or less and narrow sweep width (a few meters for cameras and a hundred meters or so for side scan sonar). It is here that industry is giving attention to improvements, i.e., increased speed and greater sweep width. Precision depth sonar (E) is being improved by use of narrow stabilized beams, multiple beams and towed versus hull mounted systems. Water samplers (F) are used mainly for environmental data. Navigational accuracy is obtained by ocean floor sonar beacons (G), surface radio beacons (H) and satellite navigation (I).

Exploration vessels are becoming increasingly more sophisticated with the use of shipboard computers and techniques being developed not only for use at sea but ashore for the analysis of the data. The manganese nodule deposits represent a sufficiently attractive potential to encourage the development of improved exploration equipment and techniques. To many in the field these improvements are not coming rapidly enough.

The manganese nodule deposit is rather unique in that it is basically two-dimensional. Since the deposit is on the surface of the seafloor and covers hundreds of thousands of square kilometers, topography is all important. Our knowledge of the topography of the ocean floor is minimal compared to our knowledge of the topography of the land masses of the world. Accessibility explains the difference.

Charts of the ocean floor are created through the use of deep towed vehicles equipped with camera, TV and precision sonar. Only a small fraction of the area of interest can be covered in any reasonable time. The slow speed and narrow sweep width give at best a sweep rate of a few square kilometers a day. The area of interest is on the order of tens of thousands of square kilometers or more. Therefore one has to plan on a statistical basis. What is the probability of occurrence of an impassable object in a given area?

Nodule Exploration and Survey Techniques

NAVIGATION

BATHYMETRY

SURVEY OF ORE DEPOSITS

OCEANOGRAPHIC/
METEOROLOGICAL

ENVIRONMENTAL

1000
2000
3000
4000
5000

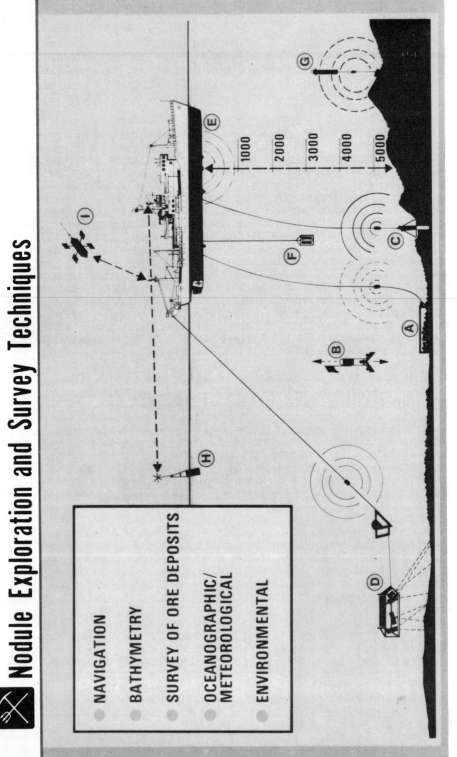

FIGURE 1

Another factor, besides the topography, is the nodule abundance. Contours of nodule abundance reveal large patches with dimensions up to several kilometers or more. The relationship between topography, scarps, obstacles, and nodule occurrence is not too well known; neither, for that matter, is nodule grade which in itself is considered the most important factor.

III. Mining Development

As is the case with many new development programs, the principal objective is to determine the problems and to minimize the attempted solution of the wrong problems or in some case non-existing problems. The principal objective of the follow-on pilot plant stage is the satisfactory solution of the problems. One has to make many assumptions at the beginning of a program, and system analysis and operations research applied to conceptual designs can provide useful guides.

The development of deep ocean mining is a revolutionary process, not an evolutionary one. Ocean mining takes place today with conventional dredges at water depths of less than 30 meters. There is little in the state-of-the-art of conventional dredging that is applicable to deep sea mining in water approximately 5000 meters deep. By contrast, the excellent development of the offshore oil industry has been an evolutionary process. The increase of water depth from a few meters to 300 meters or more took place over a period of thirty to forty years.

Perhaps ocean mining may experience a reverse process. Once the technology and operational experience is developed in the deep ocean, the know-how will be extended to the shallow water deposits. One of the deposits for which this may be true is phosphate nodules at water depths out to several hundred meters.

Industry has virtually completed the first phase R&D program and thus we have confidence of technical feasibility. To get to this stage, however, it was necessary to make a number of assumptions.

Initially many years ago, a number of simplified assumptions were made about the design of the equipment necessary to mine the nodules in quantity. Serious conceptual design studies and scaled down experiments on land quickly dispelled many of these illusions. It became apparent that a simplified dredge approach would not provide the quantities of nodules needed for commercial production and that economy of scale was a very important factor in the design. Economics required several million tons of nodule production per year.

The design of a technically advanced system is an iterative process. At each stage in the design evaluation, not only must feasible technological factors be considered but also the economic impact and potential markets can not be ignored. The high capital and operating costs of marine systems place a premium on utilization and efficiency. In spite of this, the vast extent of the manganese nodule deposits led early designers to the conclusion that mining efficiency was not of great importance. Nothing could be further from the truth. Even though the total tonnage of nodules on the ocean floor can lead to extensive mining for a century or perhaps several centuries, there are limits to the economically recoverable deposits at any particular time.

Throughout history the economical cutoff grade of any particular ore has steadily decreased leading in most cases to an increase in the total resources. There is no reason to believe that the case will be different for manganese nodules. The exploration costs involved in delineating the nodule ore body, however, combined with the limits placed upon the total area obtainable under an exploration license and the need to meet production goals, strongly suggest that the mining operations must be carefully planned and executed with great efficiency.

The combination of large scale operations and high efficiency has a dominant influence upon miner system design (Welling, 1979)). First of all precise control of all major functions at the miner is necessary. This, in turn, requires maximum real time information on the activities of the various miner elements. The major control functions required of the miner include, speed and direction, depth of cut of pickup head, and sizing and feed of nodule particles to the lift pipe. The large vertical pipe length of approximately 5,000 meters places a speed limit of approximately one to two knots on the ship and miner which necessitates a miner width on the order of thirty meters or more.

In order to obtain the engineering and operational data necessary for the design and construction of a commercially feasible deep sea miner, an approximately one-tenth scale miner was tested at sea from the Glomar Explorer. An illustration of the miner in the well of the Glomar Explorer is shown in Figure 2. The most prominent features of the test miner are the large Archimedes propulsion screws on each side. TV cannot provide sufficient visual coverage as it is limited to approximately 30 meters. Extended coverage forward and to the sides is obtained by use of a high resolution sonar.

IV. Economics

The industry has essentially completed the preliminary R&D stage and is preparing to initiate the pilot plant stage which will take approximately five years and cost two hundred and fifty million dollars. Required is a demonstration at sea of a scale-up miner that can mine a thousand tons or more a day of nodules. The miner should be able to operate many days, perhaps a month or more to provide the necessary operating knowledge and reveal any reliability weaknesses. The engineering design and construction of the miner plus the conversion of a suitable ship could cost one hundred and fifty million dollars. The pilot processing plant is estimated to cost approximately fifty million dollars and require approximately twenty thousand tons of nodules for testing. An additional fifty million dollars is required for supporting activities for both the mining and processing during the expected five year period.

FIGURE 2

95

Provided that a successful pilot plant stage has been completed in the planned five years and that the economics and political environments are still favorable, the engineering and construction of the commercial plant can begin. It is estimated that an additional five years and approximately one billion dollars are required for this phase. The costs are based upon a mining system providing three million dry metric tons per year to the processing plant. The costs are made up of three major subsystems. The mining system, i.e., ship and mining equipment--three hundred and fifty million dollars; the nodule cargo vessels and port facilities--one hundred and fifty million dollars; and the processing plant, land and tailing disposal facility--five hundred million dollars.

Government policy decisions which impinge on these costs are listed below:

o   Environmental regulations;

o   Domestic taxation/international payments;

o   Depletion;

o   Depreciation;

o   Investment credit;

o   Production limitations;

o   Technology transfer.

Revenue forecasts for a period of 10 to 20 years in the future are difficult. Over half the revenue is projected to come from nickel production in the nickel, copper, cobalt (three metal) system. Estimates of investment and operating costs are based upon projected designs which, in turn, are based upon the results of the research and development program. While the effects of inflation are taken into consideration, it is more important to study the sensitivity of the projected return on investment to variations in the assumptions made. One of the most common problems encountered in large programs is time delays either during development or in having the commercial plant reach planned operating capacity. As an approximation, a two year delay in the program after the R&D phase would lower the expected internal rate of return from 10 to 8 percent.

Another important economic factor is the comparison of projected ocean mining costs with land based producers. Figure 3 illustrates the estimated nickel equivalent price required to obtain a 15 percent internal rate of return on investment. The data are in terms of 1979 dollars. For the land mines the data is plotted in dollars vs. the cumulative percent of free world production. In other words, when nickel was below $3.00 only about half of the world nickel land mines were in the 15 percent or more internal rate of return category. For the high cost land mines, the price of nickel would have

96

FREE WORLD NICKEL

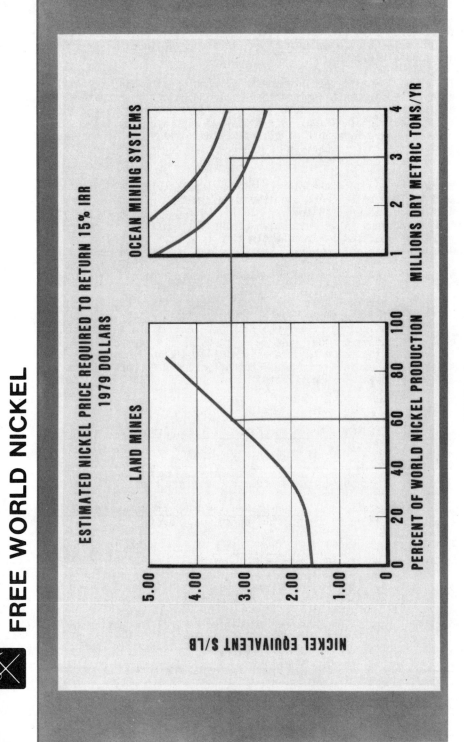

ESTIMATED NICKEL PRICE REQUIRED TO RETURN 15% IRR
1979 DOLLARS

OCEAN MINING SYSTEMS

LAND MINES

NICKEL EQUIVALENT $/LB

PERCENT OF WORLD NICKEL PRODUCTION

MILLIONS DRY METRIC TONS/YR

FIGURE 3

to be about $4.00 in 1979 dollars for reasonable profitability. The price would have to be even higher to encourage investment in most new land nickel mines.

The comparison with expected costs of deep ocean mining systems, especially for the three and four million ton per year systems, indicate that manganese nodule mining would be competitive with new land-based nickel mining. Ocean systems have high capital costs, but, they have favorable direct operating costs. One of the factors influencing this comparison is the expected lower energy requirements for ocean mining.

Because of the unsettled international legal environment, it could well be 1984 or later before investment in non-fuel ocean mineral development occurs. A ten year period is required for attaining full operations after initiation of the pilot stage. Therefore the mid-1990s represents a reasonable time frame for the beginning of a deep ocean mining industry. It is logical then to assume that it could well be the turn of the next century before the knowledge developed in the deep seabed is expanded and applied to other areas.

Possible other incentives will develop before then, such as certain critical metal shortages, vastly improved exploration tools, or accidental discovery of a large rich ore body within the 200 mile exclusive economic zone. The 200 mile exclusive economic zone is the area of the seabed under national jurisdiction that would not be subject to the control of the International Bed Authority established by the Law-of-the-Sea Treaty.

References

1.   D.S. Cronan. Underwater Minerals 1980, Academic Press. New York.

2.   Mero. The Minerals Resources of the Sea, 1965 Elsevier Publishing Co., Amsterdam-N.Y.-London.

3.   United Nations. Manganese Nodules Dimensions and Perspectives, 1979, D. Reidel Publishing Co., Boston.

4.   Heezen, Tharp. World Ocean Floor, Lamong-Dogherty Geological Observatory, 1977 - U.S. Navy Office of Naval Research.

5.   Welling. "An Advanced Design Deep Sea Mining System," OTC 4094 Offshore Technology Conference, 1981, May 4-7.

6.   Welling. "The Economics of Marine Mineral Production--A Private Sector Profitability Analysis," University of California, Santa Barbara, Marine Sciences and Ocean Policy Symposium, 1979.

Oil and Gas Resources

Arlon R. Tussing

I. Offshore Oil and Gas in the Energy Economy

Petroleum,[1] including both oil and natural gas has become the industrialized world's dominant fuel in the Twentieth Century because
fluid hydrocarbons have been the cheapest sources of energy for
most purposes. Though these substances are produced from depths as
great as ten kilometers beneath the earth's surface, natural or
artificial hydrostatic pressures will push them up towards the surface. Man, in other words, does not have to take himself into the
bowels of the earth in order to mine petroleum but, rather, relies
on a combination of geological and geophysical interference, luck,
and the ability to pierce the earth's crust with thin tubes of
steel, to find oil and gas and induce it to come to him. Once
brought to the surface, moreover, fluid hydrocarbons are among the
cheapest of all substances to transport long distances, either by
pipeline or by waterborne tankers.[2]

Notwithstanding their "depleting" nature, oil and gas are still the
cheapest energy sources on a global scale, reckoned according to
the resource costs of extracting, transporting, and converting them
to final products. To date, most of the world's petroleum has been
produced--and is still being produced--from a handful of "supergiant"[3] fields for which the resource cost of discovery, development, and production are only a few pennies per barrel.

The outlook for finding many more deposits of conventional oil or
gas of such large size and low production cost is rather dim in the
United States (and particularly onshore in the Lower 48). On a
world scale, however, the resources of conventional petroleum in
supergiant fields that have already been discovered (but in large
part not yet developed into "proved reserves") could sustain current levels of consumption for several decades--and at a marginal
economic cost (the unit cost of producing a given added volume) no
higher than pre-1973 (constant-dollar) world prices.

During the 1970s, however, a combination of circumstances conspired
to make Middle-Eastern and other potentially low-cost supplies

unavailable at prices that had any recognizable connection with economic costs. In addition, because the resources of low-cost petroleum in the United States had been explored, extracted, and consumed at an increasing pace for over a century, they were already depleted to a point where there seemed little prospect that new domestic supplies of conventional oil and gas could eliminate the need for oil imports at any foreseeable price.

As a result, the economic cost of new domestic oil and gas, and the administered price of imported oil, both appeared to be significantly (and permanently) higher than the cost of several alternative sources of energy, including electricity from coal and nuclear-fired steam turbines, and liquid or gaseous fuels synthesized from coal, oil shale, or vegetable matter.

The effect has been nearly a decade in which the marginal cost of energy for the United States as a whole has been determined by the rising price of imported oil. By the late 1970s, virtually all parties had come to assume, however naively, that this price would continue to rise (even in constant-dollar terms) without limit. Consumers, investors, and energy producers have been adapting to these higher costs, realized and anticipated. In several ways, among them by:

- Reducing total energy consumption;

- Substituting some conventional energy forms for others (e.g., coal and natural gas for fuel oil);

- Exploiting conventional resources more intensively (e.g., recovering a larger fraction of the "oil-in-place" from developed reservoirs; searching for and developing smaller, less productive, or otherwise high unit-cost oil and gas fields);

- Revising energy forms and technologies (e.g., synthetic gas from coal and wood heat) that had been displaced by hydrocarbon fluids;

- Adapting familiar energy forms to new uses (e.g., alcohols and compressed gases as transportation fuels); and

- Exploiting previously uneconomic kinds of resources (e.g., liquid fuels from oil shale and tar sands; and methane from tight or deep formations, Devonian shale, and geopressurized aquifers).

Each of these adaptations to higher prices has been a way of accepting higher economic costs for petroleum fuels. There are, however, two kinds of adaptations, not totally separable, that have the potential of at least in part circumventing diminishing returns to human effort and capital in producing fluid hydrocarbons--technological advance and geographic advance. The United States still has at least two major geographic frontiers for oil and gas production:

100

Alaska and the ocean bottom (for which the bulk of the promising acreage is adjacent to Alaska).[4] The chief economic significance of the new frontiers is their endowment with conventional oil and gas resources that are yet largely undepleted and, in most cases, unexplored. Unlike the onshore basins of the Lower 48, in other words, it is not necessarily true of the Outer Continental Shelf (OCS) that "all of the easy oil and gas has already been found."

On the average, geologists do not consider today's exploration frontiers to be quite as favorable geologically for petroleum as the onshore territories of the Lower 48 have proved to be. Among the OCS provinces, moreover, the most promising still seems to be one where the most activity has already taken place: the Gulf of Mexico off Louisiana.

Nevertheless, the great acreage of sediments that remains untouched by the drill almost guarantees some pleasant surprises. The on-shore area of Alaska is equivalent to about one-fifth of the land area of the Lower 48; while the area of the U.S. continental shelf and slope having a sea depth of less than 600 meters is equivalent to about half the nation's onshore land area. On both the Alaska and offshore frontiers, moreover, the oil and gas-producing industry is only two decades old, and returns to exploration effort, measured in reserves added per foot of exploratory drilling, remain an order of magnitude higher than the onshore Lower-48 average.

So far, only the Upper Cook Inlet basin, which contains only about 4 percent of Alaska's onshore and offshore sedimentary acreage, and a part of the submerged lands of the Gulf of Mexico containing less than 4 percent of the nation's total OCS acreage, have been explored intensively enough to show diminishing returns to exploration and development effort (and even there the statistical evidence is ambiguous). Both the United States Geological Survey (USGS) and oil-industry geologists, moreover, regard certain frontier pro-vinces--offshore Louisiana and Alaska's Arctic Slope plus the adja-cent shallow waters of the Beaufort Sea--as the most promising petroleum-exploration targets under the American flag.

The OCS therefore offers a fresh beginning for oil and gas explora-tion on U.S.-controlled territory, an opportunity to find and de-velop bigger and more productive deposits of conventional oil and gas than most petroleum geologists think remain to be found onshore in the Lower 48.

Obviously, searching for and producing oil and gas under the ocean entails costs for equipment and procedures that are not required on land--very large added costs in the case of deep stormy waters like the Gulf of Alaska or the North Atlantic, or shallow ice-stressed waters like those off Western and Northern Alaska. In 1980, the average offshore Louisiana oil or gas development well cost $3.0 million or $293 million or $293 per foot drilled; the average onshore well in Arctic Alaska cost $4.1 million or $386 per foot. These costs are, respectively, about 9 and 12 times as much per well and 4.2 and 6.2 times as much per foot as the average onshore well in Texas. Thus far, the unit cost of drilling in the Beaufort Sea appears to be on the order of $10 million per well and $1,000 per foot.[5]

On the other hand, we can still expect a new offshore Louisiana gas well to produce about forty times as much gas, and a Beaufort Sea oil well to produce on the order of one hundred times as much oil per day as their onshore Texas counterparts. On balance, then, the great appeal of exploration for petroleum in frontier areas is as a repository of nearly untapped resources that offer some hope of producing substantial amounts of energy whose marginal economic cost is low compared with either the price of imported oil or the cost of non-petroleum domestic alternatives.

The best indicator of the economic promise that major and independent oil and gas producers and others (gas transmission companies, chemical manufacturers, etc.) see in the OCS is the billions of dollars in cash that they have paid in recent lease sales for drilling rights on unproved acreage. (In the 1981 Louisiana offshore sale, Exxon alone exposed more than $700 million.) Industry's optimism about the offshore oil and gas frontier contrasts dramatically with the general reluctance of the same companies to invest in synthetic fuels unless they receive hundreds of millions of dollars in federal subsidies, price supports, or loan guarantees.

II. The Burden of Justification

The social justification for finding and producing offshore oil and gas is identical to the social justification for economic activity generally--it is a means of producing something that people want at a cost no greater than the value people put on it. A reasonable first approximation of the value of OCS petroleum is the price of its energy equivalent in imported oil. For this reason, expectations regarding future foreign oil prices are clearly crucial parameters both in explaining the great sums that oil companies are willing to gamble on OCS exploration programs, and in projecting the net social benefits (the present value of the stream of benefits less the present value of the stream of costs) from OCS production.

For most goods, the demonstration that their production generates substantial producer surpluses or economic rents--that their market value exceeds their resource cost, in other words--justifies a powerful presumption that production is a Good Thing. Likewise, the need for a subsidy--the fact that resource costs exceed market values--normally justifies a negative presumption. Either of the two presumptions might conceivably be rebutted by a showing of significant "external" costs or benefits--social costs that are not paid by direct consumers of the goods, or benefits that the direct consumers do not receive--and that these benefits and costs do not cancel each other out.

The prices companies are willing to pay for oil and gas exploration rights, and the prices final consumers are willing to pay for fuel, do indeed leave out certain identifiable costs and benefits of OCS production. Some of these "externalities" can be measured or estimated with some degree of confidence, while others are nearly immune to quantification. The public debate on offshore oil and gas exploration and production is an unusual one, however, because it focuses primarily on comparing external benefits and costs (like national energy self-sufficiency, or damage to fishery resources); secondarily on the means by which the federal government can maximize the rent it extracts from a given acreage, and hardly at all on the problem of maximizing the first-order or "internal" net benefits to society of developing offshore hydrocarbon resources, or of optimizing the total combination the resource makes to social welfare.

If my unsystematic personal observations about public attitudes are accurate, the attitudes themselves are a worthy object for social-scientific research. Why, indeed, is there a general presumption against developing offshore hydrocarbons? Some parts of the answer are clear:

- It is hard for most people (including many professional economists) to see how a market for rights in unknown quantities of hydrocarbons in unspecified mixtures, producible (if at all) at costs that are currently unknown and unknowable, can be relied upon to allocate or value oil and gas exploration rights with any degree of efficiency or accuracy.

- The resource is controlled by the federal government under a regime which makes it unavailable for development, so that an oil and gas lease sale appears to be an affirmative "public" act that requires a "public" justification--a justification, that is, in terms of externalities.

  The usual presumption that the existence of a market incentive to produce OCS oil and gas truly reflects society's preferences is often absent in this debate. Even among professional economists with a strong free-market bias, the dominant attitude seems to be that offshore petroleum leasing must serve some exceptional social "need" that is not reflected in the price of fuel.

- Almost all parties to the public debate, along with the scholarly authorities that provide their ideological armor, explicitly or tacitly assume that OCS oil and gas will be "price-takers" at the OPEC-equivalency price (in the absence of wellhead price controls, at least). As a result, the savings to society that result from substituting OCS oil and gas for OPEC oil, synthetic fuels, or other higher-cost alternatives, are not expected to affect the prices paid by final consumers.[6]

- Not only do the prevailing market models predict that OCS petroleum will create no consumer surpluses, but the leasing system has been designed expressly to allow the government as landowner to expropriate any producer surplus generated in production, and thus to capture the whole social increment in the form of lease revenues (bonuses, rentals, and royalties) and taxes.

- The federal government is everybody and hence nobody, and thus public enthusiasm for its fiscal interests is scant. The objective of maximizing federal leasing revenues if and whenever leasing is otherwise in the "public interest" is, however, approved of by a large number of educated and articulate citizens who view oil-company profits and producer surpluses exactly as they would "exploitation" or "the private appropriation of surplus value" if they had been educated in the Marxian language. To many progressive-thinking Americans, that is, it is less important that OCS petroleum can increase society's total product than it is to prevent some of the increment being captured by the hated oil companies.

  At bottom, the main permanent constituency for OCS leasing is the government itself. The fact that OCS petroleum generates revenue without requiring Congress to levy a tax on anyone guarantees it the patronage of at least some Congressmen, plus, of course, the Treasury Department and the Office of Management and Budget.

  The leasing system is not totally efficient in expropriating producer surpluses and economic rents, however; if it were, not even the oil companies would bother to advocate OCS development. But imperfect as the leasing system may be, it is effective enough to restrict the private constituency that actively campaigns for offshore petroleum development to something far smaller and far less zealous than the income it generates would suggest.

- State and local governments do not share in federal OCS revenues as they do in the revenues from onshore mineral leasing and sales, timber sales, and the like. Affected communities thus seem only to bear the external costs, real or imagined, from offshore petroleum development, and receive none of the direct benefits. It is not surprising, therefore, that California, Massachusetts, and Alaska politicians have been in the forefront of opposition to acceleration of OCS development.

It is instructive to compare the power and determination of the lobbies that support protection and subsidies for the merchant marine (which reduce the national income) or the tobacco growers (who may rank first among all industries in the negative externalities they generate), with the near-invisibility of the political forces advocating OCS development for private or sectoral gain, despite a potential contribution to the national product that is greater by two orders of magnitude.[7]

III. Politics of the Research Agenda

The polemical parts of this paper emphasize that economic research which is relevant to policy is by definition political, in at least two senses: (1) Definition of a research problem, choice of vocabulary, definitions, and model structure are inevitably infused with the cultural and political values of the investigator, his discipline and that of his peers, and his social environment; while (2) the acceptability, influence, and impact of intellectual effort depend at least as much on its timing and apparent salience to the time, and on the interests it serves (or seems to serve) as upon those formal qualities that scholars would list in a discourse on scientific method.

Any plausible agenda for economic or public-policy research related to offshore oil and gas has certain inevitable components. Some of the most conspicuous issues are marine-resource issues only incidentally, or relate to offshore petroleum in exactly the same way they relate to petroleum generally. The projection of national and global energy demand, or the level of world oil prices; analyses of petroleum industry structure and behavior; and the effects of oil or gas price controls and petroleum-industry tax policy, are all such instances, and I have not rigorously segregated them here from those that are chiefly or wholly marine-resource issues. The chief categories of research relevant to the offshore petroleum resource include:

1) The character and size of the resource base, and the supply function (i.e., the schedule of production rates or volumes vs. costs) that flows from the character of the resource;

2) The schedule and pace of resource development;

3) The system of assigning exploration and production rights, and for structuring and allocating resource rents. (Under present institutions, these issues are largely summed up by a consideration of "the leasing system."); and

4) The external costs of offshore petroleum exploration and development, largely in the form of damage or the risk of damage to fisheries and other living resources of the sea and its estuaries, shorelines, etc.; aesthetic values; and the social stability of small coastal communities.

While most scholars would likely agree that these four categories contain most of the vital issues of economic analysis and social policy, any ordering of the detailed research agenda is an intensely political task, which cannot help but reflect one's ideology and predispositions. Better information about the offshore petroleum resource base, for example, can have several legitimate analytical and policy purposes.

For example, the notion that it is desirable for the government to "take an inventory" of OCS oil and gas resources or "know what's out there" prior to leasing are almost axiomatic both in systems which view offshore petroleum development as a "public good" (or "bad") and whose necessary justification is an ability to serve some exceptional collective "need," and in policy models where the chief objective is for the federal landowner to extract the last measure of rent from each acre it leases.

A supply function for offshore oil and gas would, similarly, have many analytical and policy uses, but the most insistent clients for such information have been, on the one hand, industry spokesmen seeking a "scientific" cloak behind which to argue for higher prices or lower taxes and, in the opposite camp, public servants, public-interest lawyers, and others whose aim is to design an ideal leasing scheme, or minutely stratified tax and price-control measures (like the so-called windfall profits tax and the Natural Gas Policy Act) in order to fine-tune the federal government's capture of economic rents generated in production, or their transfer to consumers.

A theoretical case for providing more geological information to the government's lease administrators or to the public might rest on a finding that something about the bidding system or the structure of markets for exploration rights prevents effective competition in OCS lease sales, or that successful bidders in lease sales are systematically averse to exploration risk (or significantly more so than society).

The first proposition is one of the most intensively worked-over in petroleum economics, and the literature leans heavily toward support of the hypothesis that OCS lease markets are effectively competitive. The second proposition, that oil companies individually are risk-averse with respect to investments in acquiring individual lease tracts, is intuitively unappealing, and even if it were accurate, it would not necessarily follow that bidders were risk-averse in the aggregate, much less the set of successful bidders with respect to the tracts on which they were successful.[8]

Subject to these caveats, it seems to me that the willingness of oil companies to pay up-front cost for drilling rights establishes a prima facie presumption that society will indeed benefit from leasing the tract in question. If effective competition for the tract does exist among bidders, how much geological information was in the files of the Interior Department or what the Geological Survey (USGS) thought about the probable reserves contained in each tract is of little relevance for lease administration.

The relative importance of the various other categories of information or analysis concerning OCS petroleum depends, similarly, on the policy purposes for which one wants them. Subject to this warning, the remainder of the present paper surveys some of the salient issues.

IV. The OCS Petroleum Resource Base And Its Supply Function

Estimation of the Petroleum Resource Base

Most petroleum geologists believe that all of the "petroleum" fluids found in the earth's crust are products of organic sediments that have been subjected to great heat and pressure. Such deposits occur only where suitable "source rocks" occur in the right relationship with suitable "reservoir rocks" having an effective "trapping mechanism" to prevent the hydrocarbons from escaping into the atmosphere and/or oxidizing.

The total hydrocarbon resource base in areas with a long petroleum-producing history is usually estimated by plotting cumulative production or additions to proved reserves against time or (in the more sophisticated variants) some proxy for exploration effort such as the number of feet of exploratory-wells drilled; this function is then fitted to a logistic curve or other function chosen a priori, and the curve is then extrapolated to a point which corresponds to the complete exhaustion of the resource. The area under the curve represents the total original endowment of recoverable resources, and the area to the right of today's date (or the cumulative level of exploration effort to date) represents the remaining recoverable resource.

In many developed petroleum-producing areas, the fit of such curves and their predictive power has been excellent. Unfortunately, the same family of curves can readily be scaled to fit any trend in which a positive rate of increase declines over time, and there has developed an influential school of zealous curve-fitters who purport to build forecasting tools by fitting such two-factor functions to continental and global exploration experience extending over many decades. The practitioners of this technique have had little inclination to consider how the aggregate production history might be affected by differences among areas, and changes over time, in exploration and extraction technology, relative prices, and development institutions.

The volume of economically recoverable oil and gas in frontier areas is generally estimated by "geological inference," whose systematic component is based upon multi-factor analogies with well-studied portions of already-explored and largely depleted regions, on the basis of the estimated volume of various categories of source rocks and the presence or absence of suitably situated reservoir rocks. The most ambitious resource-assessment program of this kind is that of the USGS, which publishes basin-by-basin projections of ultimately recoverable oil and gas for onshore and offshore regions of the United States at 5 percent, 50 percent, and 95 percent confidence levels.

The basin-by-basin projections of the USGS are revised periodically on the basis of new information, new definitions (the cut-off water depth in offshore areas, for example), changes in the professional staff's theories of regional geology, and changes in methodology. The USGS also makes estimates for smaller areas--including single lease tracts for use by the Bureau of Land Management (BLM) in administering lease sales--employing essentially the same procedures, but using more location-specific data.

Both steps in the estimation process--extrapolation of total reserves in regions with a substantial production history, and the process of analogizing to frontier areas--deserve critical scrutiny. To my knowledge, however, no one has attempted a retrospective evaluation of the USGS forecasting methodology on the basis of the results of subsequent exploration. In the meantime, the USGS estimates should be viewed only as a ranking of various areas by one competent team of geologists in terms of their relative attractiveness for exploration.

Even apart from the apparent absence of systematic retrospective evaluations of USGS performance, there are several reasons not to take anyone's projections of absolute resource volumes for offshore and other frontier areas too seriously. The estimates are for an arbitrary but only vaguely defined fraction of the "in-place" hydrocarbons in each region. Methane, for example, is found everywhere in the earth's crust, including volcanic rocks--in apparent contradiction to the dogma that crude oil and natural gas are exclusively of biological origin. The Devonian shales of the Appalachian region alone, and the geopressurized aquifers along the U.S. Gulf Coast, are each believed to contain about three orders of magnitude more methane than the USGS estimates of the total remaining domestic resource of "natural gas."

One problem, therefore, is that the resource-base estimates expressly refer only to that part of the in-place resource which is discoverable and economically recoverable with current technology, under current economic conditions. The meaning of both of these phases is nebulous, and the phrases become hopelessly ambiguous in connection with the ultimate size of a resource, most of which will inevitably be produced (if at all) with different techniques and under different economic conditions from those that prevail today.

In this context, the Survey's recent decision to publish its estimates in probabilistic terms is both a service and a disservice. Posting a broad range of plausible resource values between the 5-percent and the 95-percent confidence levels indicates clearly that such projections are essentially guesses, and reduces the tendency of unsophisticated readers to accept them for planning or policy purposes as if they were precise accounting measures. The use of percentage confidence intervals, on the other hand, tends to mislead more sophisticated readers by suggesting that there is actually a 90-percent probability that the oil or gas ultimately recovered will actually fall between the two estimates.

This is not a correct inference, because the method the USGS uses to arrive at its numbers does not treat all its variables, parameters, and structural relationships as random variables. The

basic geological theories behind the method (that petroleum is exclusively of biotic origin, for example) do not vary, nor do the
chemical and physical boundaries of the substances it considers as
"crude oil" or "natural gas," nor does the content of "current
economic conditions" or "available technology."

While the volume of oil or gas that is recovered can be expected to
depart somewhat from the USGS estimates because of theoretical
errors, changes in the physical or chemical characteristics that
define the limits of "crude oil" or "natural gas," the development
of geophysical techniques for locating "stratigraphic traps," or
future changes in real energy prices, the probability of such developments is not incorporated into the USGS method for establishing the "probable" range of resource volumes.

The Link Between the "Resource Base" and the
Outlook for Discovery and Extraction of Hydrocarbons

Even if the estimates of the economically recoverable oil and gas
resource in each region by the USGS or some other institution were
both unambiguous and accurate--say, within a factor of two--these
estimates themselves would still be of little use for economic
analysis or policy formation, except as an index of the relative
attractiveness of different regions as exploration targets. We
would still have little systematic knowledge about the effects of
deciding to lease a given OCS area on the time profile of exploration, development, and production effort, or on the volume of
hydrocarbons that will be produced over a given period.

Other variables besides the total resource of a whole region (or
even its average resource volume per unit of area) are vital for
projecting discovery and production costs or the timing and rate
of future production. It is crucial, for example, to know whether
surface geology and seismic surveys indicate that the 1-billion
barrels of crude oil in the "median" estimate for a given OCS area
is likely to be contained mostly in one or two already identified
and precisely located giant "structural" traps, in a few large
"stratigraphic" traps that today's technology can not locate from
the surface, or in dozens of smaller fields and reservoirs of
various kinds.

While contemporary geological science does have a great deal to say
about these issues, this knowledge does not seem to be a systematic
input to the Interior Department's development and production
scenarios for the current generation of OCS lease sales. Organization; manpower, materials, and equipment procurement and mobili-
zation; exploration and information-processing sequences; and
institutional rhythms (including formulation of impact statements,
permitting, and litigation) will interact with the geological
peculiarities of a particular area to dictate the pace of exploration and development. The effect of all these factors will be
modified at random, moreover, on the basis of early discoveries
or the lack of them.

Microeconomics of Petroleum Exploration and Production

Estimates of ultimately recoverable offshore oil and gas resources may not have much usefulness for economic analysis or policy formation, in light of their definitional and methodological uncertainties and the murky process by which they have to be translated into variables that have operational consequences--proved reserves, for example, or barrels per day of production over a given period. The most useful microeconomic data are those that could be assembled to make up a series of supply functions for offshore hydrocarbons--in other words, the expected combinations of fixed and variable costs at various plausible rates of production.

Different dimensions of these supply functions can be viewed as mapping the long-term marginal costs of OCS oil and gas production instantaneously and in response to movement along several successive variables:

- Additional development and depletion of known reserves on tracts that are currently under lease;

- Additional exploration investment on currently leased tracts, and on other tracts currently or presently available for lease;

- Exploration and development of the latter tracts;

- The availability of additional tracts for lease;

- The increase in knowledge (including geological knowledge obtained in the exploration and development of earlier prospects) and the improvement of technique; and

- The depletion of prospects that are "easiest" to find and produce.

Unfortunately, we do not even have a satisfactory recent point estimate for the marginal economic cost of OCS oil or gas. Even a single-point marginal resource-cost estimate based upon information from all post-1970 lease tracts would be the beginning of wisdom in comparing the social cost-effectiveness of OCS leasing with conservation, coal-conversion, synthetic fuels, or whatever, or in assessing the supply effects of the Windfall Profits Tax, natural-gas price deregulation,etc.

In principle, one can impute the marginal costs which petroleum-producing companies expected for oil and gas from the more-recently leased OCS tracts--acreage still without significant discoveries--but only by analyzing the successful bids in the light of what is known about the geology of individual tracts, and only with insider information (or by making heroic assumptions) about the discount rates used by the companies, and what they in turn assumed about the course of future oil and gas prices. Mapping successive

dimensions of the OCS oil and gas supply function in the order set
out on page   would require increasing amounts of geological and
engineering information (or increasingly arbitrary assumptions),
much of which would have to be presented and processed in probabilistic form.

The work required to produce such supply functions would be stupen-
dous. Exploration effort, for example, is not homogeneous. The
process of adding to reserves is a sequence of analytically-separable
phases--surface geophysical and geological exploration, stratigraphic
testing, new-field exploration drilling, delineation drilling, and
field development--the mix and relative costs of which are highly
variable. Before these stages can be comprehended in the construction of oil and gas supply functions, however, we need a better
theoretical understanding of the relations among them, and the way
in which expected petroleum prices, the current reserve-to-produc-
tion ratio, the availability of "wildcat" acreage, tax treatment,
and regulations regarding unitization and conservation, bias the
mix of current exploration investments toward one phase or another.

The supply functions for inputs to petroleum exploration and development, and particularly the lags in their supply response, also require better analysis--if only because the alleged shortage of
drilling rigs, tubular goods, and petroleum engineers is a frequent
weapon in the ideological armory of those who deny the possibility
of significant energy-supply responses to accelerated OCS leasing
or price decontrol.

In each phase of exploration, moreover, different teams of geologists and engineers interpret the same data very differently, and
approach a given exploration play with a different geological theory
and a different exploration strategy. There are many anecdotes
about instances in which one exploration team has made a big discovery on a play that has been thoroughly worked over and rejected
by many others. Such differences in judgment are also reflected
dramatically in the fact that a single tract will receive bids
differing by one, two, or even three orders of magnitude in a single
offering.

I am not aware of any systematic analysis of the importance of
"multiple perspectives" in petroleum exploration, or of its policy
implications. To what extent do variations in the number of bidders
on oil and gas lease tracts and the range of bids on individual
tracts truly reveal the existence of different geological evaluations, or different exploration strategies?

If multiple perspectives do indeed have a powerful effect on the
discovery outlook, perhaps the duplication of effort involved in
competing pre-leasing geophysical programs, and the fragmentation
of control over prospective petroleum-bearing structures through
leasing small tracts, are not as uneconomic as some scholarly com-
mentators have assumed. The same issues are of course central to
any evaluation of proposals for a "two-stage" leasing systems or
pre-lease governmental exploration programs.

A greater number of competing exploration teams will surely increase the likelihood of exploratory success; but there are surely diminishing returns to this effect as well. Where, for example, does duplication of effort or fragmentation of the target acreage begin to offset the advantages of multiple perspectives? Increasing the number of teams working a single frontier play from one to two probably has a powerful effect on the expectation of success, but what about an increase from seven to eight, or seven to fifteen?

V. The Long-Term Demand for Natural Hydrocarbons and the Optimum Rate of Depletion

There is a body of orthodox economic theory that deals with the optimum rate of depletion of a mineral resource. Decision rules that flow from that body of theory depend, inter alia, on (1) the choice of a discount rate, (2) the expected long-term price trend for the resource product (reflecting growing scarcity or abundance of the product and/or its substitutes), and (3) the rate at which depletion raises the marginal cost of the resource product.

The lack of consensus on (2) and of useful information on (3) would make the existing analytical apparatus practically useless for making policy about the rate at which OCS acreage should be leased, explored, or depleted, even if the real-world analytical problem were not complicated by nonmarket price determination, royalties and Windfall Profits Taxes, trade barriers, questions about the national-security or foreign-exchange premium to be imputed to domestic production, etc. Yet no intellectually respectable alternative is in sight.

In the absence of an appropriate body of theory, even professional economists often tend to speak casually of the alleged failure of market prices to take account of the "user cost" of exhaustible resources (the present value of depleting the resource some time in the future, rather than today), and the imperative for saving a supposedly appreciating stock of goods for "future generations" or for "a time we really need it."

Perhaps we can excuse biologists and engineers this kind of nonsense, but economists ought to be aware that:

- There are already several acceptable long-term substitutes for every use of conventional petroleum at costs in the vicinity of, if not lower than, its current world price;

- The world's known resources, and the known U.S. resources, of "near-petroleum" (heavy oil; oil shale; tar sands, methane in deep basins, Devonian shale, geopressurized aquifers, and hydrates, for example) are equivalent to hundreds, thousands, and sometimes tens of thousands of years of consumption at present rates;

- Technical advance will undoubtedly widen society's technological options regarding both the production and the consumption of energy; and finally

- Future generations will probably be richer than we are.

A related truism found in the classical economic literature, but whose relevance to the present is doubtful, is the notion that the discount rates private firms apply to decisions regarding the exploration, development, and production of exhaustible resources are higher than society's true rate of time preference and that, as a result, private firms would deplete OCS oil and gas resources too rapidly. The notion that industry, left to itself, would develop hydrocarbon resources too rapidly is implicit in the very idea that the government should have a "leasing schedule."

In the absence of that questionable assumption, however, poor Mr. Watt is almost right, notwithstanding his lack of finesse, in trying to make the entire OCS available for leasing now, with tracts put up for auction or otherwise disposed of whenever serious interest appears. His approach has a more respectable theoretical foundation than the previous policy of the Interior Department, which has been deliberately dribbling out a mixture of good, bad, and indifferent prospects selected on wholly noneconomic criteria.

The assumption that industry's discount rate is higher than that of society has a certain intuitive appeal, as does the notion that it is the "social discount rate" that ought to be reflected in the exploitation of publicly-owned resources. These propositions have no operational meaning, however, in a world where no consensus is possible on the true discount rate for either private or social decisions, and in which "society's" only operational proxy is the federal government. What reason is there to believe, in particular, that elected officials or public servants--say, either Mr. Andrus or Mr. Watt--have time horizons that are longer, closer to that of "society as a whole" (whatever that may be), or more rationally based than those of the multinational oil companies?[9]

VI. Leasing Policy

Strategies for leasing oil and gas exploration rights have received exceptionally intense scrutiny in the last decade, and a massive theoretical and analytical literature exists comparing various bidding systems for their effect on investment, the time profile of production and the volume of hydrocarbons ultimately recovered, and above all, the present value of the landlord's income.

One part of this literature seems to confirm the superiority of conventional cash-bonus bidding (with, perhaps, a shift from an ad valorem royalty to a net-profit-share royalty), but the larger part of the recent theoretical effort seems to present a strong case for radical changes in bidding and leasing arrangements--two-stage leasing, for example, and royalty or net-profit share rates as the bid variable. These analyses have provided the foundation on which Congress and the Alaska legislature, for example, directed their respective resource-management agencies to experiment with several different bidding systems.

It appears, however, that the responsible personnel in both the government land-management agencies and in the industry abhor such innovations, and that independent exploration companies (who were among the purported beneficiaries of the lower front-end charges under the new system) shun royalty-bid sales just as much as did the major operators, and certainly no less than they did cash-bonus bidding. The reasons for the nearly universal opposition of those who must operate the leasing system are not clear, but they may be as interesting and as important as the outcome of the various mathematical models that provided the justification for the new procedures. (Some of the potential mischief that multiple bidding systems and variable royalties can create is about to surface in the Beaufort Sea, where the companies will surely propose to establish production units that include tracts leased under several different arrangements.)

Government lease administrators, like industry explorationists, tend to hold traditional views and to favor the conventional system of sealed bonus bids. The case for the traditional leasing system includes the practical considerations that it is the easiest to administer and to understand, and the most difficult to corrupt, as well as the theoretical/empirical proposition that bidders regard geological risk as a fair gamble.

Thus, if the traditional view is valid, wider dissemination of geophysical and geological information among prospective bidders before each lease sale is not likely to have a significant long-run effect on either the aggregate value of the winning bids or on the outlook for exploration success. The same view also implies that the amount of geophysical and geological information the government as lessor has for its own use will not significantly enlarge its lease revenues, unless the number of bidders on each tract is very small.

Both Federal and State land-management personnel seem to favor this analysis with respect to the bidding system but, paradoxically, they constantly seek authority to require lease operators to disclose more and more proprietary information, on the ground that "we need to know what we're selling," and that such information is necessary in order to decide which bids to reject as too low. If the companies truly regard exploration as a fair gamble, and the market for exploration rights is workably competitive, however, it is not clear to me just how official behavior would or should be affected by the possession of additional geological information, or what effect it would have on the aggregate outcome of the leasing process.

Other leasing-policy issues that are amenable to systematic analysis but which have received far less attention than bidding systems include the optimum size and number of tracts to be offered in a sale, and the term a lease may be held prior to commencement of drilling, unitization, development for production, or commercial production.

VII. External Costs of Offshore Petroleum Operations

Evaluation of the adverse effects of offshore oil and gas exploration and production is an area that is not particularly amenable to rigorous economic analysis, because it involves a comparison of uncertain but quantifiable commercial resource values with uncertain and nonquantifiable environmental, aesthetic, and emotional values. It is, of course, an ideologically charged area, in which the case for commercial oil and gas production is handicapped by the factors I enumerated early in this paper.

The most conspicuous issues under this category relate to (1) the short- and long-term effects of discharges of oil and other materials into water or the air on the marine environment, and to the size-frequency distribution of discharges from various types of petroleum-related offshore activity in various environments; and (2) the short- and long-term effects of disturbing the ocean bottom, wetlands, estuaries, beaches, and the onshore coastal zone by drilling, dredging, laying of pipelines, platform and terminal construction, and the like.

In the absence of dramatic new findings regarding cumulative damage from hydrocarbons discharges, the potential economic benefits from oil and gas production almost certainly probably swamp out the expected value of all quantifiable damages that might result from such discharges. In many cases, indeed, they are likely to overwhelm the gross economic value of the assets placed at risk.

Even if the expected quantifiable economic damages per unit of output (e.g., per billion barrels of oil produced) are significant, they still may not be large compared to the expected damages from alternative energy-related activities, the most conspicuous of which is shipment of onshore-produced or imported oil by tanker, but which include onshore oil and gas production, the mining and use of coal, and the production of synthetic fuels. A number of studies have compared the volume of residuals produced by various modes of energy production, transportation, and conversion--in each case I have examined, offshore petroleum comes out as the second cleanest (after, ironically, nuclear electric generation, which is inferior only with respect to waste-heat discharges). I have not seen any systematic analyses, however, of the marginal rates of exchange among various energy alternatives in terms of their environmental impacts.

VIII. Containing the Oil (Research) Glut

Energy was the great public-policy problem of the 1970s. During this period, no domestic energy resource appeared to have a better potential than offshore petroleum for increasing the nation's self-sufficiency in energy. Unlike (say) nuclear power, fusion, synthetic fuels, or central-station solar power, OCS oil and gas could displace oil imports at lower rather than higher marginal economic costs, and with organization and technology that was already proved and in place. The money that was at stake in OCS leasing policy amounted to billions annually.

The 1970s also brought a record high tide of environmental con-
sciousness, environmental activism, and environmental legislation
and regulation. Protection of marine life and ecosystems, and the
aesthetic integrity of the seas and coasts, was a major focus of
this movement. Offshore oil and gas development was an apparent
threat to these values and a major object of environmentalist
lobbying and opposition.

The strategic considerations, economic stakes, and environmental
controversy attached to national policy toward offshore oil and gas
made it one of the most extensively debated, researched, and written-
about concerns of our era. The literature generated by this concern involves the physical, biological, and social sciences; engineering; economics; law; ecology; community planning; etc.; and every
conceivable permutation and combination of these disciplines.

The result of this concern is an enormous library in hard covers,
and in scholarly, professional, and trade-journal articles, conference proceedings, and professional papers. This conventional
literature is, however, only a minor fraction of the serious research and analytical literature about offshore petroleum. There
exists as well a good deal larger body of public, semi-public and
nonpublic "ephemeral" literature.

There is no complete catalog of bibliography of research and
analysis about offshore petroleum economics and public policy, and
there is no human being who comprehends even the general scope and
content of more than a few subcategories of the literature I have
mentioned here. Therefore, perhaps the most crying research need
at present in the area of marine oil and gas resources is simply
a systematic and responsible review and synthesis of the already
existing literature on the subject.

Notes

1.   The term "petroleum" has two common meanings. In the narrower
      but more popular usage, the word refers only to certain liquid
      hydrocarbon mixtures: crude oil and the liquid products re-
      fined from it, like gasoline and fuel oil. The more general
      usage, which we adopt here, includes all of those naturally-
      occurring hydrocarbon fluids (both liquid and gaseous) that
      are commercially produced today from oil or gas wells: crude
      oil, natural gas, and natural-gas liquids (NGL's or "conden-
      sate").

      Natural hydrocarbons vary considerably in molecular size and
      structure, and each hydrocarbon compound can take a solid,
      liquid, or gaseous form depending on the prevailing pressure
      and temperature. Crude-oil fields or reservoirs are those
      petroleum deposits which contain hydrocarbons that are liquid
      at atmospheric pressures and temperatures, while natural-gas
      fields or reservoirs are deposits containing only hydrocar-
      bons that are gases under atmospheric conditions. However,
      most commercially recoverable petroleum deposits contain

mixtures of liquid and gaseous hydrocarbons that have to be separated near the wellhead into two or three streams for transportation and processing.

2. Crude oil is almost an ideal cargo for large ocean-going vessels. It has just the right density--slightly lighter than water so that the entire hull-space can be filled with cargo and the vessel will have a low center of gravity, which improves its stability. A liquid at atmospheric pressures and temperatures, crude oil does not require closely controlled conditions on board, is easy to load and unload, and is relatively insensitive to contamination.

    Shipping gases by tanker is a wholly different matter. Vapors must be chilled and liquefied in costly facilities that consume substantial amounts of energy as well. The lightest hydrocarbons such as methane, ethane, and ethylene have especially low boiling points, and vessels designed to carry them feature expensive cryogenic (refrigerated or super-insulated) compartments.

    Pipelines are the ideal transport mode for gases. In a pipeline, extremely high pressures can be used to squeeze even the lightest hydrocarbons into dense-phase fluids which contain nearly as much energy in a given space as liquids, and these fluids can be pumped long distances with a relatively modest loss of energy in the form of compressor fuel.

3. We can think of an oil or gas field as a supergiant if its commercially recoverable reserves are on the order of 109 cubic meters (or 1010 barrels) of crude oil, or an energy-equivalent volume of natural gas (2 x 1012 cubic meters or 6 x 1013 cubic feet). Examples in the United States are the East Texas (oil), Prudhoe Bay (oil and gas), and Hugoton-Anadarko (gas) fields.

4. We might also note two other geographical (or geological) "frontiers" that petroleum geologists have generally recognized only in the last decade: (1) the "overthrust belts" of the Rocky Mountains (including Alaska's Brooks Range) and the Appalachians--potentially oil-and/or-gas-bearing sediments buried under unpromising (often igneous) rocks; and (2) very deep (ten kilometers or more) sediments beneath strata that were previously considered to be "basement."

5. This estimate was derived from proprietary accounts of total 1980 and 1981 on-site expenditures by two companies in the area of the December 1979 joint federal-state lease sale, coupled with the estimates of total footage drilled by these two companies from scouting reports (oil-patch jargon for industrial espionage) by two other companies. The ratios may be misleading, because the expenditure categories in the total may differ significantly from those included in the JAS survey and because of possible inaccuracies in either set of

figures. More important, these ratios attribute to the initial exploration wells the whole cost of constructing gravel pads and access roads that will ultimately accommodate many more wells, particularly if (as is likely) some of the prospects are developed for production.

6. The model in most people's minds seems to be a nearly perfect market that joins world petroleum supply and demand functions, the sum of whose price elasticities is nearly infinite, so that the expected consumer surplus from OCS petroleum production is approximately zero. Even the most committed partisans of OCS leasing and development reason from models which allocate the whole social benefit between producer surpluses and land rents, with a ritual salute, perhaps, to national security benefits that they typically measure by the savings to the federal treasury from the nation's ability to get by with a smaller Strategic Petroleum Reserve (SPR).

   So long as this model dominates scholarly, official, and popular thinking, we should not look for any labor, liberal, or "consumer-advocate" constituency in favor of accelerating OCS petroleum production. And since the popular economics of the American elite does not recognize economic rents or producer surpluses (under any name) as respectable concepts or legitimate sources of private income, OCS petroleum can not hope to gain a broad "public-interest" constituency either.

7. Consider, on the one hand, the Congressional ban on exports of Alaska oil. The tiny maritime lobby has been consistently successful in defeating "big oil" and "big government" on this issue, perhaps because few Americans recognize producer surpluses or resource rents as social benefits if they accrue first to oil companies or the federal government.

   Contrast the outcome of this contest with the division of economic benefits from OCS petroleum production. Here, the revenue-maximizers in Congress and the executive branch have nearly always triumphed over sectional and private sectoral interests. They have avoided having to share any offshore oil and gas leasing revenue with the States and have persuaded the courts to prohibit state or municipal taxes on OCS production, producing properties, or on the landing or transportation of OCS oil and gas.

   The federal fiscal lobby has also beaten back "location" (claim-staking) systems like the general mining laws, the lotteries and other noncompetitive allocation systems which prevail in federal offshore oil and gas leasing, and the work-commitment bidding system used in some countries to maximize on-site inputs to exploration and development (rather than the excess of outputs over inputs).

In 1973, moreover, the federal government reclaimed authority over offshore oil and gas conservation from the coastal states (Louisiana and Texas) which had previously been able to restrict federal OCS production in order to protect the market for onshore oil, which was produced on state, county, and voter-owned land, mainly by small companies, and (unlike OCS oil and gas) subject to state taxation.

The revenue-maximizers have, indeed, suffered political defeats, but only by consumer rather than producer or sectional interests: Congress refused, for example, to exempt OCS crude oil from the petroleum price controls that were in force between 1973 and 1981, or from the ceilings that still remain on natural-gas prices, despite the fact that the federal government could expect to capture in royalties and taxes at least 57 percent of the incremental revenue from old leases and at least 100 percent of the incremental revenue from new leases through its capitalization into lease bonuses.

("At least," because exemption from price controls would also tend to shift the expected and realized economic margins, increasing the acreage apparently worth exploring, the apparent optimum intensity of exploration, the number of prospects deemed worth developing for production, and the volume of hydrocarbons economically recoverable from each developed reservoir.)

8. The evidence implies that the discounted-cash-flow (DCF) rate-of-return on investments in OCS petroleum exploration and development (including lease-bonus outlays) has not been significantly above--and appears in fact to have been lower than--the return on other oil-industry investments. If the OCS lease market were less-than-effectively competitive, successful bidders must have a tendency to be risk-seekers rather than risk-avoiders. (Or, is it plausible that the bidding system, by selecting the highest bid from a range that may vary by one or two orders of magnitude, systematically select bids that are too high?)

9. The opposite hypothesis has just as much a priori appeal to me: it may be government which has the steepest time-preference function, reflecting the mind-set of civil servants who think in terms of one, two or, at most, three-year budget cycles, acting under the direction or prodding of elected or politically-appointed officials preoccupied with the next election. There are good intuitive grounds to suspect that this tendency, if it exists, is not a peculiarity of democracies and that third-world tyrants, for example, would typically have shorter planning horizons and higher subjective discount rates than major oil companies.

Research topics raised during discussions include:

Bidding and Leasing

1. Compare expected net present value of revenues and distributional effects from various bidding systems such as the present system (risk share); the old system, profit share; or bid plus percentage of price on international market.

2. Analyze the economic consequences of varying limits on the time between leasing, exploration and development.

3. Analyze the impact of an accelerated leasing schedule on exploration, production, the level of competition in the industry, consumer prices, foreign exchange, public revenues from bids and royalties and dependence on foreign crude.

4. Evaluate the net effects of biases (including subsidies) which accelerate or slow the development of OCS petroleum.

Regulation, Environment, Fishing

5. Analyze the impact that alternative forms and levels of regulation (performance, design, etc.) have on incentives for development and environmental protection.

6. Attempt to ascertain if there exist situations permitting simple regulation systems which can, once in place, decrease the need for government intervention.

7. Estimate the expected costs and benefits of requiring a "front end environmental impact statement (EIS)" and the EIS required prior to drilling.

8. Estimate the value of environmental damages from alternative sources of crude at various sites.

9. Estimate the contributions of OCS drilling and resource extraction activities to other uses (e.g., effect of rigs on fishing).

10. Evaluate means of distributing revenues at the federal, state and local level, as well as to various administrative areas.

Oil and Gas Resources

Mason Gaffney

Arlon Tussing's paper[*] impresses one at first as too casual. No
sources are cited for sweeping, controversial allegations; subjective preferences are commingled with objective reasoning; the ex-
position is often foggy, terms loosely defined and variously used;
tendentious codewords and catchwords creep in to shift from analysis
to exhortation; and so on. One needs a very good opinion of Dr.
Tussing to accept on his authority various judgments and evaluations
advanced to be facts. But I do hold such an opinion, even though
the present work is not the basis for it. His attitudes and judgments, formed from experience during a distinguished career in this
field, carry weight and deserve serious review.

Further, the casual style is itself an artful form of persuasion.
He wins our confidence by reciting standard economic premises, and
by appealing to our group loyalty against ill-advised natural scientists, before leaping over to controversial doctrinal views and derivative policy ideas. The offhand style lets him martial arguments
on one side of an issue without our, and perhaps his noticing that
he is screening out the other side. The result can be disarmingly
persuasive, the more so when new topics and subtopics fly by with
bewildering acceleration.

To bring some order, I list below ten doctrinal positions and seven
policy positions which form the core of the paper. I comment on
most of them as they go by.

A.   Tussing's doctrinal positions.

      (Tussing's position in caps; Gaffney's comment in lower case.)

1.   THE DISTRIBUTION OF WEALTH AND INCOME IS UNIMPORTANT, SO LONG
      AS GOVERNMENT DOES NOT GET TOO MUCH OF IT. OPTIMAL ALLOCA-
      TION IS ALL THAT SHOULD CONCERN ECONOMISTS. The damage done

---

[*]   The revision of Arlon Tussing's paper was submitted too late
for the discussants to make any modifications of their comments in
light of the new version.

to good men by an education at Chicago and its colonies (in this case, both) can last a lifetime; post-hypnotic suggestions keep popping up. But we need not press this point, for Tussing moves to a worse position: he laments that "The public debate...focuses on...the means by which the federal government can maximize the rent it extracts...and hardly at all on...maximizing...benefits to society... ." Thus he presumes a conflict between a landlord collecting the market rent, and efficient allocation of land. Again, "...the size of the welfare benefit (is)...a higher concern than the ability of the federal treasury to capture the whole of that benefit." To most economists these objectives are at least compatible; to some of us they are inseparable.

Tussing also tells us that we (I obstinately refer to the U.S. Government as "we" in this context) should not have a leasing schedule, but transfer all the OCS to private hands right away, unless we believe society has a lower discount rate than private "individuals" (corporations in this case). May we not also dislike the distributive results of mass transfer of undrilled structures?

a) The financial strength to gamble on possible cash flows several decades after bidding is limited to a few giants of the Exxon class. The effect would be further to concentrate key resource control, in an industry whose competitive structure is parlous at best. That aside, advance sales effectively screen out most potential bidders because few investors today can tolerate payback times as long as 10 years, let alone 30 and more as mass sales would require. Massive advance sales would quickly exhaust most buyers and turn into a giveaway to a very few of the super-rich.

b) Among speculators, the gains to wealth would be distributed more by chance than by functional contributions to the commonwealth. The results of gambling are inherently regressive.

c) We will sell or lease more advantageously if we, rather than the buyers, choose the time and place of sale or lease--a privilege accorded almost all other owners of real estate, so why not us, too?

d) The industry already carries hundreds of millions (sic) of acres of undeveloped leases, well beyond its capacity to use for years, held for speculation, for sequestering private information, for preemption, and for tax shelter games.

e) With every passing year that we hold back disposal, we and they all know more on which to base reasoned bids and hold-back prices, and to optimize the time of exploration and severance. We gain the spillover benefit of information from tracts that are drilled, and cash in on drainage sales.

f)   The long term evolution of land disposal policies in most countries is progressive, offering real hope for better future ones, if not posthaste at least post-Watt.

g)   If our government be viewed as alien--as "them," not "us"--it is less so than the multi-national oil corporations whose influence in Washington is the cause of our alienation. We cannot even learn who owns their shares, but we do know many large owners are foreign, and that whoever owns and controls them cares not for us, but uses us for naval protection, a national base, and subsidies.

2.   "FINDING AND PRODUCING OFFSHORE OIL...IS IDENTICAL TO...PRODUCING SOMETHING... ." DEPLETION IS EITHER INCONSEQUENTIAL OR UNKNOWABLE AND HENCE TO BE OVERLOOKED. But, to many of us, finding something that already exists, and in limited quantities on a small and shrinking planet, is significantly distinguishable from producing things by labor using renewable resources. For one thing, it often entails territorial expansion, with military costs and risks, and displacing other claimants. Few of us today (I hope) would follow the ultimate Chicago guru, Frank Knight, who wrote that the cost of "killing or driving off previous occupants" of land is just another investment. For another thing, each discovery depletes the world stock of undiscovered resources to be found by later seekers. For yet another, the business of severing natural goods from the ground involves an element of stripping, so some people justly object to the word "producing." "Exploiting" may be loaded the other way, as Jerry Milliman has complained, and "severing" may be a properly neutral term. Whatever the word, a charge for depletion is in order, and Tussing treats this with extraordinary insouciance.

As to macro-economics, payments for bonuses and royalties to landowners, private or public, are not payroll payments that make jobs in the same sense as payments to ordinary producers. Rent aside, the business is highly capital-intensive because of the uncommonly long lag between investment and recovery of capital. In a capital-short era, this trait warrants unfavorable notice. In a time of high unemployment, the passive investment in accruing values in situ is clearly inferior to the active investment that creates payrolls.

3.   IF "PRODUCTION GENERATES SUBSTANTIAL ECONOMIC RENTS...PRODUCTION IS A GOOD THING." True enough with renewable resources, but it makes sense to hold back exhaustible oil and gas while their value in situ is rising faster than money in the bank. Rent is good, but more is better. And if someone plans to hold out for the rise, why should we turn this rent over to others on the rapid part of the growth curve? One could make the case by demonstrating that government is bad at calculating optimal sales schedules, but very good at auctioning, and this is the case the industry pushes and Tussing is endorsing.

But is it not suspiciously selective to argue that government is inept at doing what you want and efficient at doing what I want?

4. PRICE SIGNALS TELL US WHAT CONSUMERS REALLY WANT. This sounds like a theory of first best, with no recognition that demand for energy is heavily encouraged by various consumption subsidies. Subsidies to urban sprawl are a case in point: they may more than double the demand for gasoline in the U.S., which has created in our times the most energy-using settlement pattern ever known to man. Roll-in pricing by power utilities is another subsidy to consumption, and one could go on, and on. On the cost side, the partial repeal of the old depletion allowance has barely scratched the surface of tax preferences to oil and gas, a subject so vast that I modestly refer you to my forthcoming article in the summer 1982 Natural Resources Journal. One theme there is that the tax treatment of leasehold abandonments (an ordinary loss deduction) is outlandishly preferential and creates a powerful tax-induced motive to play the game of leasehold acquisition. Whether I be right or wrong, the question of tax subsidies and other subsidies surely wants a look before anyone interprets industry bids for OCS leases as reflecting consumer sovereignty. Tussing seems to be following along in the pattern set by Potter/Christy (1962), and then Barnett/Morse (1963), of taking market prices at face value as indicators of resource values, ignoring subsidies. Not surprisingly, it leads him toward the same anti-Malthusian resource optimism that led us into the OPEC trap ten years ago.

5. THE WEIGHT OF INSTITUTIONAL BIAS IS AGAINST USING THE EXTENSIVE GEOGRAPHIC MARGIN, SPECIFICALLY OCS OIL AND GAS. While Tussing advances a good case, I believe the weight of bias goes the other way. Space prevents expanding. See my chapter in M. Crommelin and A. Thompson (1977).

6. CONSERVATION IS NONSENSE. SYNFUELS AND NUKES ARE ALREADY CHEAPER THAN NEW DOMESTIC OIL AND GAS, (he alleges early in the paper, on what basis I cannot imagine, as these two industries emit death rattles; later, he reneges on synfuels.) The future will be richer than we are and smarter, too, in spite of plummeting student performance. Here is a strong heart indeed, uninfected by the gloom of our times, still singing songs of the soaring sixties. Singing thus, he overlooks what is perhaps the best argument against conservation, that there may be no market for oil and gas during the coming depression. But this, if a good forecast, would not lead us to sink more national capital into OCS development at this time.

Depression or not, as I read America in Ruins I am persuaded that our future capital needs will far exceed the supply. Tussing's resources optimism is silently premised on there being plenty of cheap capital to develop all the new resources

he lists. That premise is dangerously, demonstrably, un-
equivocally wrong.

7. POTENTIAL BENEFITS FROM OIL AND GAS PRODUCTION SWAMP OUT ALL
    ENVIRONMENTAL DAMAGES THAT MIGHT RESULT. "All"? Surely that
    is overreacting to Jane Fonda. "May," perhaps "most," but
    an economist recognizes margins where small net benefits from
    oil and gas must yield to large environmental values.

    But, Tussing continues (pulling a Kissinger), if you suppress
    OCS oil you will get worse, e.g., tanker imports, which is
    the alternative. But this industry refrain overlooks the
    alternative of using less oil and gas, one that reduces
    damages in production, transportation, refining and consump-
    tion. In the hot summer of 1967 Mayor Maier of Milwaukee
    shut down all the gas stations and sealed the city from cars,
    to forestall arson (remember those days?). As an interesting
    by-product, the muggy summer air became sparkling crystal
    clear, such as never seen after. I would welcome more holi-
    days for cars, and from cars.

    But note how damages must be "quantifiable." Given the indus-
    try mindset betrayed throughout this paper, that sly word
    implies that the burden of proof of environmental damage is
    with the damaged (assuming they get standing in court) and
    limited to provable quantities. Evnironmentalists can be
    annoying, I know, but without their continual fussing what
    kind of a hell would this world be when greed and irresponsi-
    bility, vanity, stupidity and immaturity command modern
    technology? May the protestors not be squelched under impos-
    sible measurement burdens. They fight our battles, and not
    for profit.

8. NUKES ARE OUR CLEANEST SOURCE OF ENERGY. If you overlook con-
    tingent hazards, rapid decay, decommissioning, and ultimate
    waste disposal, I suppose you could believe that.

9. GEOLOGICAL INFORMATION SHOULD HAVE MORE ECONOMIC CONTENT.
    D'accord, and bless the memory of Orris Herfindahl. But geo-
    logists know on which side bread is buttered, and there is no
    danger that fundamental research will crowd out "economic"
    content from our industry-oriented schools of mines. The
    wonder is that fundamental research survives, and it seems
    that the single-minded profit approach, common to everyone in
    business, might benefit by the stimulus and challenge of re-
    search done to a different drummer.

    The true shortage is of economists who look into geology from
    a public viewpoint, to work out tax and leasing plans to pro-
    tect the public. Recent research on this topic, which Tussing
    finds so "massive," "radical," not "responsible," full of
    "mischief" and "not clear," would not consume the profit of
    a good oil well. It is worth remembering that energy indus-
    try sales in 1981 were some $600 billions, which really is

massive: it is twelve times the sales of steel, for instance, six times sales in non-food retailing, seven times food retailing, and so on. Yet, for every economist writing on oil leasing and taxation, there are a dozen Doctorates in the Philosophy of mixing hog feed in Iowa. Profit will be served, never doubt it; but who will guard the common weal?

10. SELECTIVE NIHILISM. THE ECONOMISTS' ANALYTICAL APPARATUS IS "USELESS" WHEN USED BY GOVERNMENT, BUT THE CORRECT BASIS FOR PRIVATE DECISIONS. THE SOCIAL DISCOUNT RATE IS NOT "OPERATIONAL," BUT PRIVATE DISCOUNTING IS: I once voted Libertarian myself, but this is ridiculous. If we are to have government at all, let us order it to act rationally. If we are not to have a government, forget about those leases, for some other government will discover a claim to our OCS and act "appropriately."

Early Libertarians like Albert J. Nick and Frank Chodorov, let us remember, were Henry Georgists. Let government collect and distribute land rents equally, and <u>then</u> proclaim liberty throughout the land. Latter-day Libs promote the conclusion but forget the premise, without which the theory will never fly. And you cannot collect rent without applying the economists' analytical apparatus.

B. Tussing's Policy Positions

1. BONUS BIDDING IS BEST. (This follows from Doctrines 1 and 9, and from deference to "responsible personnel in both...government...and in the industry... ." Foot-dragging bureaucrats become "responsible personnel" where we like the status quo, but I am not persuaded. No one ever reformed an agency without kicking butts and raising squawks.

We do indeed need more study of the optimal size and number of tracts in a lease sale, but I wonder why Tussing should care since he wants it all leased "now." Lease terms before drilling also need review, but Tussing clearly would have us lengthen them towards infinity, for how else could we sell all the OCS now before the industry could develop it.

2. THE ENTIRE OCS SHOULD BE AVAILABLE FOR LEASING "NOW." This follows from Doctrines 3 to 7, Q.V.

3. THE TIMING OF LEASE SALES SHOULD BE AT INDUSTRY INITIATIVE, "WHENEVER SERIOUS INTEREST APPEARS." Who will be the first to show serious interest? The few with the most patient money. When? When they know something others do not. Where? Wherever is best for them. I cannot imagine a surer formula for rooking the public, coupled as it is with repeated strictures against public collection of useful information. You would never guess from Tussing that Alberta, with its systematic data gathering, is prospering with a bulging treasury; or that Alaska's limited success in tapping lease revenues was won with the leverage of data from well logs required by law.

4. ENVIRONMENTAL DAMAGE NEED BE ACCORDED LITTLE WEIGHT. Tussing would evidently leash David Brower, unleash the roughnecks, and rely heavily on Red Adair. This derives from Doctrine 7, Q.V.

5. GOVERNMENT SHOULD ABANDON ITS FOOLISH QUEST FOR INFORMATION. (Look what happened to Eve). THE "INSISTENT CLIENTS" FOR INFORMATION ARE "THOSE WHO WANTED TO CREATE COMPLICATED SCHEMES...TO EXTRACT THE LAST MEASURE... ." (Shylocks, probably). LET US BE DONE WITH SUCH FOLLY: TRUST THE INDUSTRY. THIS VIEW FOLLOWS FROM DOCTRINES 1, 3, 9 AND 10, Q.V., AND IS AT THE HEART OF THE PAPER.

6. IN MATTERS OF LEASING, SIMPLE IS BEAUTIFUL, SO TAKE A BONUS WHEN IT'S OFFERED AND DO NOT PARTICIPATE. Beautiful for them, yes, but not us. If we had a good tax system I would agree: sell the title and walk away. But we do not, so we need a good lease. Leases and other contracts get complex in order to anticipate contingencies, most of which never arrive. I would not go abroad without one. The normal cinema lease, producer-distributor, is more complex than an oil lease, for smaller stakes, and I doubt that the $600 billion energy industry cannot handle a little boilerplate.

7. "GEOGRAPHIC ADVANCE" INTO THE OCS IS THE CHEAPEST SOURCE OF OIL AND GAS FOR THE NEAR FUTURE. Maybe so, maybe no: we would never know from the fragments of fact and anecdote presented. THE "BEST INDICATOR" IS INDUSTRY BIDS ON TRACTS, but this indicator is not compared to bids in the Overthrust Belt or elsewhere, so we have little to which to hold fast.

C. In closing, I offer some reasons why the distribution of rents is important.

Rent as public revenue substitutes for taxes without the disincentive effects of most taxes and the regressive impact of many. Rents from oil and gas are ones which the public recognizes for what they are and is willing to socialize. Five percent of all state revenues now come from severance taxes, and the trend is up. The Federal Windfall Profits Tax (WPT), badly structured though it is, brings in billions. The public correctly perceives that these collections are not mainly shifted forward, but tap fat in the private sector, i.e., rent.

The beneficiaries of rent are highly concentrated. This follows a priori from the nature of most rent-sources: they yield cash flows more deferred than do most other assets, because they last forever. Oil and gas do not last forever, but leases sold well in advance of use yield cash only after long holding periods, which gives the same effect. Only the well-heeled can afford to apply.

Surpluses, like rent (perhaps the only true surplus), privately-received, cushion beneficiaries from the full pressure of market forces. The beneficiaries can afford to coast and often do. If aggressive, they can commit extinction pricing. They can plow back earnings into acquisitions, augmenting market shares at the top. Rents divide the industry (and the world) into Haves and Have-nots, with profoundly destructive economic, sociological and political effects.

When anyone gets unearned income and wealth, it weakens the effect of marginal work incentives. It also hurts social morale, by destroying faith in the market system. It is used to rationalize inefficient devices like price control and roll-in pricing which distribute rent by processes which promote waste. Worst of all rent corrupts, both in the getting and the spending. Let government sell lands to speculators and we get incidents like the recent restitution of the Pauley lease off Santa Barbara--an abandoned lease was revested in Pauley after a neighbor found oil. On the spending side, privately-received rent becomes the mothers' milk of politics, and gives recipients a huge edge over ordinary people.

Let us not, therefore, disregard the functional distribution of wealth, as Chicago has long urged. Classical political economy rightly put distribution at the center of our discipline. J.B. Clark and Frank Knight bade us forget all that, but we cannot escape the basic historical fact: "Custer died for our sins." If we forget, the dispossessed do not, and with the rising concentration of economic power on one side, and unemployment on the other, more and more of us fall among those dispossessed.

References

Barnett, Harold J. and Chandler Morse (1963). Scarcity and Growth, The Economics of Natural Resource Availability (Baltimore: Johns Hopkins Press).

Crommelin, M. and A. Thompson, eds. (1977). Mineral Leasing as an Instrument of Public Policy (Vancouver, B.C.: University of British Columbia Press).

Potter, Neal and Francis T. Christy (1962). Trends in Natural Resource Commodities (Baltimore: Johns Hopkins Press, for Resources for the Future).

Discussion

Oil and Gas Resources

Robert J. Kalter

The Tussing paper leaves this reader with mixed emotions. The
topic is approached in a conventional, if somewhat superficial,
manner. The precepts of economic efficiency provide the basis for
both the introductory remarks and the general topics suggested for
a research agenda (although broader economic and political issues
are raised at several points). Most economists can readily identify
with not only the objective function but the rather narrowly defined microeconomic focus which such an approach requires.

The result is a series of recommendations for a research agenda of
substantial interest in interpreting private sector decision making
with respect to the Outer Continental Shelf (OCS), but of little
direct relevance in understanding or changing the broader political
and social rules of the game. By largely ignoring the interaction
of economic forces with the political/legislative/legal setting
within which OCS development takes place and the equity, as opposed
to economic efficiency, arguments relevant to establishing that
framework, Tussing has excluded those factors which will ultimately
be the major determinant of his chief interest; namely, optimizing
"the total contribution the (OCS) resource makes to social welfare."

Nor can we dismiss lightly Tussing's admonishment that "any ordering of the detailed research agenda is an intensely political task,
which cannot help but reflect one's ideology and predispositions."
Although obviously true, this should not serve as an excuse to
ignore or put aside the issue of research priorities. Clearly,
those of us familiar with the OCS leasing and development process
need to provide the public at large with our thoughts and views
concerning such priorities.

Given the lead times involved in OCS development (particularly in
frontier areas); the serious long term economic and national security threat of moderate to high levels of oil imports; and the
uncertainty involved in OCS exploration, the optimal public policy
would appear to be that being advanced by the Reagan administration.
Rapid acceleration of the leasing schedule is necessary both to

develop undiscovered conventional fossil fuel sources for use in the next decade and to obtain improved information on our perspective inventory of such fuels. Only the latter will permit rational planning and public decisions with respect to the timing, magnitude and type of alternative energy sources which will be needed in the future.

Research, and especially economic research, should be structured to support this broad objective. This implies a multifaceted research agenda which differs to a large degree from that suggested by Tussing. The remainder of these comments discuss these issues and the directions for research on the political economy to which they lead.

I. A Short Critique of the Tussing Agenda

Four general areas of research are suggested by Tussing. They include additional research on the character of the resource base and the potential supply function relating to that base, the schedule and pace of resource development, the leasing system, and the external costs of OCS development.

Use of subjective probabilities to forecast the size, location and character of the potential resource base has reached the point of diminishing returns and, as has been shown in instance after instance, is an idle exercise for micro-planning purposes. In his long discussion of this point, Tussing essentially admits the failure of this research and the difficulty of improving on it. To hold public policy captive to these results or await "improved" estimates would be a serious mistake. The only sure means of acquiring better information on our potential offshore energy inventory is to expand drilling activity in an unrestricted atmosphere. Whether from weak analogies or from more sophisticated statistical techniques, efforts to "fine tune" estimates of oil and gas by geological province, by field size, by water and geological depth and, correspondingly, by economic cost are misleading when used to guide the actual administration of a leasing program. It would be far more cost effective and less time consuming to permit the private sector to develop its own exploration agenda on the basis of geological data available to the respective participants in OCS development.

Likewise, concern over the external effects of OCS energy development has been over-researched. Often the environmental studies now required by law are meaningless since they are carried out prior to the discovery of actual resources. Because of the limited nature of past experience with environmental damage from OCS development, many years and millions of dollars are expended on studies of areas later found not to contain energy resources (witness the Gulf of Alaska and Destin Dome experiences). Yet the concern for environmental studies continues despite the lack of any creditable evidence that OCS energy exploration causes long term environmental damage and despite the documented advantages of OCS energy sources over other alternatives in this regard (Travers and Luney (1976).

Our noble experiment with alternative leasing systems should also be phased out. With perhaps one exception, that experiment does not appear to have met the objectives set out for it. For example, competition for OCS resources has not been noticeably enhanced, while transactions costs of development have been substantially increased for both the public and private sectors. The private sector has not responded in the anticipated manner to having the public assume a greater portion of the risk and uncertainty associated with exploration and development (Kalter, Tyner and Hughes (1975)). Only in assuring an adequate portion of economic rents for the public in times of rapid structural change do systems like profit sharing appear to have merit. A general economic analysis of these points is now called for, and if the above contentions are correct, the proliferation of leasing systems and approaches should be phased out in favor of the traditional cash bonus system in areas of relative certainty and possibly the cash bonus with a fixed profit share approach in frontier areas. Most studies have shown that the difference in the public share of economic rent under such systems is probably not substantial and, consequently, equity considerations would not be greatly affected by such a policy (Mead et al. (1976); Dougherty et al. (1979); Kalter, Tyner and Hughes (1975)).

Finally, if the research community has been unsuccessful in providing more accurate information on the potential resource base, the supply functions involved in exploiting that resource base, and the impact of alternative leasing arrangements on optimal development, we are unlikely to provide meaningful data relevant to the optimal schedule and pace of resource development. For any detailed attempt at influencing public policy in this area must depend on this type of underlying data to be successful (U.S. DOE (1979)). If the necessary micro-data is unreliable and the likelihood for improvements in that data base is not near term, leasing policy cannot afford to wait if real world problems are to be solved.

What then are the important areas for research focus and public policy debate? To understand the determinates of OCS activity, one must consider the legal and administrative framework within which it operates. If desired objectives relating to the OCS are not being met, changes in this framework may be desirable. Research, which ultimately influences public attitudes, should then be designed to ascertain the most effective approach to modify the rules of the games. In essence, I am suggesting that we look more towards the political economy of the situation when formulating our research agenda (Commons (1924)). With that in mind, let us briefly review the statutory and administrative basis for past and current leasing policy.

II. The Statutory and Administrative Framework

The basis for all recent development and exploitation of energy resources located on the United States outer continental shelf was established in 1953 with the passage of the Outer Continental Shelf Lands Act (OCSLA) (43 U.S.C. 1331-1343). That Act, formulated in an era of abundant energy supplies and low prices, contemplated relatively simple procedures for leasing portions of the OCS (seaward of state boundaries) to the private sector for exploration and development.

With time, however, several conflicting constituencies were heard from. First in 1969, the Santa Barbara oil spill heightened the awareness of the entire country of possible environmental problems implicit in OCS development and provided an important impetus to passage of the National Environmental Policy Act of 1969, with its requirement for environmental impact statements for all significant federal actions.

Second, as United States oil and natural gas production began to decline in 1971 and 1974, respectively, anticipation of an accelerated production decline, from onshore and offshore U.S. oil and gas fields, led to increased pressure from some quarters to expand the pace of OCS leasing.

Third, individual coastal states became increasingly interested in the leasing policy designed to encourage development off their respective shores, demanding additional coordination and consultation prior to the development of federal leasing policy.

Finally, the 1973 Arab oil embargo increased the pressure to formulate an improved public decision making apparatus with respect to the OCS. The oil embargo accelerated interest in the OCS as a potential energy source for the country at a time when our vulnerability to oil imports had reached a critical stage.

In 1974, Congress began to consider the issue with the introduction of legislation in both Houses to reform the 1953 OCS Lands Act. Yet it would take over four years of effort to fashion an acceptable bill for passage and signature by the President. During this time, the executive branch attempted to accelerate the pace of energy development on the OCS several times, while environmental law suits and concerns by affected state governments caused delays.

The result of this long period of public discussion and debate was the 1978 OCS Lands Act amendments. The amendments consisted of 70 pages of changes in and additions to the original 1953 Act and related legislation. Virtually every aspect of energy development on the OCS was considered and brought under Federal oversight. Since 1978, further regulations have been developed by the responsible executive departments governing the behavior of affected parties.

The stated objective of the 1978 legislation was to provide a mechanism, acceptable to all parties, which would do away with further delay in OCS development, but, at the same time, make that development environmentally safe and provide affected states with additional input into federal leasing policy.

III. The Current Status and Resulting Implications For Economic Research

The OCSLA Amendments of 1978 were designed to permit OCS development while simultaneously meeting a number of conflicting social goals. Above all they were seen as a means of conflict resolution which would permit more expeditious decision making. In both respects, they must be considered largely a failure. Conflict over the pace and system of leasing has not subsided and leasing decisions can now take between 35 and 60 months (whereas an average under the 1953 OCS Act was 14 to 15 months). Moreover, the leasing of geologically promising areas for exploration continues to be stalled by the concerns of state governments and environmental groups, despite the fact that both public and private geological information strongly suggests the existence of important new fields. The political considerations which molded the new legislation have inadvertently caused increased bureaucratic delay in achieving the central goal of the legislation--rapid energy development.

I believe this situation is due to the improper design of the statutory framework which gave inadequate attention to the underlying factors motivating human behavior. As Tussing points out, there are a series of considerations which have lead to a "general presumption against developing offshore hydrocarbons," in other words, the public at large has no discernable economic stake in permitting development to take place. The role of future economic research should be to ascertain the best mechanisms for changing this gap between the public and individual private interests.[1]

This need suggests certain areas of research priority, including:

1. Design of appropriate financial mechanisms to permit the sharing of public OCS revenues with the states (both coastal and inland) and with environmental programs focused on improving the overall quality of life;

2. Cost/benefit assessments of government regulations pertaining to private sector activity on the OCS with the objective of optimizing the scope and structure of such regulations;

3. Assessment of the economic costs entailed by the decision time lags implicit in the current leasing system and design of appropriate institutional structures to reduce such costs while preserving the legitimate involvement of numerous competing public agencies interested in OCS development; and

4. Development of appropriate information designed to permit planning and public policy decisions with respect to possible economic bottlenecks that could develop under alternative leasing schedules.

Financial Mechanisms

Failure of the public to perceive a direct stake in the "internal" net benefits of OCS development stems largely from inadequate revenue distribution mechanisms. But the character and history of the OCS require innovative approaches if revenue sharing is to be extended to encompass this activity. Bordering coastal states obviously share more directly in the externality and multiplier impacts of OCS development. Cooperation with a Federal leasing program should carry sufficient compensatory rewards for these areas. Yet the publicly owned resources being exploited are not directly situated within the boundaries of a given state. The economic and political opportunity afforded by this situation should not be lost for lack of an appropriate revenue distribution mechanism. Economic research can assist by studying alternative revenue sharing mechanisms and the tradeoffs implicit in the design of such systems.

Cost/Benefit Assessments

Due to public concern with the potential environmental, safety and health problems of OCS development, over the past ten years, much of the legislative and administrative activity that has taken place has been without benefit of rigorous economic analysis concerning the potential costs and benefits. The result has been rapidly escalating transactions costs in both the private and public sectors. Rather than establishing performance standards and allowing the industry to achieve such standards in the most cost effective manner, the government often substitutes detailed stipulations on exploration and development activity.

The time has come to reassess critically such regulations with the objective of eliminating those that are not cost effective and to reform legitimate regulatory activities in a manner which would permit reductions in the resource costs connected with their implementation.

Decision Time Lags

As indicated above, the administrative and bureaucratic requirements set forth by the 1978 OCSLA Amendments have substantially lengthened the time horizon for making and implementing leasing schedule decisions. On a present value basis, the economic costs to the nation of such delays are substantial. Consequently, an accurate assessment of such costs and the design of appropriate institutional mechanisms for reducing the decision-making time-frame is needed. Again, issues of political economy will be vital to such an undertaking since a number of competing agencies, at all levels of government, have legitimate interests in OCS development. The coordination and reconciliation of these various points of view is largely responsible for the lengthened decision times involved. The critical question becomes: How can the legitimate rights be preserved and properly ranked and at the same time the economic costs involved in public discussion be reduced?

The Leasing Pace and Economic Bottlenecks

Acceleration of OCS leasing activity by the public sector must take into account potential constraints due to short and long term

economic bottlenecks (i.e., equipment and manpower shortages,
lags in the development of required technology, capital availability, etc.). A legitimate function of government is to provide
additional information concerning such potential bottlenecks and
attempt to promote their solution through private sector action.
For example, additional research and development expenditures may
be required on the part of the public sector to assist in the solution of long term technical issues. In other circumstances,
publicly available analyses may be sufficient to encourage additional private sector activity.

IV. Conclusions

In general, the agenda outlined above attempts to interest the
research community in the broader political economy aspects of
achieving a specific public objective. It is unlikely that the
list of issues presented is exhaustive or even terribly imaginative
with respect to this concern. However, it is, at the same time, an
attempt to persuade the research community that further attempts
at controlling private sector activity by "fine tuning" public
policy is no longer a productive avenue of concern. If used for
this purpose, additional research resources spent on the investigation of alternative leasing systems, on the issues of oil industry risk preferences, decision processes surrounding exploration
activity, bidding strategies or subjective resource assessments will
be unlikely to provide the payoff, in terms of meeting critical
national objectives, that will come from evaluating the motivations
of other actors in the development of leasing policy. Improvements
in our knowledge of the broad range of underlying political and
economic forces will permit the design of more appropriate institutional mechanisms for carrying out public leasing policy.

Footnote

1.   Critics will argue that accelerated development of the OCS
     for energy production cannot be taken as a national concensus
     or necessarily be in the "public interest." But the question
     of the "public interest" is an overused escape from the
     reality of making decisions. What is in the "public interest"
     can never be truly known or understood nor, in a democratic
     society, agreed upon by a clear majority. We must operate
     within the framework of our established institutions until
     and unless they are changed. In that respect, Congress has
     strongly indicated that rapid development of the OCS's energy
     potential is in the public interest and this has been agreed
     to by the President.

     The case is dramatized by the fact that though the OCS ac-
     counts for less than ten percent of domestic oil output (well
     below the world average of almost 23 percent), it contains
     possibly as much as 60 percent of the remaining undiscovered
     resource, less than seven percent of the area has been leased
     in almost 30 years of activity.

References

Commons, J.R. (1924). Legal Foundations of Capitalism, Madison: The University of Wisconsin Press.

Dougherty, E.L. et al. (1979). "The Relationship Between Bonuses Paid and Revenue Obtained for Individual Bidders in Different Federal Offshore Oil and Gas Bonus Bid Lease Sales," Proceedings: Economics of Exploration for Energy Resources Conference, New York University, May 17-18.

Kalter, R.J., W. Tyner and D. Hughes (1975). Alternative Energy Leasing Strategies and Schedules for the Outer Continental Shelf, Cornell University, A.E. Res. 75-33 (December).

MacDonald, S.L. (1979). The Leasing of Federal Lands for Fossil Fuels Production, Baltimore: The Johns Hopkins University Press.

Mead, W.J. et al. (1976). "An Economic Analysis of the Performance of the Cash Bonus Bid Leasing System for OCS Oil and Gas Resources in the Gulf of Mexico," presented at Southern Economic Association Annual Meeting, November.

Prato, A.A. and R.R. Miller (1981). "Evaluating the Energy Production Potential of the United States Outer Continental Shelf," Land Economics 57/1 (February): 77-90.

Travers, W.B. and P.R. Luney (1976). "Drilling, Tankers, and Oil Spills on the Atlantic Outer Continental Shelf," Science 194 (November): 791-796.

United States Congress, Office of Technology Assessment (1980). An Assessment of Oil Shale Technologies, Washington, D.C. (June).

United States Department of Energy (1979). Federal Leasing and Outer Continental Shelf Energy Production Goals, DOE/RA-0037, Washington, D.C. (June).

Oil and Gas Resources

Rogge Marsh

Arlon Tussing has created a very interesting and thought-provoking paper. Using his major divisions, I will first discuss the nature of the oil and gas lease market in the outer continental shelf (OCS), then present an industry viewpoint regarding Dr. Tussing's research agenda and finally propose research which I believe would be extremely interesting and worthwhile.

I. The Outer Continental Shelf Oil and Gas Lease Market

The Ideal Market

If a person were to set out to create the ideal market for offshore oil and gas leases, he likely would strive for five things. The ideal market should:

- Be Competitive and Fair--With our concept of free enterprise, Americans insist that competition be preserved because we have seen and enjoyed the effects of an economic system that sponsors competition. This means that anyone who wishes to play the offshore oil and gas game must have at least as much chance as any of the other players. Also the system by which leases are awarded must be straightforward, producing a clear and undisputed winner.

- Promote Expeditious Exploration and Development--The ideal market should be designed so that it is in the lease holder's best interest to explore and develop any resources found as quickly as is prudent. The terms of the lease should not create a situation where delay can be economically favorable to the lessee.

- Yield Maximum Return to the Public--The government has been delegated the responsibility to administer these resources so that the public receives the maximum return. Yet industry must also be kept interested in exploring and developing the remaining undrilled portion of the public's resources.

137

- Promote Maximum Development of the Oil and Gas Resources Present--Lease stipulations, laws, rules and regulations all eventually translate into costs to be applied to subsequent development by the operator of the offshore lease. If these costs are excessive, they may result in smaller prospects not receiving bids, smaller discoveries not being developed, or productive leases being prematurely abandoned. Any oil left in the ground as a result of costs generated by unreasonable lease stipulations or other requirements amounts to a waste of the public's resources.

- Have a Positive or at Least Neutral Impact on the Marine Environment--OCS oil and gas operations must not waste or impair other associated marine resources such as fisheries or recreation.

The Actual Market

In practice this market appears to be one of the most competitive to be found anywhere in the world. OCS leasing began in 1954. In the first sale there were thirty-one bidders. The number of participants or individual companies in general lease sales has grown throughout the succeeding twenty-eight years to a peak of ninety-seven individual participants in the Gulf of Mexico sale held in July, 1979. Fairness has also been preserved by using the sealed bid, cash bonus system to determine the winner. Companies with different economic means can all be accommodated, some bidding alone for leases, and others bidding as members of bidding combines.

Expeditious development has been assured by the use of the cash bonus bid lease award system. This system imposes a front-end load on a project's economics, providing an incentive for the lessee to recover his bonus as rapidly as possible through exploration, subsequent development and production of the discovered resource. Speculators--those who may be interested in turning a profit only in the lease market itself and not as a result of ultimate production of discovered resources--are virtually excluded from this market, leaving it open only to companies interested in development. These facts were corroborated by a recent Department of Energy study (Gribbin, 1979) which showed that development time in the Gulf of Mexico, defined as the time from the lease sale to initial production on a lease, had dropped over the period from 1954 to 1973 from an average of 80.2 to 20.3 months.

There is very good evidence that the public is receiving at least its proper share of the economic rent for its OCS resources. Three years ago the Conservation Division of the U.S. Geological Survey (USGS) sponsored a report on "Competition and Performance in OCS Oil and Gas Lease Sales and Lease Development, 1954-1969" by economists Walter Mead and Philip Sorensen (1979). This was an exhaustive study based on an analysis of 1,223 leases issued in seventeen OCS lease sales in the Gulf of Mexico from 1954 through 1969. This study used the excellent OCS Lease, Production and Royalty data base developed and maintained at that time by the Conservation Division.

There was enough data available to do discounted cash flow analysis on each of these leases, including production projections for the leases that were productive. To my knowledge this is the most complete public study that has ever been undertaken of the economics of the OCS. Mead and Sorensen concluded that, for the 1,223 leases, the average internal rate of return was 11.43 percent before taxes. By way of expressing just how modest this return is, they go on to say that the return was "far below the average return (1954-1976) for all U.S. manufacturing corporations which was 19.81 percent before taxes." The authors estimated that a normal yield for investments having these kinds of risks would be approximately twenty percent before taxes. On this basis they were able to calculate that the average over-bid for these 1,223 leases was 239 percent what it should have been for a twenty percent rate of return. They concluded "this evidence clearly supports the conclusion that the government received more than fair market value for these leases issued under the cash bonus system. The low internal rate of return, as a measure of competitive performance, indicates that the lease sale market is intensely competitive." In addition they further determined that "alleged anti-competitive barriers to entry due to front-end payments required by cash bonus bidding, or collusive market power allegations against large firms, were not supported by the record."

Maximum resource development in the offshore has also been achieved by the government's restraint in the amount of contingency payment it requires for its leases in the offshore. In a study done by the author (1980), a comparison of all leasing systems mandated by the OCS Lands Act showed that the leasing systems that permitted bids on the smallest prospects (resulting in the greatest number of tracts receiving bids) were those that called for the smallest royalty or net profit share payments. And once a discovery has been made, the leases with the smaller royalty or net profit share rates will, all else being equal, permit development of the smaller discoveries; this means more resources are developed. Also, premature abandonment of a producing property, which wastes resources, is not a significant problem with a royalty of 1/6th or less.

In the Gulf of Mexico where industry has developed offshore resources more intensely than anywhere else on earth, we have seen a beneficial effect from oil development on the marine environment and its productivity. The presence of steel production platforms has created what is in essence an artificial reef upon and about which the entire marine community can establish itself. The place to fish off Louisiana and Texas is "around the platforms." Those who have dived around coral reefs in the Caribbean and also around established production platforms in the Gulf of Mexico see startling similarities between the two. The state of Texas is currently developing an artificial reef system by accepting obsolete production platforms from leases whose production has ceased. The goal is long-term enhancement of the marine productivity of the Gulf of Mexico. Concern over the potentially negative effects of oil and gas production in the Gulf of Mexico has been effectively allayed by an exhaustive study by the Gulf Universities Research Consortium (1974) which concluded that there has been no significant deterioration of the marine environment of the Gulf Coast even in areas where there is concentrated oil and gas production.

Conclusions

A detailed study of the reality of oil and gas production in the Gulf of Mexico, where we have substantial experience must conclude that the actual outer continental shelf oil and gas lease market is not significantly different from our ideal market. There may not be a consensus as to why the market works as well as it does, or whether the market will continue in the future to function as well as it has in the past. Certainly no one sat down in 1954 and decided to create an ideal market; a fortuitous confluence of circumstances simply yielded a leasing system that works very well. It is also possible that this Gulf of Mexico experience could be a justification of the free enterprise system as it exists in the United States. Why it works may be the most intriguing research project for the 1980s.

II. The Research Agenda

The OCS Petroleum Resource Base and Supply Function

Too much emphasis has been placed on the poor quality of the data that must be used to estimate the resource base for the U.S. outer continental shelf. It must be remembered if data of this kind is good, then you are not analyzing a frontier or an undrilled area: you are analyzing a place where exploration and development has already taken place. Estimating resources in undrilled basins is a very risky activity with orders of magnitude of potential misestimation. Tussing states that the results of resource estimation that we have seen to date are little better than guesses about the resources in the various OCS areas. To some extent this criticism is valid; however it must be remembered that these guesses are based on the experience and expertise of the geologists best qualified in the USGS to make these judgments.

USGS estimates that what we see today are much improved from the past, i.e., prior to 1975. And while there may be no empirical way to check USGS performance, we can compare their estimates with those of Exxon, Shell, the Rand Corporation, Mobil and others. This comparison reveals that there are no serious differences between the USGS and the other estimators in the field.

I believe estimates of this kind can and must be used in the absence of anything else to attempt to forecast discovery, production, revenue, etc. We as a nation must understand the potential range of resources that may be available to us in the outer continental shelf. We must also come to understand the uncertainties associated with resource estimates of this nature; this is one of the most serious problems facing those who attempt to explain resource estimates to the public at large. And finally we must tolerate incomplete information because, in many cases, it is all we have for making long-range policy decisions.

140

Long-Term Demand and the Optimum Rate of Depletion

Any gathering of experienced forecasters must inevitably agree that there is no "good" data for forecasting almost anything significantly beyond tomorrow morning's sunrise. My experience gained in creating Exxon's upstream supply forecast in the early 70s and participating in a number of forecasts since then leads me to believe that the significant variables that truly affect the future are never forecastable.

In oil industry forecasts we begin with an understanding of the geology of various areas; this includes the types of rocks, and the structures available in the area, the areal distribution of prospects within the subject basin and, in general, "the envelope" of the basin. We couple this with design concepts and cost estimates for the exploration wells, the types of production platforms that may be necessary for various water depths and water conditions, and the required transportation systems such as pipelines, single point mooring systems, tankers, etc. Putting all this together we have some concept of the timing requirements for exploration, development and production. All of these variables have a substantial impact on any forecast of resource development in the OCS. They are not the most important parts of the forecast, however.

It is the things that we do not know and cannot forecast that have the greatest impact. For instance, government policy changes with changing administrations. Who would have dreamed that a vigorously pro-development Secretary of the Interior such as James Watt would follow close on the heels of a cautious and conservationist Secretary such as Cecil Andrus? In addition geo-politics plays an enormous role in the future. In 1972, Exxon was seriously considering the possibility that oil price, which was then $2.90 a barrel, may be cut by as much as $1. There is no way we could have envisioned an Arab embargo and subsequent development of the OPEC cartel raising the price of oil not two or three times but tenfold over the next decade.

And finally, the most difficult variable of all to determine: which of the remaining undrilled basins will be productive? Over the past eight years U.S. industry has moved into seven undrilled basins; the first sales in these basins drew rather large cash bonus bids for the right to explore. To date five of these areas--the southeast Georgia embayment, eastern Gulf of Mexico, California's Outer Banks, Gulf of Alaska, and lower Cook Inlet--have turned up nothing. Industry has one gas discovery in the Baltimore Canyon area which may be too small to develop, and we are still drilling on Georges Bank in the North Atlantic with no reported discoveries.

The need to know the extent of the nation's conventional resources is unarguable. Will the Bering Sea be another North Sea or another Gulf of Alaska? If our remaining undrilled basins are barren, we must reevaluate our future energy options. We must develop alternate energy resources; yet all of the alternates waiting in the wings have extremely long lead times with enormous associated capital investments.

Leasing Policy

My most serious disagreement with Tussing's paper centers on his discussion of leasing policy in the outer continental shelf. His paper implies that in the last ten years analyses of leasing policy first confirmed cash bonus bidding and afterward, and indeed most recently, came to present "a strong case for radical changes in bidding and leasing arrangements--two stage leasing for example, and royalty and net profit share rates as the bid variable." Speaking as one who has followed this debate since 1976, I would like to set the record straight as to what the historical sequence of thought development on bidding systems has been over this period.

As mentioned previously, cash bonus bidding with a 1/6 royalty was the system that was settled on initially in 1954 for leasing the Federal outer continental shelf. There was very little question about the efficacy of this system until the early to mid-1970s when analyses appeared which questioned the ability of the cash bonus system to maintain a competitive market as well as yield maximum return to the public for its resources. This contention figured heavily in the debate in Congress to amend the Outer Continental Shelf Lands Act of 1954. As a result, the 1978 amendements to this Act included several specific leasing systems involving alternate bid variables such as percent royalty, percent net profit share and work commitment, as well as alternate means of contingency payment.

Unfortunately the Mead and Sorensen study was not available in time to figure in the debate on the amendments. Therefore Congress was unaware that there was no need for concern about ensuring competition, expeditious development, preventing collusion and systematic underbidding. After the passage of the amendments, these questions were argued by the Departments of Energy and Interior, private industry, public interest groups and affected states in response to DOE requests for comments on proposed regulations to implement the various leasing systems. In addition further studies were done by the Department of Interior, primarily by John Lohrenz with the Conservation Division of the USGS. Lohrenz was responsible for the development and maintenance of the Lease, Production and Royalty data base, known currently as LPR-24, the same one used by Mead and Sorensen in their study. Lohrenz's various studies for the Department of Interior, as well as other studies emanating from the Department of Energy, the University of Pennsylvania, Shell Oil Company and Exxon began to point up the weaknesses of the alternate systems called for in the Outer Continental Shelf Lands Act Amendments of 1978. These studies all have pointed out the inherent strengths of the cash bonus leasing system.

External Costs of Offshore Petroleum Operations

I believe the American public is little served by the environmental stridency that has dominated the discussion of the side effects of OCS petroleum development over the last ten years or so. The environmental community has focused on potentially negative impacts of OCS development with no consideration of the positive impacts.

Little positive data has been developed concerning the effects of OCS development on commercial fishing or sports fishing in the Gulf of Mexico, the opinions of land owners along the coast of Texas and Louisiana who see production facilities in the inland bays and waterways, or the value of the artificial reefs that are created by petroleum development in marine environments.

III. Suggested Research

The Mead and Sorensen report investigated only the results from lease sales in the Gulf of Mexico. Future research should initially concentrate on the inclusion in the LPR-24 data base of all of the data resulting from lease sales in the outer continental shelf from both nonproductive and productive basins. Once this is achieved, an analysis of the economics of the entire U.S. outer continental shelf petroleum development effort can be undertaken, taking into consideration the results industry has had from sales in dry basins. This analysis can also include a discussion of the extent to which government has been able to recover the economic rent from the off-shore resources. The level of competition can also be expressed with such data as has been suggested here. This analysis could include an explanation of the use and efficacy of probabilistic resource assessment. And, if the work concludes as I have that the past administration and operation of the offshore oil and gas industry has served the public and the industry well, the economic or philosophic causes for this should be identified. Maybe the "technology" is transferrable to other regulated industries.

Recreation

Gardner M. Brown, Jr.

I. Introduction

A large segment of professional economic activity follows controversy. Problems arise and resources for applied research are made
available to help resolve the issues. Theoretical inquiry more frequently follows the interests and whims of the researcher which
often is stimulated by the inadequacy of existing methods for treat-
ing a contemporary problem. A case in point is the estimation of
damages to recreation activities from inadvertent oil and gas activities such as spills. In Section II, this topic is imbedded in a
description and evaluation of the major methods for estimating
damages to beaches. Baseline studies using a variant of hedonic
analysis are highly ranked for research support.

Methods of analysis are general and problem areas have multiple
causes and consequences. Valuing sport fish and fishing is important, not only in terms of oil and gas activities, but also for making decisions about commercial and sport allocations. This topic
is given separate attention in Section III, and enters in Section V
where research needs of fishery management councils in the U.S.,
are discussed.

Research regarding the benefits from non-consumptive use is presented briefly in Section IV. How applied analysis should deal
with the cost or value of time in applied analysis, how congestion
should be treated, and a number of econometric considerations are
elements which greatly shape the empirical magnitudes of relevant
applied research. They are the substance of Section VII on model
specification. Law distinguishes between fast fish and slow fish
(shellfish). This distinction is honored in Section VI, where the
critical necessity for including density estimates in economic
analysis involving shellfish is spelled out.

How many pieces of first class applied research can you cite whose
subject matter falls within the confines of the economics of marine
related recreation? We would want to name those which had sound

144

economic theory underlying the analysis, and adequate physical and economic data for the task, and which competently utilized econometric techniques. There are not many candidates and very few that meet the further criterion of general usefulness. Part of the reason for the paucity of nominations may be the lack of many highly qualified economists attacking these problems. If this were the only cause, laying out the attractive research areas would be a simple task. Rather, I think the major reason for so little good applied economic research is the inadequacy of relevant data and very little demonstrated enthusiasm by funding agencies for establishing a data base. For a variety of reasons, physical facts of the marine environment are difficult and expensive to ascertain, but obtaining economic facts is further blocked by the reality that economics is the stepchild of the physical scientists--biologists, oceanographers--who manage the public agencies and control the purse strings for research. Funds for collecting economic data have low priority at best and often are regarded with great suspicion. Not many excellent applied economics research projects will appear until our stature as a profession improves.

There are not any econometric conundrums unique to marine oriented recreation, apart from those encountered when trying to circumvent gaping holes in information. I do not think there are major theoretical obstructions either, but this may be arguable. However narrowly or broadly we may put a perimeter around marine oriented recreation, the central features researchers must come to grips with are elements of public goods and the lack of markets. People do not acquire cleaner beaches or water in the same way that they acquire a cleaner car; they do not typically buy sport fish or purchase sport fishing services as they buy meat and wine or purchase the pleasures of eating and drinking; and they do not acquire or preserve public goods, such as beaches and ocean parks, or engage in non-consumptive, non-exclusive viewing of sea lions and whales as they purchase private beach rights and non-consumptive, exclusionary rights to view movies. Because marine-oriented recreation falls within the realm of public and non-marketed goods, we do not have the luxury of observing market prices directly. Instead, implicit prices must be discovered, which adds a layer of complication to the analysis, and more significantly, increases the cost of information. Nevertheless, there is no inherent reason why the economically efficient provision of non-market goods should not be of as paramount importance as that of market goods. Moreover, there may be extra satisfaction in solving problems which by their nature are more difficult.

II. Marine Oriented Recreation and Oil Spills

With the advent of federal supertanker legislation which provides compensation for damages, capability of estimating the recreation damage component is required. An oil spill can be expected to destroy some marine-dependent life such as fish, shellfish, their food sources, seabirds and aquatic mammals. These species either are caught by recreationists or viewed by them. Oil in some form, under unfavorable circumstances, will come ashore and diminish the quality of private and public beaches for some period of time.

Damage to beaches, will serve well as an illustration of the research which has been done. Its inadequacies provide the basis for recommending a future research program.

I am aware of only two pieces of research which directly address the economic valuation of changes in beach quality, both of them unpublished (Wilman and Krutilla (1980); Brown, Congar and Wilman (forthcoming)). Wilman and Krutilla attempted to estimate the damage from an hypothetical oil spill incident on Cape Cod and Martha's Vineyard. Brown, Congar and Wilman have estimated the non-market damages to Brittany from the Amoco-Cadiz oil spill in 1978, using both travel cost and willingness-to-pay (sell) techniques. During the summer of 1979 vacationers to Brittany were asked a variety of questions designed to elicit their value of a clean beach. In one version of the willingness-to-pay question, vacationers who had visited Brittany in 1978 were asked how much insurance they would be willing to purchase in order to provide certain financial compensation should the uncertain but probabalistically specified event of an oil spill equivalent to the Amoco Cadiz occur again. A willingness-to-sell question required the same vacationers to state the number of extra days of paid vacation necessary to compensate for the recurrence of changed beach conditions experienced as a consequence of the spill. Days were then converted into money by expressing the respondent's reported annual income on a daily basis. Answers ranged between 2 and 18 dollars per person on average.

The art is to design questions, "vehicles," which permit the respondent readily to translate qualities such as dissatisfaction into a monetary metric. It is assumed the theoretical basis for the willingness-to-pay (sell) or bidding game technique is rooted in the notion that individuals know what purchases will give them the most satisfaction. The changed satisfaction associated with changes in the terms of trade is consumer's surplus. Answers to the willingness-to-pay or willingness-to-sell (WTP or WTS) questions are the empirical counterpart of the conceptual idea of consumer's surplus.[1]

Davis is credited with authoring the original applied WTP or WTS study, followed by Mathews and Brown (1970) and Hammack and Brown (1974). Brookshire, Ives and Schulze (1976) and Rowe, d'Arge and Brookshire (1980), have used the technique more recently. Survey researchers have concluded that response bias increases as the substance of the question veers away from a respondent's direct experience. By the nature of the quest, some hypothetical aspects are inescapable in the search for non-market values through WTP and WTS techniques.

Hypothetical responses to hypothetical questions also mean that respondents may give answers which are not or would not be consistent with their actual behavior. This is vividly illustrated by the results of a recent study. In a very clever experimental design, Bishop and Heberlein (1979) found that a sample of Canada goose hunters were willing to sell a hypothetical lottery ticket for five times ($100) as much as they were willing to pay ($20) for the lottery ticket. Actual lottery tickets, giving the right to shoot one Canadian Goose in the Horicon Marsh, in fact, were purchased for $60.

Thus, judged against the benchmarks of actual market behavior, responses to hypothetical questions appear to have large biases for most purposes. If in this case all one needed was a value of $20 per ticket to tip the scales in favor of continued goose hunting, then the willingness-to-pay procedures would have been adequate for the allocation task. We note in passing that it is reasonable for answers to the WTP question to differ from the WTS questions. The formal explanation is the "real wealth effect." The informal reason is that people cannot pay more than all they own for anything but they can sell for more than this. For normal goods, however, the difference between WTP and WTS answers should be no greater than about five percent (Willig, (1976)), whereas in the Bishop and Heberlein study it is a factor of five!

Biased responses can arise because respondents behave strategically, giving larger or small answers depending on what they think it is in their interest to respond. A respondent may give a very low value to a willingness-to-pay question if he thinks answers will be used to set charges such as license fees.[2] On the other hand, a respondent may give large answers if he wants to block action. For example, Rowe, d'Arge and Brookshire use a WTP and WTS format to estimate how people valued air quality-visibility--that would be changed by the "development of large-scale networks of coal-fired electric generation plants" in the Four Corners region of the Southwest. More than one-half of their sample either would not cooperate with the surveyors or demanded an infinite price to give up some air quality (p. 9). Bias also can occur if the respondents want to please or to be helpful to the interviewer of author of the questionnaire and give answers based on cues provided (or perceived to be provided) by the questionnaire. If, for example, the interviewer initiates the possible answer to a WTP question at a particular level, the respondent may think this is the desired response and answer accordingly (Rowe, d'Arge and Brookshire).

A further criticism against the hypothetical technique is that people cannot understand the question. People have to respond in the proper context. They must know what their alternatives are, what the quality of the experience is that they are giving up or getting and they have to know the duration of the experience gained or lost--whether it is for a day, year or longer. In light of these criticisms, I would not recommend research involving WTP(S) techniques unless there are no alternative approaches.

The travel cost technique also was used to estimate losses due to the Amoco-Cadiz oil spill. The method exploits the fact that people from different origins bear different travel costs to reach the same site; therefore, they can be expected to participate at different rates. These different price (travel cost)-quantity (visits) combinations give rise to a demand curve for the recreation site. The most searching description and evaluation of the travel cost technique can be found in Dwyer and Kelley (1976). To evaluate damages from the Amoco-Cadiz spill, travel cost demand curves based on beach attendance and mileage costs to Brittany from home province were estimated for the year of the spill and for the following year. Also, in the interviews, vacationers were shown pictures of oil-polluted beaches (more severe than actually experienced) and asked their frequency of attendance at clean beaches if they were located variable distances away from the summer vacation location. The loss estimated from the hypothetical responses was much higher, not surprisingly.

The weaknesses of the travel cost technique are well known and will not be detailed here. Despite the technique's shortcomings, a revised version with prices of substitutes included may be a useful approach to use when estimating the recreational value of a site vis à vis its commercial value. I am not aware of any studies which show the relative value of mutually exclusive commercial and recreational use of a given site, but I think this conflict will grow and a well thought-out research design for it is in order.[3]

Wilman and Krutilla utilized a version of hedonic analysis in an attempt to estimate beach quality. Hedonic analysis evolved from the work Griliches (1971) and others undertook to treat quality changes in price indexes. (If a car with more safety features this year has a larger sticker price than the car last year without safety features, has the price of a car risen or has the price of a quality constant car remained unchanged and quality increased?) Lancaster put forth the case for hedonic analysis clearly when he argued that individuals purchase goods for the sum of the characteristics they provide. In the present context people are willing to pay more for rental accommodations on Cape Cod if doing so provides access to higher quality beaches, as well as better housing characteristics and closer access to beaches in general.

Wilman and Krutilla first partitioned rental accommodations into four categories; interviewed respondents regarding location and frequency of beach use and housing characteristics; collected data on beach quality such as congestion, debris on beach, and oil pollution. Second, an hedonic non-linear price equation was estimated by regressing rental value on housing and beach quality characteristics for the respondent's most frequently used beach. Third, the marginal or implicit price of the significant beach qualities was computed (by taking the derivative with respect to the characteristic). Fourth, the demand curve for characteristics was estimated using the computed implicit price of characteristics, the level of characteristics and the socioeconomic attributes of the households. A final step involved computing the loss of consumer's surplus if the quality of a beach changed in a specified way.

The results of this study are disappointing. Oil pollution and debris on beach, properly measured, should have negative and significant prices for all types of renters. Oil pollution never was statistically significant and debris was a significant determinant only in the rental value of vacation homes. The major cause of the disappointment I want to stress here is the inadequacy of data. It begins with the refusal of realtors to provide access to listings and is only exacerbated by respondents refusing to the interviewed or giving biased answers. A suitably financed research project can resolve these problems but large budgets rarely are available for social science research designs such as this one.

The other problem is measuring oil pollution. In this study it was measured by whether there was oil sheen on water contiguous to a beach, as measured by whether there was oil sheen on water contiguous to a beach, as measured by a low altitude photograph taken during a four hour interval on a given day. It is clear that the idea, if not the execution, was headed in the right direction. One needs to have a measure of oil pollution on the beaches in the water where that measure corresponds to the "consumer's" perception and response. The measure must be accurate for the period during which an individual can make substitution decisions. There must be adequate variation in measured oil pollution obtained either through time series, cross-section data or both.

To express the requirement more dramatically, it is not now possible to use observed behavior in Alaska to estimate either the effect of an oil spill off the coast of Alaska or the impact of off-shore oil and gas development much beyond present levels. A promising strategy might be to conduct a study in an area where spills or development had occurred and then make a regional translation. A third alternative is to ask people hypothetical questions about how they would react. It is important to stress that baseline studies are imperative to undertake. I will return to their importance and design below.

Several years ago Freeman (1974) argued correctly that there was a flaw in the studies which obtained the value of improving air quality by taking the product of air quality change and the marginal value of air quality obtained from regressing property values of housing characteristics, neighborhood characteristics and some measure of air quality. Freeman argued that improvements in air quality can be expected to be ubiquitous in the given residential area, not just at a single site. However, the estimated marginal value of air quality is derived from a partial equilibrium setting--the market price for a house with poor surrounding air quality is established given high air quality elsewhere in that residential market. That given is violated when air quality is changed throughout the area.

Incorporating Freeman's insight, we can explain how to estimate the value of beach (air) quality using readily available information. It is useful to assume a setting in which travel expenses, rather than rent, are the important cost component. Individuals take trips to a beach or fishing site to enjoy its characteristics. The travel cost technique focuses on only one beach, but it makes more sense to assume that if individuals at a given origin choose a slightly more distant beach, it is because the extra beach characteristics are worth the extra travel costs. For every given origin, an hedonic price equation is estimated from travel costs regressed on observed beach and/or marine characteristics, such as frequency of appearance of tar stains.[4] This first stage equation yields the marginal value of a characteristic which may or may not be constant. Since people from different origins can be expected to face different opportunities--are in a different market--we can expect there to be price variation in characteristics such as beach quality across markets.

In a second stage of investigation, demand for each qualitative characteristic is determined using the cross-section variation in hedonic prices obtained across "markets" from the first stage; observed qualities chosen by individuals; and relevant socioeconomic characteristics across the sample. A third step involves estimating the number of trips of varying length individuals take to one or more sites as a function of the price of a trip and other demand determinants. An oil spill which effects one or more beaches effectively increases the cost of acquiring a given level of beach quality. Given the demand curve for quality fron hedonic analysis, the loss of consumer's surplus due to the spill, is, to a first approximation, the difference between the cost curves magnified by the mean number of trips.

Brown and Mendelsohn (1981) developed the hedonic travel cost technique and used it to estimate the demand for steelhead density in rivers in the state of Washington. Whereas the example above keys on expenditure related to travel cost, the hedonic analysis portrayed here also will work if variations in rental rates in a market are used to determine the price of characteristics in that market, and variations in the prices observed across markets[5] are used to determine the demand functions of qualitative characteristics, such as beach quality,[6] a characteristic more relevant for beach quality.

I have spent more time discussing research approaches than many would have thought necessary. My purpose was to try to show that: quality is a critical concern for many interesting recreational research problems; past applied approaches are inadequate for valuing changes in quality; and one technique, hedonic analysis, as spelled out here, is promising but it is data hungry. Although the discussion has been mainly about oil spills, the importance and difficulty of measuring quality changes is generic. Other marine activities which change quality , such as ocean dumping, might have been used. Conversely, quality enhancing investment options would have served well.

If we are to estimate the damages to marine oriented recreation due to an oil spill or any change in the quality of the marine environment, it is important to identify the most economically important coastal recreation regions and the areas most likely to bear the brunt of future oil spills. Those who recreate in that area and in substitute areas, should be sampled and their expenditures and participation rates in substitute and complementary activities need to be ascertained. Demand functions for marine related recreation activities need to be estimated, with care being taken to include those demand determinants which will be affected by an oil spill.

It is easy to imagine focussing on six or more study areas along the Atlantic, Pacific and Gulf Coasts. It would be natural to identify: several beach quality variables; perhaps a few water quality variables to which swimmers and boaters react; and some measures relevant to fishing such as fish densities, probabilities of catch or success levels for different species. These studies would not be inexpensive. Each one could cost at least $100,000 dollars and as much as $200,000 dollars. I fail to see how recreation damage assessment seriously can be undertaken using observed--rather than hypothetical--behavior if we do not have a grip on actual recreation behavior in the absence of an environmental perturbation.

III. Sport Fishing

A major marine dependent recreation activity is sport fishing. There are a variety of reasons why it is important to know the economic value of saltwater angling, the value of fishing success and perhaps the value of species density for those fish actively sought. First, oil spills may decrease the available sport harvest throughout the period of recovery, and an estimate of the related economic damage is needed. Second, there often is a continuous conflict between the sport and commercial catch of species such as salmon. Economists can contribute to the discussion of optimal allocations if the value of sport-caught species is known. Third, investment programs can enhance fishery stocks through, for example, the construction and operation of hatchery programs. More unusual forms of investment include genetic engineering and just general research and development expenditures.

An interesting example of research payoff is the discovery that late release of salmon smelts results in their remaining in Puget Sound where a larger fraction is susceptible to domestic gear. Whether these and similar enhancement investments are worthwhile economically, requires either knowledge about the value of success and how success is influenced by density or knowledge directly about the value of density.

Most studies estimate the value of fishing days, leaving the decision maker puzzled about how to transform the value of a day to the marginal value of fish. Exceptions are Mathews and Brown (1970) and Crutchfield and Schelle (1978). There are several ways to estimate the value of added supplies of fish or added success. The first is to use hypothetical willingness-to-pay (sell) or bidding game techniques. For reasons given previously, I do not recommend funding such studies unless budgets cannot afford the development of more dependable techniques. The second approach is the hedonic-travel cost analysis just discussed, which I naturally favor. Third, when man's actions open a new site or close an old one for a period, it may be useful to use a system of travel-cost based site demand equations first developed by Burt and Brewer (1971) in their study of Corps of Engineers reservoirs and subsequently applied by Ciccetti, Fisher and Smith (1976) in their study of a proposed new ski facility, Mineral King, in California.

Following this latter approach, an individual from a given origin with known socioeconomic characteristics faces alternative salt water fishing sites, each with an estimable cost of travel and access and some measure, such as density or expected or actual success. An interrelated system of trip demand equations is estimated. Benefits from the fishing sites can be computed, with all sites included, and then with one site excluded, to obtain a measure of the loss, for instance, of an action or decision which closes a fishing site. The model works by loading all travel costs onto one characteristic of each site, density or success. If fishermen pick sites for other reasons, the technique obviously provides biased answers in its attribution of all value to the fish.

A fourth approach is exemplified by Vaughan and Russell's research (1981) on the value of water quality improvement in enhancing fresh water fishing. I can only give a hint, in a paragraph, of this book-length study, still being revised. Following Cicchetti's framework, in the first and second stages, the authors estimate logit equations, using 1975 U.S. National Hunting and Fishing Survey data, to predict the probability of being a fisherman and the probability of fishing for certain fish.[7]

In the third stage, demand for types of fish and fishing is estimated using responses to about 200 questionnaires sent out to fee fishing sites in the United States. Site characteristics or supply variables, such as acreage of available fresh water in a state, enter the estimation equations. By feats of heroism in research, Vaughan and Russell translate changes in FWPCA standards into increased water quality and increased availability of water for certain fresh water species. These favorable changes then increase the number of fishermen, induce some substitution among species fished, and increase the days fished, all of which are converted into dollar benefits using the estimated logit and demand equations. The first two stages of this model--predicting whether one fishes or not and what one fishes for--are important to include when the events studied are likely to induce substitution in and out of the fishermen's ranks and substitution among species fished. Whether Vaughan and Russell's third stage estimation of demand is superior to the hedonic approach remains an open, researchable question at this time. Regardless of the approach adopted, I would urge the inclusion of expected success as a variable which explains when and where people fish. Fishing is better in one spot than in another and fishing is better during one part of a season compared to another. Local newspapers in the Northwest and perhaps elsewhere publish information of this type. It would be tedious but perhaps rewarding to incorporate expectations in sport fishing demand analysis.

I think there does not exist research on salt water fishing values and demand functions which have a theoretical framework and data of sufficient quality to warrant publication in a respectable professional economics journal. If I am correct then research funding should be available to rectify this lack. The issues involving sport fishing are too momentous to continue to be resolved with woefully inadequate economic analysis.

IV. Non-Consumptive Valuation

Some people enjoy knowing that there is a wild expanse of undeveloped beach or recall with pleasure the color and clarity of water they experienced during a previous vacation. These are examples of existence value and a form of option value which is representative of a class of benefits people enjoy without making expenditures and often without any overt behavior associated with the benefits. By definition then, no technique relying on matching up differences in associated expenditures with differences in observed behavior can successfully discover these values. Only procedures relying on introspection can be used unless it is credible to equate in some fashion these "goods" with others which do have a known value.

Some form of willingness-to-pay (sell) or bidding game techniques will have to be relied on for answers in these circumstances. An example is the loss people incur when they learn that marine life, such as sea birds and mammals, are destroyed by an oil spill. Taking the status of the research procedures and existing national and international legal canons regarding compensation into account-- these damages are not likely to be compensable--I would not give this research very high priority unless I could be convinced that these damages are a large component of total damages. However, moral outrage is one facet of this problem which intrigues me. Can economists value moral outrage in a defensible way? Could an imaginative study of court cases provide any useful guidelines on this subject?

V. Research to Guide Fishery Management Council Policies

In recent years the Pacific Management Council has promulgated regulations which determine the ocean harvest of salmon among commercial, Indian and sport fishermen. The Council's tools for managing the sport catch are time and area closures and daily catch limitations. Whether the Council should use these policies or whether pricing policies would be superior is an interesting question to be addressed at the end of this section. Adequacy of research for accurate calibration of the physical rules first needs to be considered. Despite the fact that the Pacific Fishery Management Council has been setting regulations for a number of years and results have wildly departed from stated quantitative goals, it has shown no inclination to fund economic research which would provide it with better predictive procedures. Indeed the Council has no behavioral data to support its decisions. Each open and closed period for each area demarcated by the Council theoretically constitutes a separate market. Therefore data and analysis must recognize the differentiated markets. Yet no sport (or commercial) fishery data have been codified along the temporal and geographic boundaries imbedded in annual Council policy.

Suppose there are two ocean regions (N)orth and (S)outh and a non-ocean (I)nside sport salmon fishing area (Puget Sound). There are three time periods. S is closed during the first period (t_1);

N is (C)losed during the second (t_2) and at all other times and places the season is (O)pen as illustrated in the tableau below:

Region	t_1	t_2	t_3
N	O	C	O
S	C	O	O
I	O	O	O

It is not necessary to be very formal to make the following important point. When the Council decides to close S during the first part of the season, it must anticipate that sport fishermen will substitute open areas for the closed ones. Area substitution also can be expected to occur when area N is closed in the second period. The greater the ease of substitution, when relative travel cost, relative success, and other relevant site characteristics are considered, the greater will be the congestion and pressure on salmon stocks in the open areas. Estimating the substitution effects will entail specifying demand in each area during each period as a function of the price of travel to that area and the price of the other areas. When an area is closed, its price is set at the level which guarantees no demand. The specification might well expand if fishermen substitute between periods as they reasonably might. I have added the inside area (I) to take account of the fact that the Council regulates the maximum sport catch per day on the ocean, but permitted catch in Puget Sound is outside the Pacific Management Council's jurisdiction. Decreasing daily maximums on the ocean in one period can be expected to induce substitution between periods and between ocean and inside areas.

I know of no study designed carefully enough to aid the Council in these sorts of deliberations. There are few studies in which success even enters, and these were not designed for the task at hand (Stevens, (1966); Mathews and Brown, (1970); Crutchfield and Schelle (1978)).

While regulating sport salmon fishing is specific to the Pacific Fishery Management Council, the solution to the problem is a general one and is relevant to all management agencies who regulate a sport fishery with some combination of time and area closures and catch limits. I would give the highest priority to an applied research project designed to shed light on this problem.

Whether fishery management councils should use physical or economic regulations is a subject worthy of study if the research design is subtle enough to explain when economic policies should or should not be used. One possible direction to pursue is the application of Weitzman's approach (1974) to the fishery. In his analyis, uncertainty is acknowledged and the relative superiority of the economic or physical instruments of regulation can be ascertained using efficiency criteria. Suppose that a council sets regulations at the beginning of the season knowing only the distribution of the

demand and supply curve. Disturbances are specified to shift the
demand and supply curves in a parallel fashion. Sport fishermen
learn about the location and availability of fish as the season
progresses. That is, the supply curve of fish is more certain to
the fisherman than it is to the agency setting policies. Suppose
further, that with the population of fish fairly well known, the
cost per trip is pretty constant; i.e., the private marginal cost
(MC) of success is linear. To this must be added the marginal
social cost component of fish, to reflect the fact that associated
with sport harvest today is the economic value of foregone future
streams of physical productivity. Harvest today means marginally
less fish in the future and may also mean higher marginal harvest
costs if these vary with the size of stocks. A linear social component of the social marginal cost curve illustrated in Figure 1 is
the result of a clever proof by Koenig (1981). The proof holds
when next period's fish population is linearly related to today's
fish population in the range of management interest.

If the above rules of the game hold and demand and supply curves
are linear to a first approximation, then it can be proved rigorously that regulation by quota is superior to regulation by prices
when the demand curve is flatter than the supply curve. Figure 1
below illustrates the reason why.[8] In contrast, regulation by
price is better than a quota policy when demand is relatively steep-
er than supply. In Figure 1, I have assumed, for visual ease only,

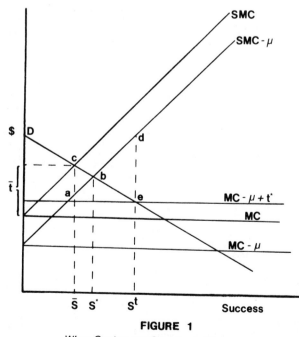

FIGURE 1

When Quotas are Superior to Charges

that the private marginal cost component is flat. The optimal level of catch ($\overline{S}$) occurs naturally where marginal value (D) equals social marginal cost (SMC). In the static world a tax of $\overline{t}$ per unit of success would achieve this outcome as would a quota of $\overline{S}$, which could be translated back to the individual demand functions (which make up the aggregate demand function (D)).

If the regulator must set a tax or a quota before the actual demand or supply curve is known, the expected value of t = $\overline{t}$ or S = $\overline{S}$ is best (because of linear demand and linear supply). If, for example, a disturbance (u) shifted social marginal cost down to SMC -u,S* would have been the best quota. But the regulator does not know the actual relations in advance, so the loss from using the quota regulation based on expected outcomes, relative to the ideal outcome, is given by the area below the demand curve and above the cost curve (abc). If, on the other hand, fishermen faced the tax ($\overline{t}$) and their costs shifted down by u, they would enjoy S^t level of success. With the tax, the loss is bde, the area under SMC and above demand. Since bde > abc, the quota is a loss minimizing regulation. The superiority of a quota regulation over price rules holds when demand is uncertain and the results could have been illustrated with an upward supply shift as well, as Koenig's proof makes clear. In which sport fisheries are supply curves likely to be steep and demand curves relatively flat? Are these phenomena the norm so that we need look no further for an explanation of the extensive use of quotas in the sport fishery? Doubtful.[9] More likely, research on regulation options will be a rich lode to explore if the analytical framework embraces greater realism. Uncertainty needs to be acknowledged and alternative strategies for pursuing one's interest in public decision making arenas need to be considered.

VI. Shellfish Research

In 1980, Massachusetts passed into law, proposition 2½, which put a limit on property taxes and effectively forced cities and towns in Massachusetts to look elsewhere for revenues. In order to raise more revenue, one small town raised its clam license fees and sadly discovered that total revenue from these license sales fell. The enemy of course, appears in the form of an elastic demand curve for clamming. Is there an existing body of empirical research which would have guarded the selectmen of this town against making such a mistake? Not to my knowledge.

The Smith, Conrad and Story study (1978) of recreational clamming, using willingness-to-pay and no measure of availability, is acceptable, given the limitations of data, but there is a need for better analysis founded on an improved data base. It is essential that stock density data be collected for at least two reasons. First, it is reasonable to believe that the number of sport clammers depends on availability of clams as does the duration of participation. When density increases, the cost of a given level of success decreases for an individual. Additionally, when density increases, utility or value is directly enhanced by increased success.

Without measures of density the important quality dimension cannot be estimated and its omission will introduce bias in the econometric models used. Second, a number of important policy issues cannot be addressed adequately if density is not estimated. The most likely source of substantial economic damage from an oil spill is the reduction of stocks of slow fish either directly or through damage to the habitat. Clamming does not cease, except in the very short run. The oil spill simply produces a lower quality experience. The only satisfactory way to estimate such a loss is by taking explicit account of density changes through time.

Recent analysis of some limited clam density data makes me confident that density indeed matters. Using physical historical data on recreational harvest (<u>Protothaca</u>) collected in Garrison Bay, Washington by Gallucci and Rawson (1979), we estimated the following relationships:

$$\text{Digger Trips} = 7.5 + 0.7 \text{ Density}, \quad \overline{R}^2 = 0.265$$
$$\text{Catch/Trip} = 0.4 \text{ Density}^{0.90} \quad \overline{R}^2 = 0.22.$$

The density coefficients were statistically very significant. Lack of economic data precluded further research which, incidentally was supported by the OMPA part of NOAA. This raises the important point which cannot be emphasized enough: the collection of economic and biological data should be a coordinated enterprise. In view of the exceptional susceptibility of slow fish to damage by an oil spill, a properly conceived study of shellfish value should have top priority.

VII. Model Specification

Most of the economic research bearing on marine related recreation has focused on particular theoretical and econometric issues such as the value and treatment of time, the role of substitutes (McConnell and Strand (1880); Wilman (1980); Scott (1965)); congestion (Deyak and Smith (1978); McConnell (1977,1980); Stevens and Allen (1980); Anderson (1980) Wetzel (1977)); the use of supply variables in reduced form equations (Hay and McConnell (1979)); heteroscedasticity in customary travel cost analysis (Bowes and Loomis (1980)); the advantage, if any, of ordinary least squares over logit analysis (Smith and Munley (1978); Vaughan and Russell (1981)); and problems of aggregation (Wetzstein and McNeely (1980)).

Time and congestion are two areas of research worthy of support, if the proper data base existed or could be created. To estimate the value of time, particularly the value of travel time, it would be advantageous to identify one or more sites accessible by several modes of travel, which vary in time and cost, and where choice of mode confers no favorable characteristics. There ought not be more pleasant sights to see if one drives rather than flies; ferries ought not be more pleasurable than rival modes; automobiles ought not have an unmeasured advantage in carrying luggage to the marine area to be studied. The analysis of a modal choice patterned after McFadden's study (1974) could then be used to estimate the value of time.

The strongest case one can make for preserving undeveloped sites today rests, I believe, on estimating the costs of congestion. If development is costly to reverse, if income, population growth and other factors, such as changing exchange rates, shift marine related demand functions out through time, and if congestion is negatively valued, then the more distant, less used marine recreation sites will become the attractive, valued places in the future and should be preserved. I am not sure of all the circumstances under which congestion is a negative good, and my research with Mendelsohn suggests that congestion is a subtle beast. When information is costly, congregations may signal a good fishing site or a good beach and attract more people on balance. So, why and how people make location selections are among the ingredients well-done future congestion studies may have to include.

Summary of Research Topics

1. Estimate regional demand or value functions for one or more beach, and water qualities such as congestion or some measure of cleanliness which bear on oil pollution. Choose important sub-regions along the Atlantic, Gulf and Pacific Coasts.

   Caution: The probability of failure is high unless the study is carefully designed and an adequate budget is available.

2. Estimate, directly or indirectly, regional demand or value functions for major sport fish and sport fish combinations, including success or fish density and price of substitute opportunities. Choose substitutes that are relevant in case of an oil spill.

3. For sport fisheries regulated by management councils, design regional demand or value function studies using the management council's regulatory geographic and temporal zones and other management variables (e.g., success) analyze creel limits.

4. Undertake a study on sport fishing valuation by location, using time series data and expectations as measured by fishing success at different sites reported by local newspapers, sport fishing magazines or other readily available sources of information.

5. Design and execute an imaginative study to estimate the existence, preservation, and option value of marine mammals and non-consumptive experiences such as undeveloped beaches, "pristine" marshes and "clean" near shore environments. (Can court settlements provide a guide to the value of some of these elusive "goods"?)

6. Analyze why management councils use physical not economic regulatory tools.

6a. Consider whether one can introduce uncertainty or asymmetric information into the environment and show when physical regulations are superior to charges.

7. Estimate sport clamming demand and participation functions, including density as an independent variable.

8. Estimate what is the value of time when one is on a vacation, driving to a marine recreation area, participating in a marine recreation activity.

9. Consider how beach congestion affects the value of a beach day.

10. Isolate the major economic uses of coastal areas which are competitive with or complementary to marine related recreation activities. (A.M. Freeman, III).

11. Determine the positive and negative economic impacts of harbor and shoreline development activities such as seawalls and channel dredging on marine recreation activities. (A.M. Freeman, III).

12. Determine in what ways and to what economic degree recreational boating activities are affected by the pollution, increased traffic congestion and other consequences of marine developments, such as the construction of sea walls, channel dredging, etc.? (A.M. Freeman, III).

13. Consider how responsive recreation activities are to promotional and advertising efforts? (Hal Lyman).

14. Estimate the economic value of more dimensions of sport fishing (and other) marine related activities. Size variation and difficulty of landing are other attributes, in addition to numbers, which give rise to value. (Hal Lyman).

Research topics raised during discussion include:

1. Analyze the effects of commercial gear and catch on sport fishing.

2. Determine the value of enhancement (hatcheries, artificial reefs) to recreational ocean use.

3. Evaluate regulation in various areas of the country for their effectiveness, redistributive consequences and the incentives created. Determine which are most effective in various circumstances (uncertainty as to catch, time of year, reproductive cycle, types of use). Determine the effect of changes in regulation on levels of compliance, enforcement costs and use patterns.

Notes

1. The loss of value incurred by those who did not come to Brittany because of the oil spill was estimated by asking German tour operators the extra cost their clients had to bear to enjoy the same satisfaction a Brittany vacation would have provided.

2. It is sometimes argued that this sort of strategic behavior can be avoided if the respondent is told that all will have to pay the average value and that the sample is too large for one person to change the mean significantly. Such a counter-vailing argument goes too far. It tells the respondent he is insignificant so there can be no reason for him to participate unless he is paid and no reason to tell the truth if the truth is guaranteed not to matter.

3. Brown and Pollakowski (1977) estimated the value of open space around fresh-water lakes where nearby development was homo-geneous using first stage hedonic techniques discussed below. The estimates are not robust for alternative specifications of independent variables. Heterogeneous shoreline use could further complicate valuation procedures.

4. This approach differs from the Wilman and Krutilla study in which observations in all towns were assumed to be in the same market, hence only one regression was run for each type of accommodation.

5. Using data from different markets is the distinguishing mark between the Brown and Mendelsohn approach and the single mar-ket proposal set forth by Rosen which is incorrect except for cases in which highly restrictive assumptions are made about individuals' preferences.

6. Vaughan and Russell proposed to obtain a travel cost demand curve for each site in question. In the second stage, the parameters of the demand curve are regressed on the character-istics of the site. There must be a set of conditions which, if true, would have the Vaughan and Russell approach give the same answers as the Brown and Mendelsohn method. This might be a useful analytical exercise for someone to undertake.

7. Davidson, Adams and Seneca also used the technique and more recently Caswell and McConnell applied the simultaneous logit model to estimate determinants of participation in salt water related activities.

8. Since the regulator must enunciate rules before the regulated respond in this model, the regulated have more accurate in-formation and this gives rise to the relative superiority of one form of regulation.

9. Surely possibilities for substitution differ dramatically across sport fisheries thus affecting the slope of the demand functions. Just as variable are intrinsic rates of growth across fish populations which affect the slope of the social cost component of the social marginal cost function.

References

Anderson, L. (1980). "Estimating the Benefits of Recreation Under Conditions Congestion: Comments and Extension," J. of Env. Man. 7 (December): 401-406.

Bishop, R.C. and T. Heberlein (1979). "Travel Cost and Hypothetical Valuation of Outdoor Recreation: Comparisons with an Artificial Market," University of Wisconsin, Mimeo (June).

Bowes, M.D. and J.B. Loomis (1980). "A Note on the Use of Travel Cost Models with Unequal Zonal Populations," Land Econ. 56 (November): 465-470.

Brookshire, D. B. Ives and W. Schulze (1976). "The Valuation of Aesthetic Preferences," J. Env. Man. 3: 325-346.

Brown, G.M., R. Congar and E. Wilman. "Non-Market Damages," Chap. 4 in currently untitled book on Amoco Cadiz oil spill to be published by NOAA through University of Rhode Island.

Brown, G.M. and R. Mendelsohn (1981). "The Hedonic Travel Cost Method," Mimeo, Dept. of Economics, University of Washington.

Brown, G.M. and H. Pollakowski (1977). "Economic Value of Shoreline," Rev. of Econ. and Stat. 59 (August): 272-278.

Burt, O.R. and D. Brewer (1971). "Estimation of Net Social Benefits from Outdoor Recreation," Econometrica 39(5) (September): 813-827.

Caswell, M. and K. McConwell (1980). "Simultaneous Estimation of Jointly Dependent Recreation Participation Function," J. of Env. Econ. and Man. 7 (March): 65-76.

Cicchetti, C.J. (1973). Forecasting Recreation in the United States (Lexington: Lexington Books).

Cicchetti, C.J., A.C. Fisher and V.K. Smith (1976). "An Econometric Evaluation of a Generalized Consumer Surplus Measure: The Mineral King Controversy," Econometrica 44 (November): 1259-1276.

Crutchfield, J. and K. Schelle (1978). "An Economic Analysis of Washington Ocean Recreational Salmon Fishing," Pacific Fishery Management Council, Portland, Oregon (October).

Davidson, P., F.G. Adams and J. Seneca (1966). "The Social Value of Water Recreational Facilities Resulting from an Improvement in Water Quality: The Delaware Estuary," in A.V. Kneese and S.C. Smith, eds., Water Research (Baltimore: Johns Hopkins University Press for Resources for the Future).

Davis, R.K. (1963). "The Value of Outdoor Recreation: An Economic Study of the Maine Woods," Unpublished Ph.D. dissertation, Harvard University.

Deyak, T. and V.K. Smith (1978). "Congestion and Participation in Outdoor Recreation: A Household Production Function Approach," J. of Env. Econ. Man.: 63-80.

Dwyer, J. and J. Kelley (1976). "Guidelines for Valuation of Water-Based Recreation," Water Resources Center, University of Illinois, Urbana-Champaign (November).

Freeman, A.M., III (1979). "The Benefits of Environmental Improvement," (Baltimore, Johns Hopkins Press).

_____ (1974). "On Estimating Air Pollution Control Benefits from Land Value Studies," J. of Env. Econ. Man. 1(2): 74-83.

Gallucci, V. and K. Rawson (1979). "The Population Dynamics and Management Modeling of Harvested Bi-Valves in Garrison Bay, Washington," Unpublished Report to Washington Dept. of Fisheries and USNPS.

Griliches, Z. (1971). Price Indexes and Quality Change (Cambridge, Mass.: Harvard University Press).

Hammack, J. and G.M. Brown, Jr. (1974). Waterfowl and Wetlands: Towards Bioeconomic Analysis, Johns Hopkins University Press, Baltimore.

Hay, M.J. and K.E. McConnell (1979). "An Analysis of Participation in Nonconsumptive Wildlife Recreation," Land Econ. 55 (Nov.): 460-471.

Koenig, E.F. (1981). "Uncertainty and Alternative Regulatory Procedures," Discussion Paper, University of Washington (November).

Lancaster, K. (1971). Consumer Demand: A New Approach (New York: Columbia University Press).

Mathews, S.B. and G.M. Brown (1970). Economic Evaluation of the 1967 Sport Salmon Fisheries of Washington, Technical Report 2, Washington Department of Fisheries.

McConnell, K. (1977). "Congestion and Willingness to Pay: A Study of Beach Use," Land Econ. 53 (May): 185-195.

_____ (1980). "Valuing Congested Recreation Sites," J. of Env. Econ. Man. 7 (December): 389-394

McConnell, K.E. and I. Strand (1981). "Measuring the Cost of Time in Recreation Demand Analysis: An Application to Sportfishing," Amer. J. of Agri. Econ. 63(1) (February): 153-156.

McFadden, D. (1974). "Conditional Logit Analysis of Qualitative Choice Behavior," in Frontiers in Econometrics, ed. by P. Zarembka. New York: Academic Press Orig. (Working Paper No. 199/BART 10, Urban and Regional Studies Institute, Univ. of California, Berkeley, 1973).

Rosen, S. (1974). "Hedonic Prices and Implicit Markets: Product Differentiation in Price Competition," J. of Pol. Econ. 82 (April): 34-55.

Rowe, R., R. d'Arge and D. Brookshire (1980). "An Experiment on the Economic Value of Visibility," J. of Env. Econ. Man. 7: 1-19.

Scott, A. (1965). "The Valuation of Game Resources: Some Theoretical Aspects," Can. Fish. Report 4 (May): 27-47.

Smith, R., J. Conrad and D. Storey (1978). "An Economic Valuation of Recreational Clamming in Massachusetts," Univ. of Mass. Agr. Exp. Sta. Res. Bull. No. 654 (April).

Smith, V.K. and V.G. Munley (1978). "The Relative Performance of Various Estimates of Recreation Participation Equations," J. of Leisure Res. 10(3): 167-176.

Stevens, J.B. (1966). "Recreation Benefits from Water Pollution Control," Water Resources Research 2(2): 167-82.

Stevens, T. and P.G. Allen (1980). "Estimating the Benefits of Recreation Modes Conditions of Congestions," J. of Env. Econ. Man. 7 (December): 395-400.

Vaughan, W. and C. Russell (1981). "The National Benefits of Water Pollution Control: Fresh Water Recreational Fishing," Draft Manuscript, Resources for the Future (April).

Weitzman, M. (1974). "Prices vs. Quantities," Rev. of Econ. Stud. XLI: 477-91.

Wetzel, J.N. (1977). "Estimating the Benefits of Recreation Under Conditions of Congestion," J. of Env. Econ. Man. 4(3): 239-246.

Wetzstein, M.E. and J.G. McNeely, Jr. (1980). "Specification Errors and Inference in Recreation Demand Models," Amer. J. of Agri. Econ. 62 (November): 798-800.

Willig, R. (1976). "Consumer's Surplus Without Apology," Amer. Econ. Rev. 66: 587-597.

Wilman, E.A. (1980). "The Value of Time in Recreation Benefit Studies," J. of Env. Econ. Man. 7 (September): 272-286.

Wilman, E.A. and J. Krutilla (1980). Hedonic Prices and Beach Recreational Values: A Case Study of Cape Cod and Marthas Vineyard, Unpublished Resources for the Future (February).

Recreation

A. Myrick Freeman III

I.

In this stimulating paper Gardner Brown identifies several management issues or conflicts and describes research that has been done
and potentially fruitful research that might provide useful information to resource managers and policy makers. As Brown says, most
of the research problems in this area stem from the public goods
dimension of marine activity and from externalities associated with
marine resource utilization. Thus a major objective of research is
the estimation of the values or implicit prices of marine resource
outputs and externalities so that appropriate prices and values can
guide resource management decisions. With all of this, I quite
agree.

Before turning to the specifics of Brown's paper, I would like to
step back for a moment and survey the terrain in an effort to provide a more comprehensive organizing framework for looking at research issues.

II.

The ocean resource is the source of a variety of service flows and
commodities: transportation, commercial fisheries, minerals, oil,
and recreation. Let us assume that the objective of policy is to
manage this resource so as to produce the maximum contribution to
human welfare. What do we need to know to achieve the objective?
Do we know it? And if not, how do we find it out?

I can see three types of questions that need to be answered if the
ocean resource is to be managed economically. The first concerns
the nature of the opportunities set. What are the trade-offs among
the rates of different service and commodity flows? Are there any
complementarities between pairs of service and/or commodity flows?
The second concerns the values of the services and commodity flows.
Third, how will users of the ocean resource respond to different
institutional arrangements and management activities?

Brown focuses primarily on the value type of question, and he gives
a couple of interesting examples of questions dealing with behavioral responses to policy actions. But he has very little to say
about research involving the trade-offs and nature of the opportunities set. It might be argued that learning more about the opportunity surface and trade-offs is more a task for biologists and
other marine scientists than for economists. But economists can
have a lot to say about how the scientific questions are formulated.
I recommend that economists be involved intimately in the design of
scientific research and data gathering efforts that are undertaken
in support of ocean resource management activities.

Turning now to marine recreation, an obvious impact that Brown discusses extensively is that of oil pollution on beach recreation.
Other ocean resource utilization activities can also affect beach
recreation adversely. Of course discharges of conventional forms
of pollution from the shore can result in the closure of beaches to
water contact recreation. Shoreline developments and changes in
coastal land use can pre-empt the use of beaches for recreation
purposes. Channel dredging or sea wall construction can alter currents and sand movements and degrade beach resources. In all
cases it is necessary to know the value of the beach as a recreation site in order to compute the benefits of protecting a beach
from these adverse impacts.

Beaches provide other services besides recreation, for example,
protection against flooding and erosion for land areas behind the
beach. These protective functions can be degraded by a variety of
activities, including over-extensive development and utilization of
the beach for recreation, alteration of sand movements, and changes
in land use. Research should be undertaken into the economic value
of the protective services provided by the beach and dune system.
These benefits may be added to the recreation benefits associated
with preserving beach areas. And these protective services may be
a significant component of the total economic value of beaches.

The extent and value of recreation fishing can be affected adversely by a variety of other ocean resource utilization activities including exploitation of the ocean as a waste sink, commercial fishing activity, and waterborne transportation. There also may be
complementarities between recreation and fishing and structures
such as oil well platforms and artificial reefs that alter the
marine habitat.

Brown does not mention boating as a separate recreation activity.
But my observation while flying over Marblehead, Massachusetts, and
Shilshole Marina in Seattle on my way to the conference suggests
that the numbers of participants in marine boating is large. I
would recommend at least some preliminary research into the number
of boating recreationists, the possible range of economic value
attached to boating activities, and the potential impacts of shoreline development, increased shipping traffic, offshore oil development, and other activities on the quality and economic value of
boating activity.

Another management issue of political significance associated with recreation boating is the nature, extent of, and source of financing for the public provision of navigation and boating safety services. The U.S. Coast Guard provides and services aids to navigation and maintains an extensive network of facilities for search and rescue activities on the coastal waters. The facilities are used not only by recreationists but also by commercial fishermen and shippers. There is controversy over the "adequacy" of the Coast Guard's search and rescue capability. And as the proposal to impose a tax on recreation boat owners shows, there is controversy over the source of financing for this system. The proposed user fees could be viewed as a form of benefit taxation. This raises some interesting research questions concerning the magnitude of the benefits provided to recreation boaters; the appropriate vehicle for financing these services; whether user fees should be earmarked for the Coast Guard; and the nature of the relationship between the cost of these services and their economic value to recreationists and other boaters.

III.

Concerning approaches to valuing beach recreation activities, it will be helpful to distinguish between the chronic, low level pollution incidental to ongoing activities and acute pollution incidents such as the Amoco-Cadiz oil spill. Brown identifies and discusses four approaches to valuing beach recreation: surveys, the travel cost technique, hedonic prices, and the hedonic travel cost technique. I have nothing to add to his discussion of bidding games, their possible biases, and problems in implementation. But I want to describe briefly an alternative survey instrument for a hypothetical valuation which has shown some promise in preliminary applications. This is the "rank order" technique in which individuals are asked to rank in order of preference alternative settings, for example, beaches, which differ by several characteristics, including some measure of pollution. The alternatives are usually portrayed by sets of photographs and other descriptive material. If one of the characteristics that varies across alternatives is a measure of price, for example an admission fee, then it is possible to impute the values of the other characteristics. Although this is a hypothetical technique, it may avoid some of the biases that threaten the bidding game approach, for example, starting point bias.

Brown recommends that in general surveys not be used to determine the damages associated with oil pollution. I agree with this recommendation at least in the case of the damages to an acute spill. But I would recommend some experimentation with bidding games and rank order surveys to determine the values of various beach characteristics, including absence of incidental oil pollution.

The travel cost technique is designed to estimate the demand curve of a specific site. As Brown makes clear, it is important to control for the availability of alternative or substitute sites. There are also basic research issues concerning the value of time as a component of travel costs, the impact of congestion at a site on its demand, and the relationship between measures of quality at the site and demand. If a site is now being used for recreation and is thought to be at risk of an acute spill, a travel cost study can provide an ex ante estimate of the potential damages if a spill were to close that beach for some period of tiem. I recommend that NOAA identify one or more recreation beaches and carry out the appropriate travel cost studies to estimate the recreation values of these beaches.

The hedonic price approach has most often been applied to the prices of residential properties to determine the value of absence of noise or air pollution. In principle, it could also be applied to the prices of shore front properties in order to determine the market assessment of potential damages to property in the event of an oil spill. Property price reflects the discounted value of the expected stream of future utilities from that site. If at any point in time oil operations such as off-shore drilling or tanker passages are ongoing, there is some probability distribution of spill events of various sizes and degree of severity. There is also some range of potential impacts that varies across properties according to their location, degree of protection, etc. If the property market is in equilibrium, and this is a necessary condition for applying the hedonic technique, then the probabilities and differential impacts will have been built into the structure of property prices. In principle the hedonic technique can identify the marginal impact of the expected damages of oil spills on property prices. But in practice, there may be a high degree of collinearity between potential pollution impacts and other desirable attributes of property, for example, view. This would make it very difficult to disentangle the pollution effects from other factors affecting property prices.

Some people have suggested that reductions in property prices following an oil spill might be taken as a measure of damages. In principle, if a spill occurs, it should have no effect on property prices since the anticipation of the spill has already had its effect on the equilibrium property prices. Some people might view this as a rather extreme assumption about rationality and foresight in property markets. But if markets are not in equilibrium and do not reflect the foresight and rationality assumed here, it is not clear what interpretation can be placed on any pattern of property prices at any point in time.

If an oil spill were entirely unanticipated, it would depress property prices. But the reduction in property prices would reflect a combination of the unanticipated damages of the present spill and the effect of revised expectations about the nature and magnitude of possible future spills.

Wilman and Krutilla (1980) applied the hedonic technique not to housing prices but to rental rates for accommodations. This was an imaginative research strategy. However, the results concerning the effect of oil pollution were inconclusive because oil pollution and

rental rate data were poor. With better data, this approach could
be useful in estimating the benefits of avoiding chronic beach pollution. It is not applicable, however, to an estimation of the
damage due to an acute spill incident. In order to apply the technique to acute spills, one would have to have data on the equilibrium pattern of rental rates during a period of acute oil pollution.
If during an acute spill some accommodations are unoccupied, this
indicates that the pattern of rental rates is not the market clearing pattern. And in the absence of market clearing, it is not possible to interpret the pattern of rental rates in the usual way. If
better price and pollution data can be identified, the Wilman-
Krutilla technique can be used in order to estimate the benefits of
avoiding chronic beach pollution.

In summary, for chronic oil pollution, the hedonic price approach
and survey instruments both provide bases for estimating values.
The travel cost model might also be appropriate, if it can be applied to a set of sites across which the degree of oil pollution
varies. But none of these approaches has yet been successfully
applied to problems of valuing chronic oil pollution damage. Furthermore, the only approach that seems feasible for estimating the
damage of an acute spill is to use the travel cost technique ex
ante to determine the present recreation values of threatened
beaches. Then these values would provide a basis for determining
the losses if a beach were closed due to an acute spill.

IV.

Turning to sports fishing, analytically it is important to distinguish between site-specific demands and demands for activity over a
large area with perhaps many points of access. The travel cost and
hedonic travel cost techniques are site-specific. As Brown says,
what is of interest is how demand and value vary with changes in
some measure of quality such as fishing success. To determine how
value varies with quality, one must either use a travel cost model
covering several sites or the same site over time when quality
varies, or utilize a hedonic travel cost model with several sites.

Willingness to pay surveys are suited to cases where the object to
be valued can be very precisely defined. Thus I think that the
survey approaches are better suited to site-specific activities than
to valuing fishing activities in general.

Finally, participation models such as those developed by Davidson,
Adams, and Seneca (1966),[*] and by Vaughan and Russell (1981) can be
used to estimate changes in activity leavels; but they do not provide a way of estimating the increase in utility to existing users.
Nonetheless, participation models represent the only well developed
technique suited for analysis of general activity rather than site-
specific activities.

---

[*]   For references see bibliography following Brown paper.

168

Brown next turns to a discussion of non-consumptive values such as
existence value and option value. Since these values, by definition
are not directly linked to present use or activity, it seems likely
that the only possible approach to estimating them is to use hypothetical instruments such as willingness to pay surveys. But there
are problems in interpreting responses to willingness to pay questions concerning non-user values.

Existence value is defined as a willingness to pay to preserve a
site even though one may not be a present or expected future user.
It is a value that is independent of use value. Users may have
existence values, but it is hard to see how one could allocate a
willingness to pay response between use and existence values. One
approach is to survey "non-users." But there is some ambiguity in
the concept of a non-user, at least at the empirical level. Suppose, as some studies have done, that we ask an individual, "Do you
expect to visit the site during the next 10 years?" If the individual response is "no," she would be classified as a non-user. But
it seems likely that many if not most of those responding "no" could
have a non-zero probability of visiting the site. And as long as
this probability is greater than zero, the stated willingness to
pay must be interpreted as a sum of expected value of consumer surplus, option value, and, perhaps, existence value. But the technique does not provide a basis for allocating this sum among these
three categories.

In some studies, responses of users surveyed at the site have been
added to responses of supposed non-users to obtain what is interpreted as a sum of use, existence, and option values. But if my
interpretation is correct, the responses of users and non-users are
not additive, but rather are alternative measures of the same thing,
namely expected use values. What is needed here is a rigorous effort to sort out the various issues surrounding option and existence
value at the conceptual level, a reinterpretation of existing
studies that have proported to measure option and existence values,
and an effort to identify new techniques for measuring these values.

Recreation

Henry Lyman

As a specialist in halieutics, I am poorly qualified to comment upon economic aspects of recreational fisheries as presented in Gardner Brown's paper. However, that is what I am supposed to do, so in what follows I will look at his presentation through the eyes of an angling layman with the hope that my verbal mangling of economic terms will be forgiven.

What strikes me immediately is the frank admission that economic analysis of the marine angling field has been sorely neglected. I agree wholeheartedly. Lack of economic data has seriously handicapped efforts of the Fishery Management Councils and others throughout the country to place values on recreational fishing. Those involved in the multi-million dollar recreational fishing industry may claim all sorts of benefits from angling, such as relaxation and decreased dependence upon the aspirin bottle, yet basic data in the terms of hard dollars are, for the most part, lacking. "Inadequacy of relevant data and very little demonstrated enthusiasm by funding agencies for establishing a data base" are given as the major reasons for this problem.

True, but I would like to carry this a step further and mention the reasons for these reasons. They involved both politics and bureaucracy, which perhaps should not be separated into two entities. At the federal level, the agency originally responsible for marine fisheries resources of this country was the old Bureau of Commercial Fisheries. Today, it is the National Marine Fisheries Service, yet the bias towards the commercial fishing industry as contrasted with recreational fisheries still prevails. This bias in state agencies, originally influenced by the federal organization, has shifted far more rapidly towards an equitable balance simply because local politicians have been besieged by the growing army of marine anglers since the end of World War II. Bureaucrats, as is common to the breed, tend to protect their own turf and, at the state level in many cases, have found that their turf expands when they align themselves with recreational interests. In time, as sport fishermen become better organized--as they are--the federal establishment will also achieve a more reasonable balance between the two major groups involved.

To move out of their role as stepchildren to the physical sciences, economists, I submit, would do well to outline reasonable and practical programs for obtaining data bases for those Regional Fishery Management Councils that deal with recreational fishing more extensively than with commercial fishing. The Mid-Atlantic, South Atlantic and Caribbean Councils would appear to be the primary targets at this time for such an effort. As a former Council member, I recommend that the programs be designed to determine what the fisheries are worth right now rather than to attempt predictions of what they may be worth in the future.

As is emphasized again and again throughout the paper, the methodology for determining any reasonable data base for a given section of coastline is extremely difficult. Known techniques, such as willingness-to-pay and willingness-to-sell; hypothetical questions with their hypothetical responses; travel cost, and all the rest are flawed. In marine angling, the flaws are accentuated when one tries to deal with a multi-species fishery. Some sort of data base may be obtained by surveys of fishermen seeking only Pacific salmon, for example, but in New England, many fishermen temper their activities to the targets of opportunity available. Thus on a single trip an angler may start out for striped bass, shift to bluefish when the bass fail to cooperate, then to weakfish when he is tired of catching blues, and finally may end up going after anything from school tuna to cod and haddock. How can anyone evaluate either the appeal or the dollar value of any one of these species on a reliable basis across the board? It may well be impossible.

An approach which I feel has merit is mentioned in the spill discussion. "A more promising strategy might be to conduct the study in an area where spills or development have occurred and then make a regional translation." Unfortunately this strategy also presents problems because data, in the majority of such cases, are lacking on what was there prior to the spill or development. As a layman, it appears to me that this type of study might be expanded on what I call the island analysis basis--so called because it was used back in 1962 on the island of Martha's Vineyard off the coast of Massachusetts.

In those days, tourist and recreational fishing activity practically ceased after Labor Day. Sidewalks were rolled up and natives, who catered to the summer trade, settled down to a winter of politics, card-playing and taking in each other's washing. To lengthen the tourist season and boost the local economy, it was decided to conduct a striped bass derby, which would run from September 15 through October 15. The local Chamber of Commerce, bankers and tradesmen on the island submitted dollar figures on average income during this period during the years prior to the fishing tournament. At the conclusion of the first year of the derby, comparable figures were again compiled--a fairly easy operation because of the insular character of the area. The increase to the economy was approximately

171

$250,000--a tremendous boost to a comparatively small island. Incidentally, this derby, which now includes bluefish, is an annual event, the Vineyard's economy has boomed, and the tourist season now runs through Christmas.

This general approach appears sound. The author carries it forward logically when he writes of identifying economically important coastal recreational areas for study prior to an oil spill or development. I suggest going even further and studying the areas that can be most readily isolated economically to some degree without worrying about possible future oil spills or development: in brief, taking an economic inventory of what is there right now. If sites were selected carefully, I do not believe costs would be excessive. With this data in hand, the impact of a minor or major change in the supply of fish available to traveling anglers, because of natural cycles, disasters, or management restrictions, could be readily ascertained over a period of years. One fact is certain: there is no question that there will be such changes, as any fisherman will assure you!

As noted, a variable that is perhaps impossible to quantify is involved in all multi-species recreational fisheries. Choice depends upon the individual. Unhappily for easy quantification, this goes even further. Normally, anglers pass through three phases of development. First, they want to catch the most fish; next, they try to catch the largest fish; finally, they spend their time seeking the most elusive fish and even handicap themselves by using light tackle. As noted in the paper, knowledge of density of the fish supply is a vital factor in any economic analysis, but quality-- that is, large size of individuals specimens of the species sought-- must also be taken into account, particularly when dealing with the last two groups of anglers mentioned above. It is here that many recreational fishermen disagree with the concept of maximum sustainable yield so dear to the hearts of some biologists. A large number of comparatively small fish in a specific area may fill a freezer, but the advanced angler will move elsewhere for his sport. I mention this because both biologists and economists in the past have been trapped into considering numbers alone in their analyses of sport fishing potential. Quality of the catch and even availability of quality fish which are not caught have a major appeal to perhaps as much as 40 percent of the marine angling public.

I am delighted to see that mention is made of inclusion of a study in the new media of sport fishing reports, as part of a demand analysis. In my opinion, researchers in biology, sociology and economics have ignored this source of information all too long. Reports of this sort in newspapers, regional weekly tabloids, magazines, on radio and television are amazingly accurate. They have to be or the reporter will soon be out of a job. Even though Salt Water Sportsman is a monthly magazine with a considerable time lag between compiling information and final delivery of it, one of our most popular features is a "Fishfinder" column. This gives a brief rundown on fishing to be expected in every coastal state for the month of issue. For over more than 40 years, we have compiled reports on such fishing and correct them as new information arrives. Fishermen plan their trips in the long term from this information, then fine tune it for the short term from daily newspaper columns or from radio and television reports. Tracing the economic impact of a good run of yellowtail up the southern California coast might be an exercise of more than academic interest.

One word of caution: recreational fisheries in marine waters of the Pacific Northwest are not at all typical of similar fisheries elsewhere in the country. Salmon and steelhead, and those who seek these species, dominate the fisheries to such a degree that fishing for other species is comparatively minor from both biological and economic viewpoints. There may be an advantage in this because surveys and models may be obtained more readily due to the limited spread of effort. Techniques for pilot projects, which might be applied to multi-species areas, might well be developed more readily in this geographical section, yet it is dangerous to assume that research results would have coastwide application.

In passing, I am intrigued by the idea of establishing an economic value for moral outrage. This may concern sociologists more than economists, however. It certainly concerns politicans as Secretary Watt has discovered.

Section V of the paper pinpoints specific problems concerning the Pacific Fishery Management Council and, as the author points out, such problems are common to all councils. Considerable emphasis is placed upon congestion, which evidently is a major factor in the Pacific fisheries. I have seen the fleets of small craft during the salmon runs and have had the rather harrowing experience of fishing in this congestion. It should be noted that some anglers-- I am not among them--enjoy congestion of a sort. I have seen surf fishermen at various points on the Atlantic Coast leave a perfectly good stretch of unoccupied beach voluntarily to join their peers practically shoulder to shoulder. Whether they simply become lonely when parted from their fellows or whether they are moved by the spirit of competition, I cannot say. A sociologist or perhaps a psychologist might find a study of this lemming-like reaction a suitable topic for a doctorate thesis.

Since Proposition 2-½ in my own home state is mentioned by the author, I cannot pass it by without comment. The rise in fees for shellfish licenses actually has occurred in several coastal towns, primarily in the Cape Cod area. Total revenue from license fees has indeed declined, but what is worse, the resource also has declined. Not only do those who purchased the licenses feel that they have to harvest more shellfish to get their financial investment back, but also more unlicensed diggers--the term poachers comes to mine--scrabble in the sand. Since town funds to employ shellfish wardens have been cut back, these unlicensed diggers escape the arm of the law in the majority of cases. This factor should be cranked into any model that might be devised to determine the effects of an increase in license fees.

Finally, although I agree in the main with the model specification comments, I submit that the fewer variables included in obtaining a data base at the outset, the better the understanding of the whole economic problem of analysis to the layman. Council members and others involved in fisheries management already are confused enough by terminology of specialists in the many areas of marine fisheries mangement. In the early days of the New England Fishery Management Council, members spent two days at a briefing by biologists at Woods Hole as those experts tried to explain modular approaches to supply and recruitment. When the conference concluded, one of my fellow Councilmen turned to me and said: "I think I understood what was going on, but I still don't know whether they said we will have more fish or less fish."

I therefore urge that you, as economists, not only try to solve the problems outlined as soon as possible, but also that you express your findings in terms readily understood by laymen who, in the final analysis, must make the management decisions. The basic question, which has not been answered to date, is: what is the dollar value of marine recreational fishing? Pick your targets, go to work and, as all fishermen say, good luck!

Environmental Management

Clifford S. Russell

I. Introduction

Each of the uses of ocean resources discussed at this workshop (renewable and nonrenewable resource exploitation, and recreation) is linked directly to the marine environment in several obvious and not so obvious ways. For example,

- Oil exploration and production involves accidental and intentional discharges of such substances as crude oil (from blowouts, or vessel spills), drilling mud, and acid (National Academy of Engineering, 1972; Burrows et al., 1974; President's Panel on Oil Spills, n.d.);

- Deep sea mining involves disturbance of the ocean floor either mechanically by bucket lines or by hydraulic dredging. The disturbed material is to a large extent put into suspension in the water column and slowly settles again, perhaps partly in a different area. Benthic organisms will be caught up in the general chaos and a large fraction may be killed (NOAA, 1975b; Office of Ocean Minerals and Energy, 1981);

- Oil drilling, floating nuclear power plants, and the use of ocean thermal gradients (OTEC) involve the introduction of new structures either sunk onto the bottom or moored. These structures may or may not affect the ecological system, but operating through the (spatial) environment, will have a congestion effect on other users (Oceanic Engineering Operations, 1981);

- Commercial and recreational fishing involve the direct harvest of living components of the environmental system, and sufficiently heavy harvesting can have effects beyond simple depletion of one species. (And it is not only fin and shell fish that are harvested but also plants, such as kelp, and zooplankton--krill).

Other activities that take place in or on the ocean may also be rather heavy users of the environment. Again, some examples will be useful:

- The oceans, especially over continental shelves, are used for dumping of various unwanted materials: dredge spoil; industrial wastes (spent acids and bases, sludges, difficult-to-treat organics); nuclear wastes, so far transuranic material (but see Hollister et al., (1981) for an optimistic evaluation of the possibility for high level radwaste disposal beneath the seabed); municipal sewage sludge from treatment plants; and garbage and other solid wastes (tires, demolition debris) (Smith and Brown, 1971; Northeast Office, Office of Marine Pollution Assessment, 1981);

- Shipping results in both intentional and accidental spills of cargo; especially, of course, crude and refined petroleum products (Cummins et al., 1974; Burrows, et al., 1974; Institute for Water Resources, 1972);

- Along shore, and someday perhaps in deep water, ocean water is used in large quantities for cooling in electric power production. This involves heat stress on the local environment and both mechanical and heat stresses for entrained organisms (e.g., on OTEC, Oceanic Engineering Operations, 1981);

- We discharge considerable waste water directly to the oceans via pipes or through our rivers. (Officer and Ryther, 1977).

Environmental management is, then, a subject that should arise in connection with every prospective use of ocean resources. Indeed, one way of approaching the topic of this paper would be to provide a catalog of marine environmental problems, indexed by the use that gives rise to that problem, by the kind of environmental effect anticipated (species depletion, ecosystem turnover, aesthetic degradation), or the values and uses affected (public health, recreation, aesthetics).

To undertake what could be called the classical approach to each problem thus cataloged we would have to address several economic questions of greater or lesser difficulty:

- To assist in choosing management goals we would like to have estimates of:

  o benefits and costs of alternative goals;

  o distribution of benefits and costs under alternative policies.

- To assist in better achieving goals, we would like to be
  able to say intelligent and practical things about:

  o alternative implementation incentives in terms of
    static efficiency, information needs, and dynamic pro-
    spects (incentives for technical innovation);

  o enforcement needs in terms of feasibility and cost of
    monitoring backup for implementation incentives, and
    design of ultimate sanctions for "misbehavior."

All these questions necessarily involve us in obtaining and using
knowledge of the part of the natural ocean system involved in translating man's many actions into effects themselves of concern to man.
Without such knowledge, our economic reasoning can be so at odds
with physical reality as to be of limited usefulness. That, for
example, is how I would characterize some of the earliest effluent
charge arguments that failed to anticipate (or ignored) the lessons
of models of the natural world--that location of discharge matters
in establishing the efficiency conditions. (Russell, 1979).

Further, it is possible to make the case that, in any given piece
of ocean, all (or many) of the potentially damaging uses will interact directly through the environment, without benefit of market
mediation, and that therefore a problem-by-problem approach to environmental management will produce suboptimal results. This line
of thought might suggest to some the desirability of grand management models--general equilibrium models, if you will, of a section
of ocean space--in which every conceivable use is represented and
the entire set of mutual effects (conflicts and complementarities)
is explicitly modeled. In fact, those with wider vision will assert, correctly in principle, that such models should include all
land-based activities interacting directly with the oceans (such as
air pollution generation) or serving as alternatives to activities
using the ocean environment (such as land disposal of sludge) where
socially correct prices do not exist to influence choice.[1]

Were such a model to be built, in the sense that the above sketches
were translated into explicit mathematical variables and functions,
it would in principle give us the basis for evaluating alternative
equilibria and associated management policies for the piece of
ocean modeled. There would still be many practical and conceptual
difficulties--computational cost, multiple optima, and significant
income distribution effects, to name only a handful. But the modeling literature is rich with ideas for using these beasts to inform
"decision makers," whether legislative or executive. Thus, it is
mathematically possible to structure such a model to explore trade-
offs between conflicting uses, e.g., how much fishing must be given
up to get particular values of crude oil production? Or one could
concentrate on the distribution of costs and benefits over political
jurisdictions instead of uses. The model's results could be trans-
formed and transmitted to the decision makers more or less directly--
one option even being direct hands-on gaming at computer consoles.

In addition, it would be possible to use appropriately structured versions of these models to explore implementation strategies. Indeed, it would be necessary, except in very special circumstances, to have such a model if it were desired to apply optimal "effluent" charges. More broadly, we could compare technology-based standards, uniform percentage reduction rules, uniform effluent changes, marketable permits to discharge, all with the (static) efficiency optimum, as a basis for estimating the costs of our preferences for particular implementation methods. This has been done in a few relatively simple models of onshore pollution problems, and we at RFF are working on similar lines using a resuscitated model of the Lower Delaware Valley. (Atkinson and Lewis, 1974; Atkinson and Teitenberg, 1981; Spofford et al., 1976).

II. Information

Modeling and Information

It is, however, worthwhile stepping back from the above upbeat description of the conceptual marine environmental management model and its potential use to examine the information needs implied. This is true because despite the advances in data gathering technology of the past several decades; despite the millions spent on ocean research; despite the development of better mathematical methods for estimating, constructing and solving large system models; we are still a long way from being able to produce the grand management model. Indeed, I do not think it would be much of an exaggeration to say that even operationally useful and accurate versions the various key partial equilibrium or subsystem models appropriate to quantitative analysis of subproblems such as ocean dumping or the interactions of oil spills and fish populations, are beyond us.

One cannot prove this negative and intentionally provocative statement but let me begin by supporting it, as it applies to the natural system (ecological) model at the heart of any management modeling effort. A particularly pertinent assessment of the state of our knowledge in this area, appearing in a generally favorable review of a book titled, <u>Analysis of Marine Ecosystem</u>, is worth quoting at length (Pomeroy, 1981, p. 1369), emphasis added).

> The exposition leaves the reader to accept or resolve some contradictions. The unevenness and contradiction from one chapter to another accurately reflect the state of marine ecosystem research. <u>Indeed, no general agreement exists about such basic questions as the structure of food webs, the interaction of their component populations, or whether current methods successfully measures rates of ecosystem processes.</u> Various authors make a case for the special significance of large organisms in one chapter and that of microorganisms in another. The tendency toward bias in favor of certain organismal or trophic groups, which must be inherited from the days when organisms, not ecosystems, were the only formal subjects of study, is seen even in the section on modeling. Most extant models emphasize some specific

food chain, usually grazing and predation, and in that they may be less than ecosystem models. Such condensation is not a limitation inherently imposed by computing capabilities, and it tells us how little we understand ecosystem processes.

The obstacles between us and comprehensive management modeling do not arise solely in the understanding of natural systems, however. For example, we economists should be willing to admit that handling the following model components would give us trouble:

- The costs of (damages from) user congestion--i.e., how shipping density affects fishing productivity and vice versa;

- The costs of changing other spatial patterns of use, such as confining shipping traffic to particular lanes, or forcing extra consolidation of drilling and production activities into single instead of multiple platforms (Hold, 1974);

- The costs of policy elements such as: (easy) the cost of moving dumpsites; (harder) the cost of changing the probability of an oil well blowout; or (harder yet) the full social cost of substituting land disposal for ocean dumping of any particular residual;

- The damages due to interference of uses with direct consumption activities; e.g., spilled oil and beaches; ocean dumping and recreational fishing, whether from beach or deep sea boat; ocean structures and "viewing."

Note also that these latter items refer only to an essentially static model. Over time, tastes and technology change and with them relative prices. Even if our aim is only to adjust contemporaneously to change (and not to produce a dynamically optimal management path for projected changes) we must have a model that allows us to alter prices, technology and demands and to find the new optimal policies. Thus, for example, the optimal effluent charge set will change over time and not just be a scalar factor. The charge relatives will also in general change. Because so much summarization and condensation is necessary to produce a working environmental management model of any reasonably complex system, however, updating the underlying data becomes time consuming and expensive--and if the changes have not been anticipated in the model structure, one may face the necessity of complete reconstruction.[2]

Thus, at a minimum, I believe we should be skeptical of our collective ability to deliver on the promise of integrated environmental models, and even of our ability to build acceptably reliable and precise predictive models for management of individual components of the ocean environment and related human activities.[3]

Enforcement and Information

Economic analysis of the monitoring and enforcement aspects of environmental policy alternatives, in particular of implementation incentive systems, has to some extent been of the assume-we-have-a-can-opener school. This was especially true in the early literature on charges, when monitoring and enforcement were either not mentioned or were assumed away through the technological-development option clause. Later we became a bit more sophisticated, noting that monitoring was a problem for any system and that self-monitoring reinforced by random audits worked for the IRS. But there are audits and audits. The IRS operates with two very great advantages. First, it is following a semipermanent paper trail; and second, it is usually the case that one person's income is another person's or firm's deduction or expense. Therefore decentralized incentives exist for keeping up the quality of that trail.

In environmental matters this is seldom the case under present policies and commonly discussed future alternatives. In reality, then, monitoring and enforcement are complex subjects in their own rights. They involve large amounts of data, and require that we have knowledge of the characteristics of the effects we wish to manage, of the monitoring technology we have available, and of the alternative implementation incentive schemes being considered. All these ingredients must be combined with a heavy lacing of statistics (NAS/NRC, 1977).

Again, let us consider some examples in order to see the point more clearly. If the problem is monitoring observation of discharge limits at ocean outfalls from municipal sewage treatment plants (whether primary or secondary), we are on ground that is at least familiar, for it is necessary to monitor compliance with discharge (NPDES) permits at outfalls to freshwater as well. One difficulty here is that automated, continuous recording instruments are not available for some of the major pollutants of interest. And no instruments or methods are exact. Thus, bio-chemical oxygen demand (BOD) concentration must still be measured by lengthy wet-lab methods subject to variation in technician skill, using water samples pulled at particular instants in time. Flow must be simultaneously measured. Errors are introduced by the sampling and the laboratory methods (with cross-laboratory variation also inevitable). Because the samples are instantaneous pictures whereas the permits are usually written in quantities per unit time, a further source of uncertainty is introduced. (Brenchley, Turley and Yarmac, 1973). To determine that a violation has occurred with some acceptable level of assurance (avoiding false positives with one acceptable probability, while also trying to catch the real violations--avoiding false negatives--"enough" of the time) requires good planning, competent statistics, equipment maintenance and laboratory skill (Midgett, 1977).

Ocean dumping from barges is a somewhat different proposition. For significant sources, barge movements can be monitored by the Coast Guard without much additional trouble. This implies that measurement of quantities being dumped can be accomplished in part by requiring pre-sailing notification and arranging to board (audit) some fraction of barges, relying on self reporting for most loads. The location in which dumping is actually carried out is (or was, in 1971; Smith and Brown, 1971) apparently monitored by checking vessel logs, where position, course and speed must be recorded regularly, and in particular, during dumping. This information can in turn be checked, but not costlessly, for consistency with time out of port, and other reported courses and speeds. Direct monitoring of dump location requires air or sea patrols of high quality satellite photos. Or it must be required that "tamper proof" recording lorans be installed. The rate of discharge, a dimension of the dumping operation that helps determine the impact on the marine environment, is yet harder to monitor. If it can be varied, there will be an incentive to speed it up to cut down time at sea. Again logs and _post hoc_ calculations provide a tedious check, but first-hand observation or the elimination of choice of speed of release may be necessary for higher levels of assurance.

Operational dumping and accidental spills of oil at sea illustrate yet a third kind of monitoring problem. Rules limiting operational discharge in connection with deballasting and tank cleaning have been drawn up by the Intergovernmental Maritime Consultative Organisation (IMCO) in 1969. (Burrows et al., 1974). These are not binding in the sense that a NPDES permit is, but it is still possible to ask how to encourage compliance. Properly used, the "load-on-top" method of salt water ballasting is consistent with the limits on discharges, but there is no way, short of having an observer on each ship, to monitor, let alone enforce proper load-on-top operations. (Burroughs et al., 1974; Cumins et al., 1974). Again, it is tempting to wheel in the new "can opener"--a "tamper proof" recording instrument to measure simultaneously overboard discharge volume and oil concentration. Eventually this piece of equipment may become available, but for now discharges in the open ocean are essentially unmonitorable. At least for intentional or accidental spills of crude oils, reasonably close to land, there is some hope of detecting the guilty party after the fact if the spill is discovered. "Passive fingerprinting" of crude oil--that dependent on identification of the crude oil's composition by compound type and relative amount, allows identification of spilled oil by field of origin and usually by specific cargo from the field, provided that the spill has not weathered more than ten days or so and, even more significantly, that a sample of the spilled crude is on file in a registry or a finger print file is available to the authorities finding the spill. (Hunt, Mayo and Horton, 1981). On the other hand, the recommended identification methods involve looking at the entire range of crudes that could possibly be involved in the spill, suggesting that a port-by-port approach to the inventory may be desirable.[4]

I shall stop with these examples. I should, however, anticipate two objections to the prominence I have given the topic. The first objection will be that monitoring costs are very small relative to the costs of the actions required to reduce already accomplished insults to the environment. Therefore, we can have very careful and exact monitoring without significantly increasing costs of management policies, so why bother to worry about it. This is an empirical matter, of course, but I would stress that the expense and difficulty of monitoring in most real cases do not seem to depend on sophisticated instrumentation but on tedious, repetitive, and exacting lab work or on fairly sophisticated analysis of huge quantities of self-reported data.[5] These requirements put a premium on high quality personnel, exactly the place in which agency hiring limitations take their toll. Said another way, I believe that the shadow prices of monitoring resources are significantly above their market prices.

The second objection I expect is that the need for monitoring is really much less than I imply because voluntary compliance is general rather than exceptional. For whatever reasons, firms and their employers try to stay within the rules. Again, who can say this is wrong? Harrington (1981) found from New Mexico data that stationary source air pollution sources were in violation of their emission standards about 40 percent of the time on average over a number of sources (pp. 104-108). A rather large study of compliance by stationary sources of air pollution done for EPA by a group of consulting firms presents its findings in a different form and is a bit hard to interpret. (McInnes and Anderson, 1981). It appears, however, that based on quantitative data and qualitative (inspection) information, the sample of sources was out of compliance about 10 percent of the time.[6] Measuring compliance by emissions, the study group found total excessive emissions about 25 percent above the allowed total. But because the average source was "over-controlling" for the time it was in compliance, the actual annual emission totals were estimated to be less than the implied annual allowance. (McInnes and Anderson, 1981, p. iv).[7]

Implications for Research and Policy

If one is willing to take seriously the arguments above about the central and complicating role of expensive information implicit in our (economists') normal views of marine environmental policy, there are, it seems to me, four possible reactions. One is despair; but this would be both uncharacteristic of the assembled group and not especially good value for NOAA's money. A second reaction, one that might constitute model behavior in such situations, is to call for more research wherever we need more information. This has the authentic ring of self interest but it is both too easy and too unconvincing. The information "needs" we are talking about are just too pervasive and the necessary understanding too far away, or at least receding as fast as we approach. Something more--or less--is required of us. One such possibility, the one I see our sponsors at NOAA pursuing, is to seek policy formulation methods that economize on information while still retaining control at the "center." Finally, the fourth possibility I believe we have is to look for ways to use decentralized information gathering, decision processes, implementation incentives, and enforcement mechanisms; that is, to mimic the market to the extent possible.

Regulation and Limited Information

The Office of Ocean Resources Coordination and Assessment (ORCA) in NOAA is now in the midst of a large scale but nonetheless rather

inexpensive set of studies of the coastal waters of the United
States (Ehler et al., n.d.; ORCA, n.d.), the major purpose of which
is to identify potential conflicts in ocean uses. (This approach is
suggested in Epting and Laist, 1978; and carried further in Armstrong
and Ryner, 1980.) The raw materials are, by contrast with those required by the full conceptual model fairly easily available and include: Inventories of pollution sources in coastal countries and
from estuaries; simple dilution and dispersion models for large
near-ocean areas (to translate the loads into ambient conditions in
terms such as turbidity and dissolved oxygen); and information on
the spatial distribution of marine organisms, including areas in
which they spend periods of special sensitivity such as spawning
and juvenile development. As I understand the aim of these five
area studies it is to summarize all this information in the form of
maps and overlays in order to find the parts of ocean space where
waste discharge in the widest sense, including spills and intentional dumping and living resource exploitation are or are likely to be
in conflict.[8]

Where could such information, or its analogs for other environmental
problems, take us in policy formulation? Coping at the center with
limited information relevant to goal setting, choice of implementation method, and monitoring and enforcement means choosing policies
that:

- Maintain undisturbed areas to provide both variety and
  baselines for comparison;

- Seek to avoid worst cases and irreversibilities;

- Use blunt but familiar implementation instruments;

- Make enforcement as simple as possible.

In the management of the marine environment these general goals can
be translated into such specific forms as:

- Endangered Species and Marine Mammal Protection Acts with
  population and harvest limits thought to be well short of
  extinction;

- Spatial separation of uses via dumping grounds, sanctuaries, and shipping lanes;

- On-off switches for activity management (prohibitions
  versus freely available permits with no limits) rather
  than finely tuned discharge standards;

- Requirements for self monitoring even where no standards
  exist to be enforced;

- Design standards, such as tanker double bottoms and fishing gear restrictions that are easily enforced by inspection in or near port (Maritime Administration, U.S. Dept.
  of Commerce, n.d.,; Cummins et al., 1974; Hemenway, 1980).

These approaches do not generally appeal much to economists. Nonetheless, because of the lack of information about costs, ecological
systems, and benefits, it is difficult to do more than grumble about
the lack of incentives and the bluntness of the decisions. In particular, it is really impossible to tell if these policies are costing X billion more than some alternative set or if we should relax
this particular feature of that particular policy.

It would be more helpful in any case to turn our ingenuity to extending the range of marine environmental problems that can be tack-
led by information-impoverished governments which see problems but
cannot or will not, for whatever reason, shift away from regulation
by specification and prohibition toward the decentralized signalling
devices discussed in the next section. Contributions along this
line are not impossible. An obvious example is the calculation of
the costs of alternatives such as:

- Moving traditional dump sites off the continental shelves;

- Enforcing other ship-design possibilities for the reduction of operational and accidental discharges of oil;

- Establishing sanctuaries in different places with different sets of prohibited activities;

- Requiring new methods for protecting particular endangered
  species.

Another possibility for analysis is for regulators simply to attach
some more or less arbitrary prices to actions that are deemed un-
desirable, counting on the two-by-four effect to produce long term
gains, but not claiming anything about static efficiency. This
brings us rather close to my major interest, however, and at this
point I believe we should turn to the last response to lack of centralized information, one that might be called decentralizing the
decisions and hence the information needs.

An Ultimate Form of Deregulation:
Comprehensive Leases of Ocean Space

Listening to the rhetoric of the current administration, one would
be tempted to think that the new agency executives would be chomp-
ing at the bit in their anxiety to put market-like mechanisms in
place where government regulation has a legitimate role and to re-
move the government from those areas where it does not belong. We
are discovering, however, that things are not quite this simple.
It appears that some parts of the government have religion (OMB,
CEA, isolated pockets at EPA and NOAA) while others have failed to
set the light--indeed are doing the devil's work (the ICC, for
example, is rolling back deregulation of trucking, Karr, 1981). But
we need not confine ourselves to alternatives likely to be put in
place next month, and it will be instructive to begin at an extreme position. We can then move to less extreme and less comprehensive alternatives that require analysis and refinement.

Why not, then, divide ocean space out to 200 miles into large blocks and lease (or sell) those blocks to private (or public) owner/ managers?[9] Make the leases long enough that the leasees will possibly have a private interest in sustaining yields of renewable resources. Require that ocean quality at the boundaries of the lease-blocks meet certain standards. Allow subleasing of rights to mine, drill, fish and otherwise exploit. Require free rights of way for shipping and other transit traffic. Perhaps withhold some areas as sanctuaries and baselines against which to measure results periodically.

Why not, indeed? Many reasons will occur to readers. First, there is reality in the form of traditions, emotions and the politics of income distribution. For example, many feel that some matters should not be left to markets (Kelman, 1981a, 1981b). There are, in addition, too many powerful parties with vested interests in the existing hodge-podge of regulatory policies. It is hard enough to maintain political support for leasing offshore drilling rights to oil companies without throwing in fish and minerals.

Other objections will be matters of the technical problems posed by the oceans of economic principle. A few examples will convey the flavor. Fish populations are often migratory over long distances, and only the very largest lease-block definitions (e.g., the Atlantic Coastal Ocean) could "internalize" all the significant species. Smaller leases would leave a residual common property exploitation problem. But large leases, protected only by boundary water quality conditions, might not really be protected against pollution at all. Further, for resident fish populations, private decisions can optimally involve extinction (Clarke, 1973). Another difficulty would be that the market for these leases would likely be highly imperfect because capital markets are highly imperfect. Only the already big (and commercially interested) would have a chance to bid. Putting together consortia of individuals who care about oceans would involve all the transaction costs and strategic behavior problems that send the environmental quality issues to governments in the first place. An so forth.

Consider, however, some of the advantages that this system offers. It reduces the number of centralized decisions about goals. (The minimal set included just boundary quality conditions.) Information on optimal mizes of uses will be generated by individual experiments (trial and error), though this route is politically difficult for governments. Monitoring is simplified along with goals, although enforceability of the ambient quality standards is a problem because of the shared responsibility of the abutting leases.[10]

Accepting that these advantages are bought at too high a price, the next logical, and my final, line of inquiry is: To what extent can we identify intermediate systems, systems in which some information requirements are relaxed without complete abdication of responsibility and control? And, as a related matter, we should ask how and how much we pay for this information economy. In keeping with the purposes of this workshop, it is only my intention to ask, not to try to answer those questions. Hence, the final section of this paper will outline some key general issues, suggest a few specific research possibilities, and examine with some care one such possibility.

Modest Alternatives to Direct Regulation in Marine Environmental Management

One way of looking for modest alternatives is to begin by asking about the prospects for decentralizing the key activities of goal setting, decision implementation and monitoring and enforcement.

As far as goal setting is concerned, I think we can begin by dismissing most of the formal schemes for accurate preference revelation in the presence of public goods. (E.g., Tideman and Tullock, 1976; Green and Laffont, 1977; Groves and Ledyard, 1977). My sense is that these neither decentralize nor reduce information needs at the center, whatever other advantages they may have. If anything, the opposite may be their potential effect. They do not decentralize because a central authority must set up and supervise the process and must then make use of the output. This last requirement means that for significant decisions, politics (emotion, distribution) will be unavoidable, so that at best the preference revelation results can only be one more input to a centralized process. As for information, the amount required to calculate a set of "Clarke taxes," for example, for a large population (and could we accept a sample rather than the universe?) and many policy alternatives is truly awesome.

A possibility with less theoretical soundness, but I think more practical promise as a decentralizing mechanism, is one involving marketable permits to exploit (to discharge pollution), exploit minerals, or harvest fish). It is just possible that where these could be introduced, firms, groups, or individuals might enter the market with the aim of buying but not exercising permits. This possibility has occurred to some proponents of such rights (e.g., Dales, 1968; Tucker, 1981) but has never been carefully examined. A reasonable first reaction to this solution might be rejection, for it appears simply to wish away all the problems of public goods and free riders. But, on the other hand, that argument also rejects the notion that environmental groups such as the Environmental Defense Fund, with tens of thousands of contributing members, could exist and help determine environmental goals. Or, as an example, perhaps even more to the point, think of the Nature Conservancy which purchases and "retires" land.) Some literature does stress the importance of "matching" behavior and our expectations of our fellow citizens generally. (E.g., Guttman, 1978; Frolich and Oppenheimer, 1970).

The price we would pay for information economy would be the loss of political control over who gets what and who pays. This might very well strike some people as too high a price, for environmental quality and the right to harvest fish are often viewed as merit goods.

As for implementation, a possibility that seems most attractive is again the marketable permit in one or another form. This is because, while supplying a continuous incentive to economize on the permitted activity, the permits automatically adjust for growth and change by themselves changing in price. There is no need for laborious re-calculation and contentious repromulgation of prices as there would be with an effluent charge. (Russell, 1981). On the other hand, permit systems almost always have the potential for failing to pro-tect some part of our environmental goal set. This is because to be useful permit systems must often be kept simpler than the combina-tion of static efficiency and goal maintenance requires. (In en-vironmental policy, the trading of discharge permits can result in ambient quality standard violations, but decentralized trading of ambient-quality-based permits, which would maintain ambient stan-dards, would be very complex and might not work in practice without significant intervention by the public agency.) The monitoring of permit compliance would also be more difficult than for a system without marketability.

A broad set of alternatives, which to some extent combine decen-tralized goal setting with implementation incentives, is that label-led liability rules. (For example, see Brown, 1973; Polinsky, 1979; and White and Wittman, 1981.) The last of the papers discusses several alternative liability rules and zoning systems and mixes of the two in the context of two party "pollution" externality cases in which location choices are open in the long run. The authors deter-mine that a special sort of liability rule that effectively requires perfect foresight by individual decision makers, and a mixed zoning and liability rule system, can each allow attainment of short and long-run optimality under plausible assumptions about strategic be-havior. It seems likely that their results could easily be adapted to situations in which the externalities were of different types and involved simultaneous use for different purposes of the same space.

That is not to say, however, that application of the results would be easy. If goals are thought of, for example, in terms of quanti-ties of oil spilled, or quantity of damage to fishing and recreation done by spilled oil, a liability rule (enforceable) lets those re-sponsible decide how much care to take and gives them a continuing incentive to take that much care. The goals chosen in this decen-tralized way will, of course, change as incomes, tastes, technology and other exogenous forces change.

To some large extent, however, the apparently decentralized action of a liability rule is an illusion. Decisions about actual pay-ments and hence about prospective liability or insurance premiums cannot be settled in a simple market. Damages from oil spills will create damages to ecological systems and aesthetic values that will have to be argued over in a court or other forum, and some special rules about substance and procedure will amost certainly have to be centrally promulgated.

For the decentralization of information in monitoring and enforce-ment, one possibility is an incentive to mutual monitoring by users

of the environment. Most crudely and directly this could take the
form of a bounty of the sort that has occasionally been paid to
citizen monitors in pollution cases. Less crude and perhaps more
acceptable, at least in the context of marketable permits, would be
to give the buyer of a permit to discharge (or exploit) some responsibility for seeing that the seller really reduces his discharge
(use) by the amount sold. This does, however, raise the possibility
that buyer and seller would, with suitable side payments, collude
to avoid the requirement, since both can discharge the "same" number
tons of pollutant without significantly harming each other. Only
the public agency or a citizen monitor has the incentive to enforce
the trade under those conditions. Note, in addition, that decentralization by this route might actually raise costs, through duplication of effort, far more than it increased benefits by encouraging compliance. Perhaps this area is one from which it is very
difficult for governments to withdraw, though certainly much more
thought and effort would be needed before any such conclusion could
be defended.

Specific Suggestions for Research

The discussion above implies a wide range of potential research
topics, from attempts to build better pieces for the classical models (trusting to scientists to prove me unduly pessimistic about
their capabilities on the national system side) to fundamental research on the applicability of liability rules in cases of conflict
over ocean uses, or the potential for nonuser demand for marketable
discharge permits. The following list of promising topics represents an attempt to choose from this range projects that seem do-
able for budgets on the order of $100,000, and over time scales of
one to two years. Even within this restricted universe, however, I
provide only a sample of the possibilities, though I have tried to
find examples illustrating useful points or general methods. The
list is divided into "Traditional building blocks" and "Alternatives
where information is scarce."

Traditional Building Blocks

  1) An empirical study of the effect of oil exploration and
      production, via congestion and pollution, on commercial
      and recreational fishing. (A careful study would con-
      trol for other exogenous shocks to a fishery during a
      period when an offshore field was developed. Because
      no two areas may be alike in terms of ecological system
      and fishing methods, more than one case study would be
      valuable. The North Sea and Louisiana Gulf Coast
      fisheries are obvious candidates--so obvious that per-
      haps only a compilation of various existing results will
      be in order.)

  2) A study of the costs of altering offshore oil operations
      to reduce congestion and pollution. (This would include
      costs of reducing the number of above-water and seabed
      structures, and of building into those structures, and
      into exploration and production methods, smaller

188

routine discharges and lower probabilities of accidental spills. I believe the necessary technologies are well known, but the costs are not discussed in the easily available sources.)

3) A study of the costs of mandatory shipping lane maintenance and enforcement. (These costs include navigation aids, charts, communications, patrols, and, one suspects, increased probability of accident.)

4) Synthesis of existing studies on the land and sea alternatives for sludge disposal. (These methods include landspreading, composting, use of abandoned mines, and of course, ocean dumping from ships and barges of varying designs.)

5) Estimation of benefits from the maintenance of higher marine water quality. This is a broad subject and not easy to break down into pieces that are at once conceptually satisfactory and related to potential policies. For example, the benefits of oil pollution control accruing via marine fisheries may not be independent of policies toward ocean dumping. Nonetheless, some breakdown is necessary, if only for the list.

   a. Benefits to commercial fin and shell fishermen of reducing or moving out to sea ocean dumping of sludge, dredge spoil, and industrial waste.

   b. Benefits to recreational fishermen of the policy changes in (a).

   c. Benefits to commercial fishermen of policies reducing pollution of land-based sources--especially direct discharges and riverborne loads.

   d. Benefits to recreational fishermen of policies in (c).

   e. Benefits to swimmers and users of beaches of the several types of pollution control.

   f. Benefits to boaters (sail, power) of the several types of pollution control.

It is possible, as has already been observed, that existing data will not allow us to separate out the effects of the several policies mentioned above in (a,b), (c,d), and item 1. The best we can do may be to estimate the benefits of cleaner oceans from a mix of all three policies run at specified levels of strictness. This at least will be a start and will be a check on the rather amazing numbers now quoted (e.g., those in Freeman's summary of pollution control benefits, Freeman, 1979).

Alternatives Where Information is Scarce

1) Estimation of the costs of existing marine sanctuaries. (For example, one would want to count the fishing yield or oil or mineral production actually foregone as well as the costs of administration, boundary marking and enforcement.)

2) Estimation of the costs of marine mammal protection in specific cases. (The outcome, so far, of the tuna-porpoise controversy is well known and, I believe, well documented. Other controversies over whales and turtles could also be investigated to try to determine what we are paying to reduce the threat of extinction in specific cases.)

3) Investigation of the costs and performance specifications for alternative ocean dumping monitoring schemes aimed at quantity, location, and rate of application.

4) Case study of alternative harbor dredging cost allocations and likely effects, including possibilities for collective decisions by users.

5) Feasibility study of true liability systems applied to accidental and operational oil spills. (This would necessarily focus on monitoring possibilities and costs and on prospects for estimating damages for specific spills.)

6) Investigation of possible decentralized monitoring schemes for various activities affecting the marine environment.

7) Investigation of potential for use of marketable permits in the control of ocean dumping of sewage sludge and industrial waste.

It should be clear that there is no lack of potentially useful things to do. But at a more fundamental level the needs are for new ways of approaching the political, social, economic, and technical problem that is marine environmental quality management. More of the same is not the prescription for long run success, I think. I hope that someone, somewhere, can find the money to support imaginative, if risky, projects seeking ways around our great information problem.

Research Topics Raised in the Discussion Include:

1. Determine if there are uses of marine resources which could result in irreversible environmental damages of a magnitude and with a probability that warrant remedial policy.

Notes

1. An argument exactly analogous to this led RFF in the late
    1960s and early 1970s to support the Lower Delaware River
    modeling project (Spofford, Russell, Kelly, 1976). Here the
    attempt was to include air and water pollution and solid
    waste disposal with their several interlinkages. My exper-
    ience with that project will be reflected more clearly later
    in this paper. This framework was suggested for several
    ocean problems explicitly in Russell and Kneese, 1973. Along
    with other bromides, the Tenth Annual NACOA report (NACOA,
    1981) recommends such an "integrated approach to waste man-
    agement." (p. 37)

2. For example, to keep our Delaware model of manageable size
    we reduced the row sizes of our industrial control-cost LP's
    by a process of repeated constrained solution and summariza-
    tion using only the discharges and costs from each solution.
    To update the regional model then, would require respecify-
    ing of every individual LP, redoing the multiple solutions,
    resummarizing and reentering the results. Not conceptually
    hard but tedious.

    A more difficult problem arises if in the original construc-
    tion an influence that subsequently turns out to be impor-
    tant was buried in the assumed constants. Thus, for example,
    if energy using technology had been largely chosen before
    the 1970s, the model might well lack scope for adjusting to
    the new reality.

3. I do not mean to suggest that modeling efforts should be
    abandoned. They have value, at least as guides to data
    gathering, and may one day bear real fruit. It does, how-
    ever, seem unrealistic to base policy and implementation re-
    commendations on the assumption that defensible models are
    (or will be soon) available. An extreme version of this
    position may be found in Hollick, 1981.

4. I do not know the extent to which this technique can be ap-
    plied to refined products. I would guess the refining pro-
    cess would wash out much of the difference. In addition,
    blending usually occurs in refining or storage. Active tag-
    ging of cargoes with radioactive tracers is possible and
    could presumably be applied to either crudes or products at
    some non-trivial cost.

5. That is, looking for a violation in months of discharge data
    is never simply a matter of noting every number above X.
    Measurement and sampling errors and differences in sampling
    timing relative to permit averaging times and errors to-
    gether mean that each record is sui generis and tailored
    statistical analysis could be necessary depending on the
    choice of error probabilities and assumptions about the
    process itself.

6. The time of compliance is given in the study in terms of numbers and duration of "incidents" of noncompliance per year. On average the product of these two figures was about 290 hours. The report does not state a corresponding average number of working hours, but the 10 percent estimate would correspond to 365 days of about 8 hours, or 220 days of 13 hours.

7. The report does not make clear the terms of the permits applicable to the several plants, but one would expect them to involve allowed rates (e.g., pounds of particulates per 10^6 Btu or per ton output), or perhaps quantities emitted per day. It is unlikely, therefore, that the annual average results are a useful measure.

8. Ehler et al., n.d., page 6, Table 1, list the maps contained in the "East Coast Data Atlas." Under five major headings (Physical Environments, Living Environments, Species, Economic Activities, and Jurisdictions) are listed 125 individual maps. For a related approach see Weyl (1976).

9. This is a didactic extreme example and takes no notice of such parts of reality as the contention over the nature of our claim to the 200-mile zone and the conflict between our management interests at home and our freedom-of-access interests abroad. (Shapley, 1973; U.S. Department of Commerce, 1977; Hammond, 1974).

10. Nelson, in a provocative article on the argument over the relative virtues of markets, as opposed to central direction of economic activity, stresses that information, its gathering, processing, and use in decisions, is one of the key matters separating the two extreme possibilities. (Nelson, 1981).

References

Armstrong, John M. and Peter C. Ryner (1980). Ocean Management: Seeking a New Perspective (Washington, D.C.: USGPO). (Prepared for U.S. Department of Commerce, Office of Policy/Office of Ocean, Resource, and Scientific Policy Coordination), Stock No. 003-000-0055707.

Brenchley, David L., C. David Turley and Raymond F. Yarmac (1973). Industrial Source Sampling (Ann Arbor: Ann Arbor Science Publishers).

Brown, John P. (1973). "Toward an Economic Theory of Liability," Journal of Legal Studies, Vol. 2, pp. 332-349.

Burrows, Paul, Charles K. Rowley and David Owen (1974). "Operational Dumping and Pollution of the Sea by Oil: An Evaluation of Preventive Measures," JEEM, Vol. 1, No. 3 (November), pp. 202-218.

Clark, Colin (1973). "The Economics of Overexploitation," Science, Vol. 181, pp. 630-634.

Cummins, Philip A., Robert D. Tollison, Dennis E. Logue and Thomas D. Willett (1974). "Oil Tanker Pollution Control: Design Criteria vs. Effective Liability Assessment," Unpublished paper from U.S. Treasury (July).

Dales, J.H. (1968). Pollution, Property and Prices (Toronto: University of Toronto Press).

Edsall, Thomas B. (1981). "President's Users Fees Fall on Face," Washington Post, August 15, p. 1.

Ehler, Charles N., Daniel J. Basta, Thomas F. LaPointe, James A. Dobbin, Michele Lemay, G. Carleton Ray and Geraldine McCormick-Ray (n.d.). "Strategic Assessments of U.S. Coastal and Ocean Regions: Preliminary Results of the East Coast Project," Unpublished Discussion Paper.

Epting, John T. and David W. Laist (1978). "Perspectives on a Developing Ocean Management System," Unpublished paper, Washington D.C., The Center for Natural Areas (August).

Freeman, A. Myrick, III (1979). "The Benefits of Air and Water Pollution Control: A Review and Synthesis of Recent Estimates," A report prepared for the Council on Environmental Quality.

Frolich, Norman and Joe A. Oppenheimer (1970). "I Get By With a Little Help From my Friends," World Politics, Vol. 23, No. 1 (October), pp. 104-120.

Green, J. and J.J. Laffont (1972). "Characterization of Satisfactory Mechanisms for the Revelation of Preferences for Public Goods," Econometrica, Vol. 45 (March), pp. 427-438.

Groves, T. and J. Ledyard (1977). "Optimal Allocation of Public Goods: A Solution to the 'Free Rider' Problem," Econometrica, Vol. 45 (May), pp. 783-809.

Guttman, Joel M. (1978). "Understanding Collective Action: Matching Behavior," American Economic Review Papers and Proceedings, Vol. 68, No. 2 (May), pp. 251-255.

Hammond, Allen L (1974). "Manganese Nodules (II): Prospects for Deep Sea Mining," Science, Vol. 183 (15 Feb.), pp. 644-646.

Harrington, Winston (1981). The Regulatory Approach to Air Quality Management: A Case Study of New Mexico (Washington, D.C.: Resources for the Future).

Hemenway, David (1980). "Performance vs. Design Standards." A paper presented in the Series of Colloquia on Alternative Regulatory Approaches, Arlington, Virginia. (Paper dated October 1980; Harvard School of Public Health).

Hollick, M. (1981). "The Role of Quantitative Decision-making Methods in Environmental Impact Assessment," Journal of Environmental Management, Vol. 12 (January), pp. 65-78.

Hollister, Charles D., D. Richard Anderson, G. Ross Heath (1981). "Subseabed Disposal of Nuclear Wastes," Science, Vol. 213 (18 September), pp. 1321-1326.

Holt, J.A. (1974). "Some Difficulties Inherent in Applying Congestion Theory to Marine Problems," Maritime Studies Management, Vol. 1, pp. 207-214.

Hunt, Gardner S., Dana W. Mayo and Donald B. Horton (1981). "The Feasibility of Identifying Mystery Oil Spills." A report to the Municipal Environmental Research Laboratory of U.S. EPA, April (EPA Report EPA-600/2-81/060; NTIS Number PB81-184947.

Institute for Water Resources, U.S. Army Corps of Engineers (1972). U.S. Deepwater Port Study Conclusions (Washington, D.C.: U.S. Army Corps of Engineers).

Karr, Albert R. (1981). "New ICC Chairman Reese Taylor Moves to Halt Trucking Industry Deregulation," The Wall Street Journal, August 5, p. 50.

Kelman, Steven (1981a). "Economists and the Environmental Muddle," The Public Interest, No. 64 (Summer), pp. 106-123.

_____ (1981b). "Cost-Benefit Analysis: An Ethical Critique," Regulation (Jan./Feb.), pp. 33-40.

Maritime Administration, U.S. Department of Commerce, (n.d.). Draft Environmental Impact Statement: Maritime Administration Bulk Chemical Carrier Construction Program (Washington, D.C.: U.S. Department of Commerce, Maritime Administration).

McInnes, Robert G. and Peter H. Anderson (1981). Characterization of Air Pollution Control Equipment Operation and Maintenance Problems (Washington, D.C.: U.S. EPA).

Midgett, M. Rodney (1977). "How EPA Validates NSPS Methodology," Environmental Science and Technology, Vol. II (July), pp. 655-659.

National Academy of Engineering (1972). Outer Continental Shelf Resource Development Safety: A Review of Technology and Regulation for the Systematic Minimization of Environmental Intrusion from Petroleum Products (Washington, D.C.: NAE, Marine Board) (December).

National Academy of Sciences (1971). Marine Environmental Quality: Suggested Research Programs for Understanding Man's Effect on the Oceans (Washington, D.C.: NAS).

National Academy of Sciences/National Research Council (1977).
Analytical Studies for the U.S., Environmental Protection
Agency, Vol. IV: Environmental Monitoring (Washington, D.C.).

National Advisory Committee on Oceans and Atmospheres (NACOA)
(1981). A Report to the President and the Congress
(Washington, D.C.: NACOA) (June 30).

National Oceanic Atmospheric Agency (1975a). A Conceptual Representation of the New York Bight Ecosystem (Boulder: Marine
Ecosystems Analysis Program Office), NOAA Technical Memoran-
dum ERL MESA-4.

National Oceanic and Atmospheric Administration (NOAA) (1975b).
Draft MESA Project Technical Development Plan: Deep Ocean
Mining Environmental Study (DOMES) (Seattle, Washington:
Pacific Marine Environmental Laboratory).

Nelson, Richard R. (1981). "Assessing Private Enterprise: An
Exegesis of Tangled Doctrine," The Bell Journal of Economics,
Vol. 12 (Spring), pp. 93-111.

Northeast Office, Office of Marine Pollution Assessment (1981).
New York Bight Project: Technical Development Plan for F.Y.
1981 (Boulder, Col.: U.S. Department of Commerce, NOAA,
OMPA).

Oceanic Engineering Operations (1981). Draft Environmental Impact
Statement for Commercial Ocean Thermal Energy Conversion
(OTEC) (Anaheim, Calif.: Interstate Electronics Corp.),
Contract No. NA 81 RAC 00015.

Office of Ocean Minerals and Energy (1981). Deep Seabed Mining:
Draft Programmatic Environmental Impact Statement (Washington, D.C.: U.S. Department of Commerce, NOAA, OMPA).

Office of Ocean Resources Coordination and Assessment (ORCA) (n.d.).
"Mission Statement," (Washington, D.C.: NOAA).

Officer, Charles B. and John H. Ryther (1977). "Secondary Sewage
Treatment versus Ocean Outfalls: An Assessment," Science
(9 September), Vol. 197, pp. 1056-1060.

Polinsky, A. Mitchell (1979). "Controlling Externalities and Protecting Entitlements: Property Right, Liability Rule, and
Tax Subsidy Approaches," Journal of Legal Studies, Vol. 8,
pp. 1-48.

Pomeroy, Lawrence R. (1981). "Marine Ecology: Status Report."
A Review of Analysis of Marine Ecosystems, Science, Vol. 213,
pp. 1368, 1369 (18 September).

President's Panel on Oil Spills (n.d.). The Oil Spill Problem
(Washington, D.C.: U.S. GPO).

_____ (1969). Offshore Mineral Resources (Washington, D.C.: U.S. GPO).

Russell, Clifford S. (1979). "What Can we Get From Effluent Charges?" Policy Analysis, Vol. 5, No. 2 (Spring), pp. 155-180.

_____ (1981). "Controlled Trading of Pollution Permits," Environmental Science and Technology, Vol. 15, No. 1 (January), pp. 24-28.

Russell, Clifford S. and Allen V. Kneese (1973). "Establishing the Scientific, Technical and Economic Basis for Coastal Zone Management," Coastal Zone Management Journal, Vol. 1, No. 1, pp. 47-63.

Shapley, Deborah (1973). "Ocean Technology: Race to Seabed Wealth Disturbs More than Fish," Science, Vol. 180 (23 May), pp. 849, 851, 893.

Smith, David D. and Robert P. Brown (1971). Ocean Disposal of Barge-Delivered Liquid and Solid Wastes from U.S. Ocean Coastal Cities (Washington, D.C., U.S. GPO), Stock No. 5502-0035; EPA Solid Waste Management Series SW-19C.

Tideman, T.M. and G. Tullock (1976). "A New and Superior Process for Making Social Choices," Journal of Political Economy, Vol. 84 (December), pp. 1145-1159.

Tucker, William (1981). "Marketing Pollution," Harper's (May), pp. 31-38.

U.S. Department of Commerce (1977). "Background and Options Relating to the Development of Ocean Policy" (Washington, D.C.: The Assistant Secretary for Policy, Office of Energy and Strategic Resource Policy).

Walsh, James P. (1981). "Statement on Ocean Dumping Before the Subcommittee on Oceanography," Committee on Merchant Marine and Fisheries, United States House of Representatives (Washington: NOAA).

Weyl, Peter R. (1976). "Pollution Susceptibility: An Environmental Parameter for Coastal Zone Management," Journal of Coastal Zone Management, Vol. 2, No. 4, pp. 327-343.

White, Michelle J. and Donald Wittman (1981). "Optimal Spatial Location Under Pollution: Liability Rules and Zoning," Journal of Legal Studies, Vol. 10 (June), pp. 249-268.

Young, Peyton, N. Okada and T. Hashimoto (1980). "Cost Allocation in Water Resources Development: A Case Study of Sweden," IIASA Research Report R12-80-32 (Laxenburg, Austria: International Institute for Applied Systems Analysis).

Environmental Management

Blair Bower and Dan Basta

Before commenting directly on Russell's insightful paper, some characterization of the context or setting of his discussion in order.
After delineating that context and discussing a few of the points
raised by Russell, I will pose some other questions which are relevant to the "economics" research agenda.

I. Context or Setting

An off-shore region can be defined as an area bounded roughly by
the 3-mile and 200-mile limits; north and south limits determined by
geologic-hydraulic characteristics, political boundaries, ecosystems,
or some combination; and the seabed down to at least the economic
depth of mineral recovery (seabed mining). Within a given off-shore
region, activities can include: oil and gas development; marine
transport; minerals development; fisheries development; marine ecosystem sanctuaries; and residuals disposal via ocean dumping, including disposal of dredge spoil, radioactive materials, sludge from
municipalities, and via municipal and private outfalls. Residuals
are generated in the first three activities in amounts which depend upon the combination of factor inputs chosen. Most of the
residuals, along with those from planned ocean dumping, are presently discharged directly into the marine environment, with vary-
ing--and often not yet well defined--short-run and long-run effects
on that environment.

The residuals are affected by, and in turn may affect, various physical, chemical, and biological processes which transform the time
and spatial pattern of discharges of residuals from the various
activities into short-run and long-run time and spatial patterns of
ambient environmental quality. Ambient environmental quality re-
lates to the ambient quality of a natural system, in this case the
ocean, as measured by a specified set of indicators. The indicators used to characterize ambient environmental quality depend on:
(1) existing knowledge about the effects of residuals represented
by the indicators; (2) ability to measure the indicators, i.e.,
the technology of measurement; and (3) available data.

The resulting time and spatial patterns of ambient environmental quality directly affect the various biological species residing in a coastal/ocean region and the ecological processes of the region, as well as various human activities in the region, e.g., marine-based recreation, commercial fishing. These impacts, as perceived by humans, and the responses of individuals and institutions to the perceived damages, provide the stimulus for activating the institutional system. The extent and form of this action, as expressed in a specified resources management strategy, depends on the institutional structure in and value system of society and competing demands for scarce resources to produce other goods and services desired by society.

Given the foregoing, the first problem for marine resources management is to determine the "best" mix of products and services to be produced from any given management region over time where "best" satisfies an objective such as maximum net social benefits over the time horizon considered (constraints also may be imposed for example, such as preserving the critical habitat of species or the requirement that a specified quantity of a specified product or service (e.g., fish) be produced in a region over time. The management strategies developed would have to: limit or preclude the production of products and services which inhibit attainment of the fish catch requirement; specify technological modifications to their associated production processes; or some combination. For example, a technological modification might be specified involving changes in processes for handling the disposal of drilling muds and fluids and formation waters discharged from oil and gas exploration or development activities in the region.

To produce some mix of products and services will be the logical management objective in almost all regions except for regions where the management objective is the protection of some species/species habitat or of some unique scenic or geologic resource. Determining the best mix of products and services to be produced in a given coastal/ocean region is a dynamic problem. What constitutes the best mix will change over time, assuming that prior decisions have not resulted in irreversibilities that would preclude, subsequently, the production of certain outputs from a region. The mix of outputs desired from any region will change as a result of:

- Changing interests of society, as interpreted by Congress, the courts, and the executive branch, and as reflected in legislation, policy statements, rules and regulations, guidelines, plans, and programs;

- Increasing knowledge of the basic physical/chemical/biological processes in coastal and ocean ecosystems and of the interrelationships between and among the various products and services which can be produced in a region;

- Changing technology of producing produces and services;

- Changing values of products and services in relation to other sources of the same or substitute products and services.

- Changing demands for products and services which can be produced from a region; and

- Changing governmental regulations, export and import policies, adherence to international conventions.

Russell's assignment did not include the task of addressing the problem of how to determine the intertemporal and intratemporal mix to be produced over time from any given region. Yet that problem is critical. It is a problem analogous to the management problem on a national forest, from which multiple outputs can be produced, not all of which may be amenable to rigorous valuation in monetary terms. Economists have something helpful to say about how to determine that mix, for example, by goal programming as has been used by the U.S. Forest Service, or by some other technique or set of techniques. The determination of the mix is a particularly difficult problem because of the uncertainties involved, with respect to:

- Demands;

- Quantity and quality of resources available, e.g., manganese nodules;

- Natural variability of the biological system;

- How varying management inputs can affect the quantity and quality of the resource available, e.g., a particular species of fish;

- Effects of various activities on ambient environmental quality, which in turn is related to the uncertainties with respect to tradeoff functions among outputs;

- Values of the outputs of products and services over time; and

- Costs of exploration/development/production over time, including changes in technology and factor input prices.

Two other points merit mention: the multiplicity of tasks of which marine resources management is comprised and the problem of determining tradeoffs between or among various outputs of products and services.

Functions of Marine Resources Management

To produce any given set of products and services from a given region involves a multiplicity of functions too numerous to list in detail here.

These functions, which include various aspects of analysis and planning, research, exploration, monitoring, leasing, construction and cleaning up, are carried out by a multiplicity of agencies with

direct and indirect responsibilities for assorted pieces of the
action. The institutional milieu involved might be characterized
as follows:

Off-shore: (3 miles to 200 miles)--multiple federal
agencies;

Near-shore: (Up to 3 miles)--often multiple state agencies
plus some federal agencies, e.g., U.S. Coast
Guard;

On-shore: --multiple state and local agencies; federal
agencies with respect to, for example, siting
of certain activities and setting standards
for residuals discharges.

In addition, there is a multiplicity of private and public "actors"
engaged directly in productive activities, e.g., shippers, commercial and recreational fishers, minerals--including oil and gas--
extractors, liquid and solid residuals disposers.

Given the above, at least two relevant questions can be posed. How
do governmental agencies react with one another, and how do they
relate to the private and public actors? What effect does this
complicated institutional milieu have on the economic efficiency of
management of any given region, granting--as Russell implies--that
economic efficiency is not a cause which brings men cheering into
the streets?

Tradeoffs Between and Among Outputs

A basic characteristic of marine resources management is the occurrence of physical and economic interactions among and between users
of the resources in the processes of producing products and services.
Occasionally these interactions are beneficial, as might be the
case when the disposal of domestic sewage increases food availability
in fishing areas, thereby increasing fish production. More often
the interactions are detrimental, in terms of the production of one
output having an adverse impact on the production of another output.
Discharge of sewage through ocean outfalls can--but does not always--
adversely affect shellfish and recreation; facilities for oil and
gas production potentially interfere with shipping movements; accidental spills and operational discharges from marine transport
can--but do not always--adversely affect fisheries.

Developing tradeoff relationships requires first the defining of
a "level of activity-cost relationship" for each product and service which can be produced from a given region, including marine
sanctuaries. Producing some of these products and services results
in the generation of residuals which must be disposed of in some
manner. For example, offshore oil and gas development--neglecting
the leasing procedure--involves exploration, drilling, production,
and transport of output to facilities on shore. Each of these is
affected by economic and technological variables which change over

time, and each results in the generation of residuals. There are various measures for reducing the generation of residuals or for modifying the residuals after generation before discharge into the environment.

Given these relationships, the next step is to assess interactions between and among various possible outputs. Examples include: impacts on habitat and species of interest of a specified time pattern of dumping specified quantities of residuals at a specified location; impacts of increased commercial marine transport through the region on recreational boating in the region; impacts of increased commercial marine transport on intensified fish management/harvesting in the region. Various possible relationships between two outputs are shown in Figures 1A, 1B, and 1C, where the outputs can be in physical units or in equivalent monetary units. Figure 1D is a plot of the value of the sum of the two outputs shown in Figure 1A. Figure 1E shows an interrelationship among three outputs. Economics has an important role in developing these relationships.

Approaching the Management Task

In the context of the management task as described above, Russell states the basic economic questions which must be addressed. These questions require understanding the effects of man's activities on the ocean ecosystem and the linkages among activities. One would like to have an overall management model which simultaneously or sequentially generates all of the desired information. Russell comments on two relatively comprehensive studies sponsored by NOAA-- MESA and DOMES--which were pointed, at least to some considerable degree, in this direction.

Russell concludes, based on his review of the NOAA efforts and on his own experience with large-scale regional modeling at Resources for the Future, that the capability is lacking at this time either to put together such models--because of lack of quantitative understanding of some of the component parts--or to interpret the numbers which such models can generate in profusion. I would also add that I am not certain it is possible to present the mass of data so generated in a manner understandable to decision-makers. The presentation of data problem is one that is rarely addressed explicitly.

Russell is rather negative toward the two NOAA studies and the "grand approach," but in my view, formulating the problem in all of its complexity is useful in and of itself in at least two respects. First, a comprehensive study illustrates the interrelationships among the mix of outputs, the technologies for producing the outputs, and the effects on the natural system, and can highlight segments of the analysis where ignorance is largest. One is forced to ask which variables are the most important and if all the relevant variables have been included. Second, given the first, questions can be asked about: the design and imposition of implementation incentives to achieve the products and services mix and the ambient environmental quality levels desired; and the economic implications of alternative institutional arrangements.

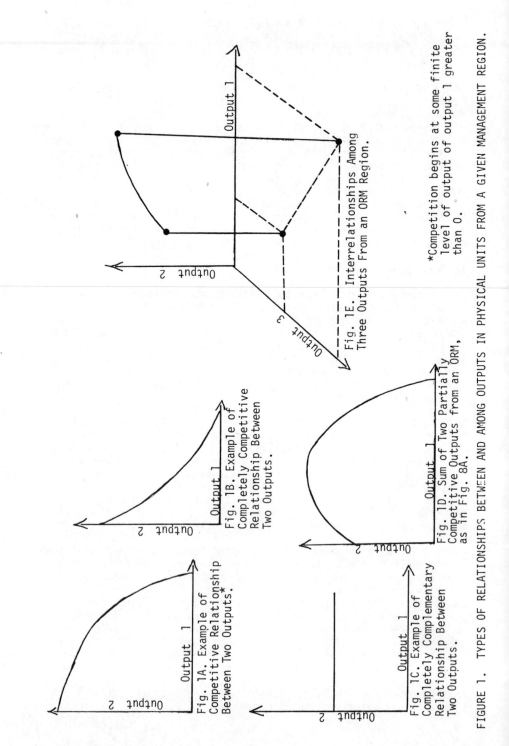

Fig. 1A. Example of Competitive Relationship Between Two Outputs.*

Fig. 1B. Example of Completely Competitive Relationship Between Two Outputs.

Fig. 1C. Example of Completely Complementary Relationship Between Two Outputs.

Fig. 1D. Sum of Two Partially Competitive Outputs from an ORM, as in Fig. 8A.

Fig. 1E. Interrelationships Among Three Outputs From an ORM Region.

*Competition begins at some finite level of output of output 1 greater than 0.

FIGURE 1. TYPES OF RELATIONSHIPS BETWEEN AND AMONG OUTPUTS IN PHYSICAL UNITS FROM A GIVEN MANAGEMENT REGION.

202

Having discarded the global models as residuals have substantially less value than the costs of their development and use, Russell turns his attention to the monitoring and enforcement aspects of marine resources management. Implicit in his discussion of these aspects is that the mix of outputs already has been determined and that the management task is to induce the relevant actors to produce that mix in the socially desired manner over time.

Russell describes the information problems inherent in monitoring and enforcement, particularly given the variety of activities involved, some of which are highly mobile. Information for marine resources management is expensive, with respect to both collection and analysis. In the given face of that fact, Russell proposes seeking policy formulation models that economize on information while still retaining "control at the center," and looking for ways to use decentralized incentives, information gathering, and decision processes to replicate the market to the extent possible.

I have no quarrel with his suggested approach or objectives, but would add two suggestions.

First, be imaginative in broadening the range of implementation incentives. For example, is there a role for "performance bonds"? Associated with the development of implementation incentives is the need for measures of performance and for developing of costs of different methods and levels of monitoring performance. Can estimates be made of how the "actors" will respond to the various implementation incentives? Simply assuming that they will "behave," as has often been done with respect to discharge standards in air and water quality management, is obviously insufficient.

Second, consider explicitly the problem of sanctions. How should noncompliance be defined in relation to specific activities and their performance? How should sanctions be related to noncompliance? The history of air and water quality mangement in the continental United States indicates that there are some actors who are truly recalcitrant, for whatever reasons. Some governmental agencies are particularly notorious in this respect.

Summary of Additional Research Topics

One way to try to develop an economics research agenda in relation to marine resources management would be to identify economic issues in relation to different elements of the management system. A generalized schema of that system is presented in Figure 2. The following list is based on that schema.

> 1) Estimating the demands for products and services, e.g., tanker movements over time, as a function of international supply and demand for petroleum and petroleum products; and demand for sand and gravel from within an on-shore economic region, over time, as a function of the time pattern of construction.

Figure 2. Generalized Ocean Resources Management (ORM) System

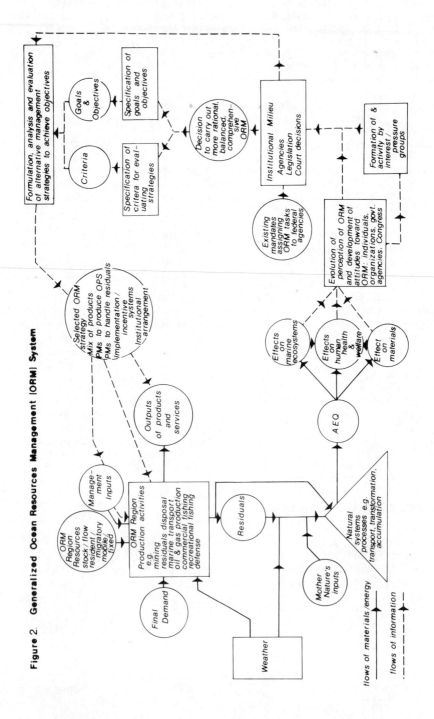

Note: The demand for products and services from any given coastal/ocean region is, to some extent, a function of the costs of providing the same products and services from alternative sources. Ergo,

2) Estimating the costs of products and services from alternative sources;

3) Estimating input/output relationships for each product and service which might be produced from a coastal/ocean region, including residuals generation and the costs of reducing residuals discharges by various amounts;

4) Valuing the outputs of products and services (benefits).

5) Valuing the effects of residuals discharged from each potential activity in a coastal/ocean region, particularly in relation to potential irreversibilities associated with effects of residuals discharges;

6) Estimating the on-shore activities and facilities, and their costs, associated with each potential product and service produced in a given region;

7) Estimating "second round" economic impacts of on-shore activities estimated in (6);

8) Estimating the "optimal" time pattern of exploitation of non-renewable resources of a given region;

9) Developing analytical methods/computational procedures for analyzing strategies for a given region, e.g., goal programming, mathematical programming, multiple objective analysis, guided search;

10) Developing criteria for evaluating strategies for a given region;

11) Devising implementation incentive systems-institutional arrangement combinations to be applied to activities in a given region, estimating the "administrative costs" of each combination, and estimating the responses of those activities to each potential combination;

12) Estimating the distribution of benefits and costs of a specific strategy for a given region.

Marine Transportation

Stephen R. Gibbs

Maritime commerce has long been the subject of economic research in order to explain observed events and to make normative policy decisions.* The purpose of this article is to review the research undertaken to date, and to point out areas where more research is needed.

In the author's opinion most of the necessary theoretical foundation for the economic analysis of marine transportation policy problems has already been created and that the main problem faced by analysts now is to apply the available theory. The theory to be applied is that of benefit-cost analysis (Lind, 1968), which in turn is founded upon the theory of the Pareto-optimum, described by Hyman (1973). The list below contains the major marine transportation economic policy problems reviewed here.

I.   <u>Ports</u>

    1.   Regional economic impacts and the objective function of public ports.
    2.   Over-investment in public port facilities.
    3.   User charges for dredging.

II. <u>Economic Organization of Shipping</u>

    - Liner conferences and cartels

     o   UNCTAD Code of Conduct and cargo preference.
     o   U.S. open conference policy.

---

*Comments on various drafts of this paper were received from Bill Beyers, Doug Fleming, David Fluharty, Steve Kinnaman, Henry Marcus, Bob Stewart and Bob Stokes. Tom Dowd, Derwood Hall, Al Hammon and Curt Marshall discussed with the author current shipping and port issues, and Bob Stewart suggested the topic of decision-making for transportation facilities. This assistance is gratefully acknowledged. All errors of fact or interpretation are the author's alone.

- Bulk Cargo Fleet

    o Market analysis.
    o UNCTAD bulk fleet code and cargo preference.
    o Flag of convenience vessel registries.

III. Multimodal Transportation

    - Intermodal competition.

IV. Additional Topics

    - Growth of the Soviet flag fleet.
    - National shipbuilding and operating subsidies.
    - Decision-making for transportation facilities.
    - Maxims of marine transportation economics.

Some of the results of research on these problems has either not
been understood or else research recommendations have not been politically acceptable. Political unacceptability has often been caused
by the policymakers' desire to trade-off real income to other policy
dimensions. Detailed comments upon the current state and prospects
for further research of the listed problem areas follow.

I. Ports

Regional Economic Impacts and the
Objective Function of Public Ports

One of the oldest issues pertains to the economic impact of public
ports. Most public port authorities are only weakly accountable to
the public (Walsh, 1978). Nevertheless, port commissions are
usually anxious to prove the value of the port to their constituency.
If the port has a large regional economic impact, this may streng-
then the stature of the port management, help raise bond revenues
or legitimatize state or local taxes paid to the port. Most commissions try to prove beneficial impacts by citing the number of
port-related jobs and by estimating the value added to the goods
shipped through the port or the value added of the service industries that function within the port's larger boundaries. As a rule,
these efforts over-estimate the value added contribution of the
port because they are overly generous in their attribution of relevant port activities. Furthermore, it is not clear that value
added and employment are the right variables on which to focus.

The question here is, by what measure should the merits of a port's
administration be measured? Ports would exist and activities there
would go on whether port management was good or bad. One must de-
vise a measure of merit of commission decisions if the impact
statements are to accomplish their purpose.

The first steps are to define a proper objective function for the
port and then to assess the effect of commission decisions on that
objective function. A port's objective function may be multi-

dimensional, including economic welfare, environmental quality and national security, for example. But whose economic welfare is to be served?

One possibility is maximum real world income, or more precisely, Pareto-optimality with respect to the prices prevailing external to the port. This will be achieved by:

- Pricing port services so as to recover marginal costs, including in this cost the revenues foregone from demand which could not be served due to the capacity limit of the port;

- Investing in those increments to port capacity which will just pay for themselves under the port's pricing policy.

In other words, have the port's investment and pricing decisions mimic those which would be followed were the port functioning as a profit maximizer in an environment of pure competition. It has been argued that profit maximization is the proper objective for ports in developing countries (Bennathan and Walters, 1979). Adopting this as a port's objective assumes that prices external to the port reflect the societal income foregone from alternative factor employment and that the prevailing income distribution is just. A measure of merit of a commission decision, while it is pursuing this objective, would be the net discounted consumer surplus created by commission decisions. Alternative, because it is not uncommon for ports which are controlled by a central body to possess some monopoly power, one could choose monopoly profit maximization as the port's objective. Profit would be the commissions' measure of merit. Devanney, et al., (1972b) have a fuller development of these two objectives, and this material has been extended for the case of a multicommodity port in Devanney and Tan (1975). A third possible objective for the economic dimension would be maximization of real regional income. As yet, no one has succeeded in defining an algorithm for achieving this through port investment and pricing decisions.

What about pursuing an objective consisting of two or more policy dimensions? If accomplishments toward the various dimensions are quantifiable and if it can be agreed a priori what value weights the dimensions should bear, it is probable the methods employed by Devanney can be extended to this case. If weights cannot be agreed upon, then a multi-objective analysis which is described by Major (1977) will be necessary.

Real income gains would probably result if port commissions were to clarify their goals. Actual port practice in the U.S. has been to pursue an objective of through-put maximization, or in some cases employment maximization (Goss, Vol. 1, p. 20, 1979). Few port constituents are aware that maximizing employment or through-put is inefficient when measured with any reasonable objective function.

Because the federal government long ago relinquished authority for port development to the states which, in turn, relinquished it, with

a few exceptions, to locally defined public bodies, the choice of
a port's objective function now resides at the local level. Presumably local citizens would opt for their port to maximize regional income, along with some other possible non-economic objectives.
Therefore, useful research endeavors would be:

- To assess quantitatively the regional income gains created
  by one or several ports' actual decisions;

- To develop an operational definition of regional income
  maximization as a port objective; and

- To determine what the port(s) should have done to maximize
  regional income and determine the net regional income loss
  of foregoing the better management choices.

Over-Investment in Public Port Facilities

One consequence of having a weak handle on the economic consequences
of port commissions' decisions has been overinvestment in some
public ports. This is revealed by the inability of ports to earn a
return on investment or even to recover out-of-pocket costs
(National Academy of Sciences, 1976, p. 38). The U.S. Department
of Commerce (1974) has estimated that 70 percent of U.S. port's
capital funds were provided historically from sources outside net
revenues. This overinvestment has occurred mainly in the glamour
area of container facilities. Pricing wars in various port ranges
have ensued as port commissions sought business for their container
piers. Furthermore, the port wars and overinvestment can go on
indefinitely because subsidized loss-taking ports can entreat the
local tax payer to make up the losses.

The basis of the overinvestment issue is whether ports should be
subsidized from local taxes. Baltimore receives $10 million an-
nually from state income taxes, Gulfport receives $350,000 from
local property taxes, New Orleans receives $500,000 from the state
gasoline tax, Seattle receives $9 million a year from King County
property taxes (Goss, Vol. 1, p. 22, 1979). Were ports to possess
a collective goods aspect (Steiner, 1969) this might justify these
subsidies. The existence of port generated positive externalities
has not been shown. It appears that the general public does not
have reason to transfer wealth to the merchant class while incurring significant real income losses, but does so because it has not
seriously thought about it.

User Charges for Dredging

One long-standing port subsidy has become controversial of late.
U.S. ports receive free maintenance dredging from the Army Corp of
Engineers. In 1980, federally subsidized dredging totaled $600
million. It is now proposed that these costs be recovered from the
ports, which would require the latter to increase their user fees.
Dredging services are a part of the factor input needed to create
port services. Insofar as these costs and the value of these

factors are not reflected in the prices charged for use of the ports, services will be under-priced and therefore will tend to be over-consumed, with concomitant real income losses.

A 1981 Congressional proposal that ports recover their full capital and operating costs from revenues, has failed to be endorsed. Observers reported that it will be resurrected in action on the 1983 budget. The proposal has generated considerable conflict among port authorities since some ports would be less impacted than others.

Given that the present free dredging is an unnecessary drag on the national economy, why not just stop it? The economic and social problem of doing so is the immediate harm which would be done to the businesses that have grown up around these subsidized ports if national policy suddenly shifted. Estimating the amount of the total regional income loss and devising means to compensate the losers could occupy the research community for a long time.

II. The Economic Organization of Shipping

Liner Conferences and Cartels

Analysis of the liner conference market has a long history, described by McGee (1960). Significant contributions to this analysis have occurred recently, in the form of papers by Bennathan and Walters (1972) and by Devanney et al. (1972a). These show that in terms of real world income, the actions of liner conferences waste resources. Devanney et al. (1972a) estimated that the real income losses (in 1968) on one of the 300 or so cartelized conference routes was $40 million.

Others have investigated statistical relationships between freight rates and cargo value and cargo volume. They found that, on average, freight rates reflect cargo volume about as much as they reflect value, apparently refuting the accusation that cartels exercise significant monopoly power over any of the cargoes they carry. However, the key weakness of these studies was their failure to recognize that liner conferences carry cargoes over which they have little or no monopoly power as well as cargoes over which their power may be very great. In general, the power of the conferences to raise freight rates above competitive levels depends on the characteristics of the market for that particular cargo in the supplying and importing countries. The mix of these latter characteristics will be unique for each cargo type. Conferences usually have a highly developed system for determining the conferences' leverage on a particular cargo. Problems with the conferences and policies to deal with them take many forms, as discussed below.

UNCTAD Code of Conduct and Cargo Preference

Within the framework of the analyses of Bennathan and Walters (1972) and of Devanney et al. (1972a) is set the issue of the UNCTAD (United Nations Conference on Trade and Development) Code of

Conduct for Liner Conferences. The text of this may be found in International Legal Materials (1974). The evolution of the Code and its provisions are described by Bosies and Green (1974). The Code does not yet have a sufficient number of signatures to enter into force (U.S. House of Representatives, 1981). Yet it is so urgently sought by the Third World that eventually it is likely to come into force.

The Code would allot to the national shipping lines of each of two countries engaging in mutual trade, equal rights to participate in that trade. Third flag or cross-trading lines would have "the right to acquire a significant part, such as 20 percent" of the trade. The Code would require liner conferences to admit national flag lines of the two trading states to the conferences and to open up the usually secret intra-conference freight rate negotiations to government participation. The goal of these provisions is to facilitate the creation of national flag shipping lines. Simultaneously, the Code makes it possible for governments participating in the conferences to pursue a goal of reducing conference freight rates as a means of increasing the real wealth of the trading countries.

Devanney et al. (1972a) comment on the economic irrationality of these conflicting goals.

> It is patently inconsistent and self-defeating to become a shipowner while simultaneously attempting to lower rates to efficient levels which, given the present oversupply [of vessel tonnage in the conferences], means that at least some shipowners are going to go broke and all lose money.

In short, it is likely that implementing the Code will replace one inefficient system with a different but probably equivalently inefficient system. Because the Code's language is ambiguous in several important respects, especially regarding the rights in the trades of nonconference carriers, it has not been possible to make a convincing calculation of the net effect on world income of implementing it.

U.S. Open Conference Policy

The U.S. government opposes the UNCTAD Code but has other problems with liner conferences. It has long been U.S. policy to require that conferences calling in the U.S. be freely open to all entrants. Elsewhere in the world, liner conferences may close or actively exclude new entrants. Other major aspects of liner conference cartel behavior have been sanctioned in the U.S., especially collective freight rate setting. The U.S. policy is based on an inadequate understanding of the qualifications to the Pareto conditions for achieving maximum economic welfare. U.S. open conference policy assumes that it is always better to have as few departures from the Pareto conditions as possible.

Lipsey and Lancaster (1956-1957) have pointed out that if any two of the necessary conditions are violated, it is not safe to assume

that correcting one of them will result in the creation of more
real income. They demonstrate that so long as not all imperfections
are to be corrected, then more real income might be produced by
leaving the market imperfections alone or even by creating or permitting more imperfections, depending on the details of the specific
case. The Lipsey and Lancaster (1956-1957) call this the "second
best" option.

In the case of U.S. liner conference policy, the real income maximizing policy would be to bring anti-trust action against the U.S.
conferences and end the practice of overt intra-conference price-
setting. If this is not possible for some reason, the second best
option would be to permit the conferences calling in the U.S. to
close also, and become pure monopolies. This would result in more
real income to shipowners and no decrease in income to others. A
useful research task would be to estimate the savings to the U.S.
and the world of permitting and encouraging the U.S. conferences to
form monopolies.

Devanney et al. (1972a) and Bennathan and Walters (1972) suggest
that it might be desirable to create monopolies countervailing to
the conferences in the form of shippers councils. While one cannot
predict the outcome, when a monopoly opposes a monopsony, bargaining between the two may yield an outcome close to that which would
be achieved by a market in competitive equilibrium.

The proposal of letting the conferences calling in the U.S. close
and legalizing shippers' councils could usefully be more thoroughly
investigated. Suppose that the councils were strong enough to
force the cartels to lower their freight rates. What would keep
the councils from maintaining the rates they charge to cargo owners
at the pre-conference-reform level and wasting their newly gained
monopoly profits through service-based intra-council competition?
The outcome of a "closed conferences plus councils" policy could be
no better than what the U.S. now has with open conferences.

The option of trust-busting the cartels by bringing suit under the
Sherman Anti-trust Act has been repeatedly recommended (Devanney
et al., 1972a; Walters, 1973; U.S. Department of Justice, 1977).
However, that alternative has proven to be politically unpalatable,
due to the unfavorable reception accorded it by U.S. trade partners.

Bulk Cargo Fleet

Market Analysis

The bulk fleet of oil, ore/grain and combination carriers has long
been known to operate on purely competitive principles (Koopmans,
1939). Most research on the fleet has focused on explaining or
predicting price swings.

Some of the major oil companies, and some consultants, attempt to
estimate the shape of the short-run supply curve of tanker shipping.
This is based on detailed knowledge of the out-of-pocket costs of

operating some 8,000 vessels in the world tanker and combination tanker/dry bulk fleet (Lloyd's Register of Shipping, 1978). When the short-run supply curve is plotted against a forecast of fleet demand (a function of western economies' oil supply and consumption demand) it is possible to forecast future charter rates in the "spot" market, which is the market for the marginal tanker (Devanney et al., Appendix 3, 1978; Devanney, Chapter 4, 1976).

UNCTAD Bulk Fleet Code and Cargo Preference

A major policy and economic problem would arise if principles similar to those embodied in the UNCTAD Code of Conduct for Liner Conferences were extended to cover the bulk fleet, as has been discussed within the UNCTAD forum. National cargo reservation laws applying to bulk cargoes are not unknown. The U.S. Government Accounting Office (1977) has calculated that reserving 9.5 percent of U.S. oil imports to domestic flag vessels, as was proposed during the Ford and Carter administrations, would cost this nation $240 million annually by 1985. These costs arise because U.S. flag vessels are about twice as costly to build and operate as equivalent foreign flag vessels. Clearly an UNCTAD type code for the bulk fleet, which would institutionalize bulk cargo reservation worldwide, or the spread of the unilateral enactment of laws to reserve cargo to national flag lines, is an economically unsound idea.

Flag of Convenience Vessel Registries

Flag of convenience (FOC) vessels, mainly consisting of bulk cargo vessels, have been controversial since the end of World War II. Initially they were seen by some parties as stealing national maritime jobs, as resulting in the loss of revenues to national treasuries due to foregone taxes on income and due to foregone registration fees, and as resulting in a loss of national prestige. Furthermore, some thought that vessels owned by national citizens but registered under foreign flags and possessing foreign crews could not be relied on to serve the homeland when needed, and therefore that those vessels did not contribute to national security. Later, open registry vessels were perceived as the primary source of oil discharges due to inferior vessel operation and maintenance practices.

Studies have shown that FOC fleets are not uniformly vulnerable to these criticisms. Tankers under different flags differ from one another in terms of fleet average probability of spilling oil (Stewart, 1977). Nevertheless, the differences of oil spill probability among fleets are typically less than the vessel-to-vessel differences within a given flag fleet. Any particular fleet often has a wide spectrum of vessel quality in its registry. Thus, discriminating by flag is generally an ineffective method to distinguish "good" from "bad" ships.

The average vessel quality of open registry fleets could be improved without significantly affecting the competitiveness of the bulk fleet market by instituting an international regime which codified

the conditions which vessels must meet to qualify for national registry. These conditions would specify, for example, the ratings
the vessels' crew must possess and the training necessary to win a
rating, the frequency of inspections the vessels must undergo and
the standards to be obtained. The creation of such a regime was
agreed to in principle by a vote taken in June 1981 in the UNCTAD
forum. The principles agreed to will eventually be incorporated
into an international convention. Some have speculated that the
June 1981 UNCTAD vote "might just mark the beginning of the end of
the (flag of convenience) system" (Seaward, 1981). Were this to
come to pass, it would end some of the basis of criticism of FOC
vessels.

Much of the Third World support for the proposed FOC code is based
on its provision requiring that natural persons of the flag state
hold equity in the vessels. The FOC code is being used as an alternative to cargo preference, but the consequences for the economic
operation of the bulk fleet market are not likely to be as pernic-
ious as would be the case if cargo preference were applied instead.

The complaints about oil spills from FOC tankers could be answered
by creating an authority which quickly and predictably fined parties
responsible for spills. The fine would be paid to the damaged party
as for that party's right to the damaged environmental amentities
(Pearson, Chapter 1, 1975). The size of the fine would equal the
social value of the resources damaged by the spill. One of UNCTAD's
objectives for the FOC code is to make FOC vessels more "trans-
parent" by making it possible to identify "owners and operators and
making them accountable for all shipping operations including maintenance of standards," (Seaward, 1981). Insofar as the proposed
UNCTAD convention for open registries succeeds in achieving this
objective it will contribute to solving the complaints.

Insurance might, at first, appear to be a means of weakening the
force of a strict oil spill liability regime. However, insuring
vessels against liability exposure would not dilute the incentive
for avoiding spills. Rational underwriters would tend to seek the
owners/operators who were most risk worthy and charge them lower
premiums than the less risk worthy owners/operators.

An international regime of strict liability has been successfully
resisted by tanker owners because, among other things, such a regime poses several difficulties of implementation. The size of
the liability fines would not be easily determined because the
value of the environmental amenities which are damaged by spills
cannot be estimated without controversy. Also, there is little
likelihood that the beneficial owners of vessels guilty of bad
practices can be reached by the enforcement authority. Furthermore,
the cargo insurance companies as well as the hull protection and
indemnity clubs, generally have not attempted to distinguish "good"
from "bad" owners, although the entire Greek flag fleet has recently come under some insurance pressure.

The contribution of the Intergovernmental Maritime Consultative
Organization of the U.N. (IMCO) to reducing the routine spillage

of oil from ship operations has been positive but moderate (Gibbs, forthcoming). IMCO's most significant action has been the passage of a 1978 Protocol to an earlier 1973 IMCO convention. The details of the Protocol and its intended versus its probable effects are described by Gibbs (forthcoming). It has been repeatedly proven that financial incentives generated organically within the petroleum transportation industry most strongly influence the operation of crude oil tankers. These incentives are largely beyond the influence of international organizations because of the latters' lack of enforcement authority. IMCO has probably succeeded in encouraging the application of new structural and equipment standards to new tankers. Yet IMCO's accomplishments would be minimal in comparison to the effect of applying strict liability to tanker owners.

An interesting research question is: Are the recent IMCO regulations being followed by all tanker owners and are these regulations actually reducing the level of routine oil spillage relative to that which would have occurred otherwise?

III. Multimodal Transportation

This section describes some current events in marine transportation. The theme of this section might be that:

- Multimodal movements of internationally traded containerized cargoes are growing;

- This growth is partly a consequence of the technological breakthrough represented by the container innovation;

- This growth is also partly a consequence of recent U.S. deregulation of air, road and rail transportation.

One industry observer has forecast that these combined events will cause the market for container transport services eventually to resemble that of a market for bulk commodity transport. Prices for transportation service will be a function of the quality of the service purchased and will be quoted on a per-box basis. Freight rate structures will be vastly simplified. Arrangements for shipment of less-than-container-load consignments will be less complex and arcane. Integrated multimodal firms will use simplified billing together with centralized control of cargo movements, while offering a range of service quality and price.

It would be interesting to investigate whether these changes will erode some of the power of the liner conferences, because price discrimination (see "Maxims of Marine Transportation Economics, below) will be less prevalent.

Intermodal Competition

A)   Intermodal transportation has becom increasingly attractive as the use of containers has spread. It has also resulted in a shift of transportation services among ports, especially in the context of the growth of the intermodal mini-bridge service. The mini-bridge is used to move containers originating from U.S. East and Gulf areas via a rail movement to the West Coast with ocean shipment on from there to Asia, and vice versa. Because most general cargoes which might be captured by the mini-bridge move from Asia to the U.S. East Coast, West Coast ports have gained business at the expense of East Coast ports. An injunction against the mini-bridge concept was sought by a group of East and Gulf Coast prots and longshore labor groups. In 1977, an administrative law judge decreed that the natural workings of advancing technology and the inevitable adjustments of the national transportation system could not be interfered with, and that a permanent injunction against the mini-bridge could not be granted (Gibbs and Meyer, 1979). This was a victory for those who believed that competition should govern the organization of the national transportation system, and that "naturally tributary" was a concept based on transportation cost and not on simpler concepts of geographical proximity, custom, or habit.

B) In 1981 the Interstate Commerce Commission deregulated the nations railroads by repealing regulations that dated to the late 1800s. This almost certainly betokens a shakeout among ports as shipping lines negotiate with railroads for service contracts to move cargoes from and to inland points. No longer will an artificial equalization of railroad freight rates between inland points and coastal ports apply. Rather, the rates will be freed to adjust to equal the opportunity costs of providing the service. This event, in conjunction with the application of dredging fees (as discussed in "User Charges for Dredging" above), would bring the price of port-inland transportation closer to equalling the resource cost of their production.

IV. Additional Tasks

Growth of the Soviet Flag Fleet

The growth of the Soviet flag commercial fleet has been a topic of worldwide controversy for about 10 years. The Soviets are one of several nations which manage one or more national flag ship lines. Many of these nationally managed lines have been making inroads into the liner conferences by quoting freight rates which are lower than conference rates. Frequently, these lines will quote per-box rates which do not discriminate among cargo types. Western shipping lines have responded to these inroads by heavily lobbying their governments for protection.

Soviet shipping has been the most common object of these complaints. Western lines argue that Soviet motives are mostly military, and that Soviet shipping is heavily subsidized. As a result, the U.S., Japan and the Netherlands have passed laws attempting to regulate Soviet flag lines calling in their countries. In the U.S. these laws place lower limits on the level of freight rates which state "controlled carriers" may charge.

216

Significant unanswered questions are:

- What are the opportunity costs to the Soviet national economy of offering liner shipping services?

- How do these costs relate to the value of the freight rates earned?

In other words, is the growth of the Soviet fleet based on government subsidy or is it self-financed? With such information one could, for example, attempt to forecast the ultimate size of the Soviet liner fleet. See the appendix for data on the size of the Soviet fleet.

National Shipbuilding and Operating Subsidies

In order to maintain a national flag fleet, some countries, including the U.S., have resorted to subsidizing their shipping. The U.S. lacks a comparative advantage in the production of shipping services. Relatively high U.S. wage scales and the outmoded physical plants of U.S. shipyards have made U.S. built and flagged ships uncompetitive in world markets. In order to maintain some tonnage under the U.S. flag, the U.S. subsidizes its slowly declining flag fleet. The subsidies have taken the form of cabotage (the Jones Act of 1920) and of operating and construction differential subsidies. U.S. flag vessels also receive special tax advantages, mortgage guarantees, and government subsidized insurance. Furthermore, government impelled cargoes are reserved for U.S. flag vessels. See the appendix for data on the recent history and size of the U.S. flag fleet.

Jantscher (p. 138-139, 1975) lists the total societal cost as of 1973 of the construction subsidy program at $1.8 billion, while operating subsidies have cost $3.6 billion to 1973. The Reagan administration has indicated that it wishes to end the 45 year old direct subsidy programs. U.S. cabotage law requires that cargoes moving between U.S. ports be carried on U.S. flag vessels. It has been estimated that this law has cost the nation about $3 billion over the period 1950 to 1970 (Jantscher, p. 139, 1975).

Decision Making for Transportation Facilities

It is now common practice for major energy and transportation facility siting issues to be litigated in regional courts or quasi-judicial councils. One example is Washington State's Energy Facility Site Evaluation Council (EFSEC) which must decide on the utility of permitting a major oil transhipment port to be sited at Port Angeles, WA.

Experience with EFSEC shows that it, and probably most of the similarly charged institutions, do not attempt to resolve conflicting testimony over such details of the facility proposal as for example, which is the most defendable of two alternative derivations of the probability of a major oil spill occurring sometime

217

during the life of the facility. Disputed aspects of siting proposals are set aside and the ultimate decision is based on non-
controversial data and testimony, since non-controversial aspects
may not be easily assailed in any subsequent court suits. Therefore, it is highly questionable whether these councils reach informed decisions.

It would be desirable to attempt to estimate the economic costs of
these uninformed decisions. Such an investigation would entail defining an appropriate system for producing informed decisions and
foretelling what the decisions would have been had that system
been employed. Were this somehow accomplished, it would then be
possible to net the outcome of the observed decisions against the
preferred decisions to achieve a cost estimate for the institutional lapse.

How does one define a preferred system and foretell its decisions?
It is well known that no social decision can be made, that does not
make interpersonal comparisons of utility and impose a value system.
Normally, imposing a value system in the context of economic research is avoided. Imposing or suggesting a value system is sometimes necessary if progress is to be made, however.

Maxims of Marine Transportation Economics

Analyses of marine transportation policies are often embellished
with sayings which have obtained credit from long use. This paper
concludes with rebuttals to the more common and erroneous of these.

A) "Hard currencies are sacred." For many reasons a country may
    get itself into a situation such that its currency is over-
    valued. The result is that, due to lack of hard currency
    reserves, domestic demands for imports exceed the country's
    ability to pay for them. The United Nations Industrial
    Development Organization (Chapter 16, 1972) explains how,
    in this situation, to estimate the equilibrium price of
    foreign currency in domestic currency terms.

    One lesson of this explanation is that hard currencies embody
    only a finite value. Therefore, efforts to earn hard cur-
    rencies cannot be undertaken willy-nilly, or losses may re-
    sult. Likewise not every act of an investor or national
    government need be interpreted as motivated by efforts to
    earn hard currency. A sample calculation of the domestic and
    foreign currency cost and revenue streams resulting from an
    investment in an ocean-going commercial ship has been provid-
    ed by Goss (1968).

B) "Trade-limiting subsidies, such as cargo preference and cabo-
    tage, waste more real income than direct subsidies, such as
    payments to ship owners to cover capital and operating costs.
    Therefore, direct subsidies are preferable to cabotage or
    cargo preference on economic grounds." In fact, both forms
    of subsidy are drags on the economy and there is no

theoretical or qualitative difference in their economic consequences. Direct subsidies, however, have the advantage of being visible and easily quantified. It is easier to make informed decisions regarding the true costs to the economy of direct subsidies and to this extent they are to be preferred.

C) Since "liner conference shipping is capital intensive, insistence on pure competition via application of the Sherman Antitrust Act would ensure that no new investments would take place because the investment costs could not be recovered from revenues, which would only be adequate to cover out-of-pocket costs in a competitive environment. Eventually no shipping service would be offered." The proportion of capital versus labor or other resources devoted to the production of a product or service has nothing to do with the long-run viability of a market. An example in rebuttal to this maxim is the market for office space in cities. Office buildings are virtually 100 percent capital, yet no supply shortfall persists. If supply fails to grow in step with demand, prices rise calling out new investment. The tanker market is likewise capital intensive, competitive and long-lived. Hence this is not a reason to foreswear application of anti-trust to the conferences.

D) "Price discrimination in the freight tariffs of liner conferences is necessary so that high rated cargoes can subsidize low rated cargoes." This maxim appears to be a justification for tariff discrimination in order to benefit some cargoes which would otherwise not be able to bear the cost of the freight charge. If interpreted literally, however, it is really an argument for a particular distribution of transportation-produced benefits. Yet, no reasons are ever given why such an equity choices are being made or, particularly, why they are being made by the liner conferences. The latter clearly have no legal competence to decide equity issues. Liner vessels offer a supply of volume and weight-carrying capacity for cargoes. If this supply sold on an auction basis, as is done in the bulk cargo market, it would be sold at a uniform price, again as in the bulk cargo market. This strategy would amount to pricing according to marginal opportunity cost and would produce maximum real world income. Decisions as to which cargoes and what ships should be subsidized are more appropriately performed by political bodies. These usually have a variety of means of transferring wealth in desired directions that are more efficient than what the conferences can offer.

E) "The availability of U.S. flag shipping promotes U.S. commerce and increases the wealth of U.S. exporters and consumers of traded goods." This maxim is often invoked as justification for the provision of government subsidies to U.S. flag shipping lines. The maxim would be true if U.S. flag shipping were the least cost alternative, in which case no subsidy would be required. The nation of registry of a shipping line has nothing to do with its contribution to national economic welfare, but the amount of resources the line consumes in providing the service certainly does. Long experience has shown that the required freight rate for a U.S. flag ship is about twice that of an equivalent foreign flag ship. Thus the U.S. could double the amount of shipping services it now consumes at no extra cost simply by employing "stroke of the pen" technology and ending its direct and indirect subsidy programs to U.S. flag shipping. Alternatively, the U.S. could purchase the same amount of shipping from foreign flags which it now obtains from domestic lines and save half the freight bill.

It is ironic that under the present system the beneficiaries of U.S. shipping subsidies are not even exporters and consumers of traded goods. These traders must obtain shipping services from U.S. flag lines in foreign trades at the same freight rates as they would pay to foreign flag ships. In domestic trades these traders must pay twice as much as they would if the service were of foreign provision, and thus domestic trade is actually depressed by the cabotage law.

The only legitimate national policy dimension possibly advanced by government assistance in the production of U.S. flag shipping is national security, and this aim will only be furthered if U.S. flag shipping is useful for that end. The utility of U.S. flag ships for military purposes is itself an issue of no small controversy, as evidenced by the maritime industries' strong resistance to proposals that the subsidy program be transfered from the Department of Commerce to the Department of Defense. Special interest pleading is at the base of the maxim that U.S. flag lines benefit U.S. merchants and consumers.

Conclusions

The causes of maritime transportation policy problems are diverse. The failure of markets to reflect the social value of goods and services accounts for a few issues such as excessive oil outflows from tankers. Problems with the liner conferences represent a different kind of market failure, one in which too few sellers have entered the market to foster competition and in which no governmental entity exists to foster competition. The absence of an appropriate international governing entity likewise contributes to the issue of flag of convenience vessels because a governing body would also nominally possess some mechanism for enforcing decisions and for transferring wealth. In the absence of such an authority, UNCTAD has been for forum wherein a FOC fleet code has been tentatively agreed to.

Government regulations which cause inefficient markets have been another source of marine transportation issues. These regulations include cabotage, railroad rate equalization (now defunct), and cargo preference (U.S.-Soviet grain). Government subsidies to ports and to shipping (some degree of these may soon be ended) also waste resources. The failure of existing federal (in the case of transportation facility siting) and state (port objectives) political oversight and review mechanisms have also been noted.

Probably the single most costly problem is that of the existence of liner conference cartels. Increasing intermodal competition, some of which emanates from nationally managed liner fleets, might end this. The UNCTAD liner code will not increase inefficiencies significantly. The end of dredging subsidies is a positive event. In summary, it seems that decreasing interference from governments in domestic transportation (deregulation and an end to unjustifiable subsidies) together with increasing efforts to influence some of the international ramifications of shipping through UNCTAD and IMCO are, with a few exceptions, desirable trends.

Summary of Research Topics

The description of the state of marine transportation economic research given here touches many of the major issues of the last 20 years. Significant research efforts are needed to:

1. Clarify the economic contribution to the country and to port regions of port activities and to determine how to improve the economic performance of ports. (The corrections of old mistakes--e.g., subsidizing a portion of port operating costs in the form of providing free dredging--will require solving new problems pertaining to compensating injured parties);

2. Provide a good estimate of the costs of the UNCTAD Code for Liner Conferences;

3. Investigate other possible U.S. regulatory schemes for liner conferences;

4. Determine the consequences of permitting the conferences to close and of facilitating the creation of shippers' councils. (Will the liner conferences lose their monopoly power over tariff rates as multimodal competition increases?);

5. Estimate the magnitude and direction the wealth transfers to citizens of developing countries which may result from the UNCTAD Code for flag of convenience vessels.

6. Determine whether the 1978 IMCO provisions are actually discouraging oil spills and whether the earnings from the sale of oil that would otherwise have been discarded have been greater or less than the cost of the provisions;

7. Establish the real costs the Soviets bear in producing their liner shipping services.

It is likely that uninformed decisions about transportation facilities are costing society a great deal. There is much to be done!

Appendix

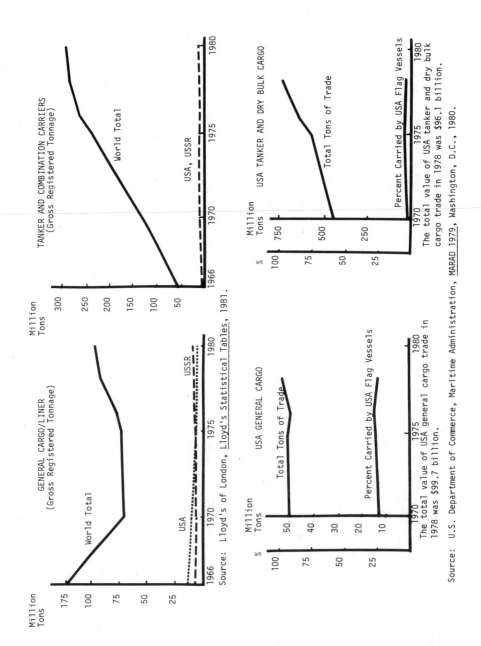

TANKER AND COMBINATION CARRIERS
(Gross Registered Tonnage)

World Total

USA, USSR

Million Tons: 300, 250, 200, 150, 100, 50

1966 1970 1975 1980

GENERAL CARGO/LINER
(Gross Registered Tonnage)

World Total

USSR

USA

Million Tons: 175, 100, 75, 50, 25

1966 1970 1975 1980

Source: Lloyd's of London, Lloyd's Statistical Tables, 1981.

USA TANKER AND DRY BULK CARGO

Total Tons of Trade

Percent Carried by USA Flag Vessels

Million Tons: 750, 500, 250
%: 100, 75, 50, 25

1970 1975 1980

The total value of USA tanker and dry bulk
cargo trade in 1978 was $96.1 billion.

USA GENERAL CARGO

Total Tons of Trade

Percent Carried by USA Flag Vessels

Million Tons: 50, 40, 30, 20, 10
%: 100, 75, 50, 25

1970 1975 1980

The total value of USA general cargo trade in
1978 was $99.7 billion.

Source: U.S. Department of Commerce, Maritime Administration, MARAD 1979, Washington, D.C., 1980.

References

Bennathan, E. and A.A. Walters (1972). "Shipping Conferences: An Economic Analysis," Journal of Maritime Law and Commerce 4(1): 83-115.

_____ (1979). Port Pricing and Investment Policy for Developing Countries, Oxford University Press.

Bosies, W.J., Jr. and W.G. Green (1974). "The Liner Conference Convention: Launching an International Regulatory Regime," Law and Policy in International Business 6(2), Spring: 533-574.

Devanney, J.W., III (1976). "Marine Transportation Economics," unpublished notes from course 13.66, Department of Ocean Engineering, Massachusetts Institute of Technology.

Devanney, J.W., III and L.H. Tan (1975). "The Relationship Between Short-run Pricing and Investment Timing: The Port Pricing and Expansion Example," Transportation Research 9: 329-337.

Devanney, J.W., III, V.M. Livanos and R.J. Stewart (1972a). "Conference Ratemaking and the West Coast of South America," M.I.T. Commodity Transportation and Economic Development Laboratory, Technical Report 72-1. (An article based on this report appeared in: J.W. Devanney, III, V.M. Livanos and R.J. Stewart, Journal of Transport Economics and Policy XI(2): 154-177, 1975).

Devanney, J.W., III, G.K. Loon and T.G. Hock (1972b). "Fundamentals of Port Pricing and Expansion," Massachusetts Institute of Technology Commodity Transportation and Economic Development Laboratory, Technical Report MITCTL 72-4, May.

Devanney, J.W., III, H. Romer and M.B. Kennedy (1978). "Alaska Tanker Fleet Economics," report prepared for the Alaska State Legislature and the Alaska Department of Revenue, Martingale Incorporated, December.

Gibbs, S.R. (Forthcoming). "New Technologies of Transportation in the North Pacific and the Problem of Tanker Originated Pollution," in The Management of Marine Regions: The North Pacific, by Ed Miles, et al., Chapter XI, University of California Press.

Gibbs, S.R. and B. Meyer (1979). "The Effect of the Panama Canal Treaties on the General Cargo Traffic of U.S. West Coast Ports," Institute for Marine Studies, University of Washington, Mimeo, June.

Goss, R.O. (1968). "Investment in Shipping and the Balance of Payments: A Case-Study of Import-Substitution Policy," Chapter 3 of Studies in Maritime Economics, Cambridge University Press.

223

_____ (1979). A Comparative Study of Seaport Management and Administration, 2 Volumes, Government Economic Service, Departments of Industry, Trade and Prices and Consumer Protection, London.

Hyman, D.N. (1973). The Economics of Government Activity, Chapter 1, Holt, Rinehart and Winston, Inc.

International Legal Materials (1974): 912-951.

Jantscher, G.R. (1975). Bread Upon the Water: Federal Aids to the Maritime Industries, The Brookings Institution.

Koopmans, T.C. (1939). Tanker Freight Rates and Tankship Building, Haarlem, Netherlands.

Lind, R. (1968). "Benefit-Cost Analysis: A Criterion for Social Investment," in Water Management and Public Policy, edited by R.O. Sylvester, University of Washington Press.

Lipsey, R.G. and K. Lancaster (1956-57). "The General Theory of Second Best," Review of Economic Studies 24: 11-32.

Lloyd's Register of Shipping (1978). Lloyd's Register of Shipping Statistical Tables, London.

Major, D.C. (1977). Multiobjective Water Resources Planning, Water Resources Monograph 4, American Geophysical Union, Washington, D.C.

McGee, J.S. (1960). "Ocean Freight Rate Conferences and the American Merchant Marine," The University of Chicago Law Review 27(2): 191-314.

National Academy of Sciences, National Research Council (1976). Port Development in the United States, Washington, D.C.

Pearson, C.S. (1975). International Marine Environmental Policy: The Economic Dimension, The Johns Hopkins University Press.

Seaward, N. (1981). "Flagging Down the Open Registries," Seatrade June: 3-4.

Stewart, R.J. (1977). "Tankers in U.S. Waters," Oceanus 20(4): 74-85.

Steiner, P.O. (1969). Public Expenditure Budgeting, The Brookings Institution.

United Nations Industrial Development Organization (1972). Guidelines for Project Evaluation, New York.

U.S. Department of Commerce, Maritime Administration (1974). Public Port Financing in the United States, Washington, D.C., June.

U.S. Department of Justice (1977). The Regulated Ocean Shipping Industry, Washington, D.C.

U.S. General Accounting Office (1977). Costs of Cargo Preference, PAD-77-82, Washington, D.C., September 9.

U.S. House of Representatives (1981). Report of the Activities of the Merchant Marine and Fisheries Committee, 96th Congress, House Report No. 96-1563, Serial No. 95-F, 96th Cong., Second Session, Washington, D.C.: 134-137.

Walsh, A.H. (1978). The Public's Business: The Politics and Practices of Government Corporations, M.I.T. Press, Cambridge, Massachusetts.

Walters, A.A. (1973). "Ocean Freight Rates, Cartels and Collusion and the North Atlantic Controversy," in J.R. Nelson, editor, Criteria for Transport Pricing, Cornell Maritime Press: 287-293.

Capstone

Anthony D. Scott

I. Capstone

"Capstone" turns out to be a well-chosen metaphor. These flat rocks were perched in celtic times atop three upright stones. Was the resulting cromlech a throne, dwelling or tomb? We cannot be certain what purpose the ancient Europeans had in mind. Neither are we sure what purpose informs the many investigations into ocean resources. What capstone can unite these studies, giving them meaning and shape?

The researches described in the papers in this volume spring from a shared apprehension that there is a political responsibility to guide the users of the oceans. Even if the public sector is to be confined to a neutral role, it must create and protect a system of laws and rights that will permit industries and small groups to pursue orderly and consistent goals. Until recently, such pursuits seemed to be constrained neither in time nor in space, so that most interventions turned out to be simply a seaward extension of well-established inland policies. The conspicuous exceptions are so simple that it is possible to contemplate revising all of them in one global convention on the Law of the Sea. The need for this codification by public negotiation instead of by evolving maritime custom is now generally accepted.

But the negotiators have not felt the need for much research. Indeed were it not for the new quest for self-sufficiency in materials and energy their attention would still be concentrated almost exclusively on naval matters, fisheries and shipping. In the past, understanding of these subjects has been provided by a nourishing mix of trial and error, leavened by vigorous lobbying. Even in the recent discussions there were few calls for research, least of all by economists.

That a research agenda is even sought today reflects an uneasy general awareness that the future will be different. The ocean will no longer offer unlimited space or time for all comers. Rationing of scarce access soon will become necessary if costly but beneficial private opportunities are to be seized.

Rationing of access is even more imperative if the public sector is to take a more-than-neutral role. Quite apart from the obvious in-adequacy of the marketplace as a mechanism for ordering private activities on the boundless main, newly-conceived public responsibility for protecting the environment, waste disposal and recreation now take their place beside naval defense. Furthermore, the recognition of the scarcity of ocean space, etc. giving rise to a potential resource rent, suggests public revenues to offset the new responsibilities. In brief, the public sector no longer is confined to policing scattered private activities, but itself is directly engaged both as owner and as user.

Thus far there is general agreement. This understanding lies behind much research already done within the public sector on behalf of municipal and regional interests on the coasts and of various pressure groups concerned with the high seas. And the private sector has carried on a good deal of its own research in response to regulations and to expected conflicts. But agreement that access to the ocean is becoming scarce is not enough to define an agreement about how or for whom to manage it. The excellent papers in this volume reveal that most researchers have been obliged to depend upon an extension of policies for allocating labor, land and capital and for protecting people as workers, owners and investors. Huppert for example asks whether existing foreign policy and international trade policy provide guidelines for ocean research: Russell whether previous river and air pollution debates offer a research agenda about ocean waste disposal; Tussing whether the well-understood principles of oil production do not apply without further research to ocean energy resources; and Sebenius whether proposed seabed institutions are sufficiently similar to land-based systems.

The process which bases proposed research on models borrowed from earlier policy problems has a serious limiting characteristic. The authors have been aware of this. Their models do not arise from a conceptual model of optimization by some identified ocean actor to whom they can attribute preferences and opportunities. The ocean unowned is merely a sump or surge tank, capable of storing its various abilities to substitute for exhausted and congested mainland resources. Its welfare is not embodied in that of any person or constituency. Put another way, while the benefits from merely good ocean research accrue to identifiable ocean-product producers and consumers, the benefits from better research mostly accrue through general-equilibrium interactions to the economy as a whole, to remote citizens who gain from improved allocation of all resources but do not perceive their dependence on ocean policy. Thus the best ocean research may have no informed clients.

It might understandably be objected that this characteristic is not a special feature of research on ocean resources but is an obstacle to planning or justifying any kind of economic research involving

227

resources. The difference here is that researchers who would serve
ocean users have a double disability. Common property denies to
users any consumer sovereignty over the resource. Perhaps worse,
their geographical dispersion greatly increases users' costs of
seeking their goals through the representative-government system, or
of finding allies for collective action.

So much is clear: ocean researchers can rely neither on market demand nor on political voice for the distillation of policy goals,
so that it is obviously difficult to design useful economic research
projects and more serious, the edge is blunted of whatever research
is undertaken. For example, research about alternative policy instruments can be inconclusive because no prior choice has been made
between alternative ends. Similarly, research about conflicting
uses may give results that merely replicate confusion about goals.

This problem is not my discovery. The need for a bill of ocean
priorities has been known, witness James Crutchfield's participation
in the "plan for national action," Our Nation and the Sea, submitted
to Congress in 1969. I have suggested above why such efforts evoke
little general response: they have no constituency. In any case,
realizing that good research requires that ends be given is only
the first of many stages in research design.

We know what the next stage is not. It is not to write endless
papers lamenting the lack of clear national purpose for the oceans.
Nor is it to substitute the researchers' own goals for those of the
political process. The lack of decision is itself to be read as a
signal, as information.

More profitably, we can attempt to narrow the field of indecision
by looking for national public choice. That is, we can ask what
we could most confidently predict would emerge if public policymakers were to concentrate on making choices about the ocean's management.

Here we can gain from examining an "actual" case study. We may consider as suggestive Dorfman's and Jacoby's models for water quality
management (as reported in the excellent Dorfman and Dorfman, eds.,
Economics of the Environment, 1977). The authors attempt to predict the "likely decisions" of a river water-quality commission
constrained by statutory terms of reference and political realities.
It is assumed that, although the various groups in the hypothetical
river basin want different things, the decision makers know what,
and how much, they want them; their dollar values are revealed and
taken into account, by the commission. Although ocean problems
are, as I have suggested, unlikely ever to be resolved by such an
information-rich process, two lessons emerge.

First, while the alternative solutions provide differing amounts of
outputs at various distributions of cost, these amounts are measured
along a constant set of "dimensions," such as water quality at
particular locations. This set of dimensions, imposed by the
questioner or searcher is a way of organizing preferences and

policies in quantitative fashion. Dorfman and Jacoby, recognizing that the political decision-making process itself changes people's perceptions and goals, nevertheless claim, reasonably, that people can be expected to persist with their original demands. If so the dimensions themselves are the medium for the expression and transmission of goals.

Second, public policies for large resources can be assumed to have some internal consistency, which makes it possible to deduce from other places or times what the same public "must" want from the oceans. We can look for consistency in final policies and for underlying consistency in a cross-section analysis of revealed preferences.

Our authors depend heavily on the lessons to be learned once the internal consistency of policies is assumed. Russell, for example, reasons from experience in controlling air and river pollution: "the same should be true of the oceans." All the authors are very cautious about the sort of analogy which claims other resources as close substitutes for the oceans. But if the ocean is a substitute (or complement), then the values of its benefits or damages are dependent on, not independent of, the values to be placed on rivers and the ambient air. But then one policy control may not be applicable to both resources. For example, solid waste problems have often been solved by policies that took into account the availability of the ocean as a receptor of last resort. The same policies cannot be transplanted, mutatis mutandis, to the ocean, for which there is no such "backstop." In general, however, the constraints perceived when analogous questions were decided on land need not exist for ocean-resource issues. Thus consistency with earlier policies can be a perverse source of ocean policies. Voters' preferences must be consulted afresh.

In what follows, it is suggested that the citizen consistently will act, if permitted, as he does in his working and investing activities. He will act like a profit maximizer. In this case he will seek to use the oceans so as to obtain (subject to constraints) the greatest possible net benefit from his property. A conceptualization of public decisions as if the voters wished to, say, maximize ocean rents has certain advantages over any other imaginable process. One advantage is discussed in the next section. In addition, this approach has the merits of providing a means of thinking about the information problem of open-access resources: if there is too little information about individual willingness to pay for use or access to the oceans, there is too much unquantified information about what selected groups would prefer. Voting and other political activities merely indicate the direction in which people wish policy to move, especially at no cost to themselves. It is a revelation for the researcher working for a regulatory agency to ask himself instead, "how much could be successfully charged this group?" To ask this question is at once to ask how other demands are to be served, how access is to be rationed, how much congestion is to be endured, and what services (of information access, facilities, enforcement and monitoring) the agency must itself provide.

Ascribing something like revenue maximizing behavior to the managers of the ocean raises other important questions in the minds of economic researchers as well. For example, what are the constraints? Two, inherent in any process of optimizing or maximizing, quickly demand attention. The first is distribution: how are the incomes and jobs of ocean users like fishermen to be weighted? That these questions have received special attention in the past, and will continue to do so, is clear. Ocean-rent maximization provides a vehicle for approaching distribution issues, when the claims of a certain region or industry are under consideration. A second constraint is the territorial boundary of "the ocean." How extensive is the area for which one country is responsible and from which one country may benefit? Let me discuss how, under their present understanding of national policy, our authors deal with the extent of the possible maximand.

Following the encyclopedic survey by James Crutchfield, the discusion is assisted by separating the almost-unbounded potential subject matter into components. These components have in common that some research, or at least speculation, has already taken place, some material been published, and some experts or specialists have become identifiable. For the most part the published work already known is mission-oriented, an element in some endeavor to solve some conflict anticipated or problem already experienced, obstructing or confusing the unfettered use of maritime capacity. Consequently, the discussions tended to center around economic problems of a fairly immediate variety, problems that do not lead many of the participants to consider what the full extent of the conceptual challenge to economists might be, or might become. Indeed some are led to imply (or assert), in their comments on the need for research, that no challenge exists. Perhaps because most economics is space-less anyway, few wish even to adapt the approaches of land economics or of agricultural economics to this new domain. Instead, a general equilibrium approach suffices to sort out the allocation of the factors of production with marketable opportunities (labor, capital goods and time), between land and water. The use of the ocean is implicitly assumed to be free, or constrained by the physical requirements of some other use for its space, depth, tides, food and other characteristics. Such an approach is not one to excite the imagination or to attract powerful researchers.

The reasons for this narrowness need not be gone into here. We are indeed fortunate that the minimal economic approach has been found robust enough to carry the research burden now under way. But we should not be surprised that it is necessary at this junction to study what the government's research agenda should be. Consider that Charles Ehler, in an informal discussion, has urged on economists the importance of applied and tangible suggestions rather than more contributions to the advance of fundamental economic theory. One can sympathize with his feeling that the ocean

economics research purse is too thin to permit much investment in
the rich theoretic proliferation that accompanied the study of
environmental problems. There is too little information, Ehler says,
and economists should do something about that first. His warnings
are certainly a useful corrective to views that the oceans provide
new nourishment for endless classificatory articles adapting old
thoughts to new decisions. But his warnings also are an impediment,
I suggest, to understanding the dimensions and magnitudes involved
in ocean conflicts, which is maybe why the authors' papers show
a pronounced lack of intensity, suggesting that these writers perhaps believe ocean problems are to be so novel as to demand the
immediate attention of the big guns of our profession.

I suggest that this lack of urgency is due to the fact that with
few exceptions, Americans did not seek and many do not yet really
appreciate the possession of the extended economic zone (200-mile
limit). The exceptions are reflected in the papers offered in the
symposium: more oil, minerals, recreation, fisheries and revenue
are now within reach. But of course, through trade, they would
have been available as imports. For many other countries, unlike
the United States, the acquisition of new oceanic territory has
made an important difference to citizens, industries, or to resolv-
ing worrisome conflicts between competing regions and classes for
the services of the high seas. Had the U.S. been a riparian of
the North Sea or the Gulf of Thailand, this might have been a more
urgent conference, with partisan economists not only pushing rival
research agendas, but anxiously attacking the interpretation of research already completed.

For the American economy most ocean research is to be justified by
remote future, not current problems. Multiple-use opportunities,
and the conflicts from which they arise, are still tomorrow's decisions. Most perceived political goals are best achieved by land-
based techniques. The economist imagining marine-allocation problems today is in the position of Gibbon Wakefield and other classical economists 150 years ago. They and their opponents attempted
to use Ricardo's slender and essentially static model to prescribe
how America and Australia should be developed. It may be that today we are attempting something just as hopeless: the application
of Pigou's insights about the conflicts between laundries and smoke
to policies for the acquisition and exploitation of the seas. It
can be argued that the problem was not theory, but facts: Wakefield
had never been abroad, and was forced to write from a prison. His
opponents were almost as uninformed. If so, more informational
research is required. But I would argue that more facts would not
help much, except to reinforce the contention that the oceans
should be seen as a resource to be analyzed in its own right, both
theoretically and inductively. In this sense the Wakefield debate
on alienation of public land should contain a lesson for today.
Can economists help decision makers to understand what the next
generation will describe as successful ocean-use administration?

Still another explanation for their serenity regarding innovative
research is that nice economic calculations seem inappropriate in

the diplomatic atmosphere today. Research may be needed, but it is overshadowed by rough international jostling, pre-emptions, and greater attention to distributive than allocative problems. Pre-occupied with other matters, Americans, to the foreign observer, seem to be repeating their 19th century expansion path, almost absent-mindedly acquiring the high seas, spending too little energy to consider costs, needs, or uses. What use is there for economic research on mining (a subject difficult enough to get supported even for conventional sources of metals and energy), when the national interest in the seafloor can still be handled by a threatened veto of the entire Law of the Sea convention? The U.S. administration also prefers a big-stick approach to oil-spills and fisheries questions involving other nations. When such policies are under consideration, they depend not on economic research, but on passions and interests.

II. A Suggested Point of View

In what follows I outline an alternative research strategy. It is based on the proposition that research projects are best selected by an ocean agency when the nation's ocean itself--not the national economy--is chosen as the unit for efficient management. The nation is the referent group in its capacity as landlord.

The landlord is the researcher's client who needs information, and can pay for it in proportion to its probable value in raising ocean wealth: the discounted net benefits from ocean use. Net benefits should be defined at their opportunity costs. For the services from a proposed ocean use, gross benefits are valued at the amounts that would have to be paid to obtain the same services if produced on land or imported; and total costs are valued at what inputs would cost if they were used in their best alternative employment. The net benefit from the use under investigation should be compared with that from conflicting uses (and the two uses combined to maximize ocean rent.)

The data required are much the same as if each use was investigated in isolation, as part of the national economy. The difference is in providing some clue as to how valuable certain data are. What is proposed is a change in the point of view of those collecting and using the data and of those making final decisions about ocean research. An agency that has been charged with ocean research has a maximand: ocean wealth, to be increased by choosing research projects in conformity with their probable returns to that wealth. Research priorities also follow automatically; the best projects are those that have the highest expected value for ocean wealth. This is an attractive feature both for projects that cast light on ocean-use conflicts and for projects that compare the use of ocean resources with alternative ways of obtaining the same services. The approach has all the operational merits of decentralization, of partial (versus general) economic analysis, and of providing research agencies with a psychological sense of motivation.

At present the abundance of nonspecific national goals becomes a source of confusion and discouragement to those who must undertake research on the oceans, and to those who must actually administer ocean policy. We can expect that two kinds of research will, on the approach, be singled out for special attention: first, help with day-to-day decisions to promote the success of long-run pro- grams; second, research and experiment among the various possible structures of management itself, including especially various de- grees of decentralized responsibility and management. Russell's discussion of charging schemes would fit under this second head, along with types of property rights and assignment of certain areas or products to communities, states, firms or not-for-profit insti- tutions.

III. Existing Research Goals

First, virtually no one among the authors here has suggested that the aim should be to broaden or deepen the general body of economic theory. I have argued elsewhere that more specialists should be- come interested in the economics of natural resources because this type of economics does throw into relief analytical problems ob- scured or glossed over when the main application of economics is to, say, manufacturing and the public sector. Nobody else has sug- gested here that exploring the economics of the sea would help to develop the already-existing corpus of economic methodology. It is apparent that NOAA and the contributors have seen the only value of ocean-economic research to be the solution of ocean-management problems. So be it.

Second, I assume, however, that no one feels the study of ocean economic phenomena for their own sake would be absolutely wasteful. Basic nonapplied studies should form some part of any research agenda.

Third, to the extent that research is to be limited to guiding ocean use, management and development, it should be valued according to its contribution to human welfare, i.e., not to water purity or fish conservation as ends in themselves. What abstract aspects of social welfare have been cited in this symposium? Below I list the major research goals identified in the papers, chiefly to illustrate that, because they are in severe need of weighting or ranking, an aggregative or comprehensive goal is required.

1) Resource development as a separate goal in itself-- especially of oil and minerals.

2) Internal industrial efficiency--especially in the fishery but also in waste disposal.

3) External efficiency in the resolution of resource-use conflicts--especially as between oil spills (and waste disposal) and recreation and tourism.

233

4)   Distribution--especially in skimming off unearned ocean rents. (Actually however, with Gaffney as an exception, most participants treat tax policy as an incentive instrument to induce efficiency or encourage development.)

5)   International division of labor--especially in mineral and fishery development. (This was rarely an "aim"; for some authors the rights or claims of foreign ocean users were taken as a constraint or simple nuisance).

6)   Stability--especially in allocation over time. Rereading the papers has suggested to me the extent to which ocean resources are a vast store of natural capital, a colossal inventory. Parts of it are fixed, like a mine or building, while others are changeable like a forest or herd of livestock. The absorptive capacity of this slowly changing stock gives it a generalized buffering potential in which living, exhaustible and waste resources can be held in stock until the economy wishes to invest in their retrieval.

Doubtless other research goals could be identified. Furthermore, those suggested above could be broken down into more specific problems. But this proliferation would only reinforce my point that the goals are disparate and somewhat inconsistent. Trade-offs are needed to guide both research and management. No one commissioning or undertaking research--even if it is only the fastidious collection of data for future use--can now be sure of the priorities. Something more immediate or proximate is needed.

This leads back to taking the ocean, not its inputs or its outputs, as the unit of management. Society becomes a landlord, whose aim, accompanied by a multitude of special definitions, constraints, lags and uncertainties, become the maximization of the present value of the ocean space. I submit that this concept, also hinted at by various contributors, does tend to order research proposals.

IV. Three Difficulties with the Suggestion

Of course, if such a simple specifying referent group or maximand neatly ordered all ocean management research problems, it would already be in use.

First, pure theory tells us that a national policy of maximizing the rent of the nation's oceans will not give us a set of outcomes differing from a national policy of efficient use of all factors of production. Further, if the outcomes of the two were greatly different, there might be reason to pick the second rather than the first. But these statements about theory apply to an economy where allocation, distribution and investment are conducted in an atmosphere of certainty. In a world of uncertainty, with technological change, resource depletion, altering preferences and capital accumulation, the ways ocean uses evolve is to an important extent a function of the amount and quality of research done in advance.

If the research is inchoate, arising from concerns about the different goals mentioned above, little will be learned about the ocean as a resource in its own right. My suggested ordering principle would tend to make research harmonious, the clients having in mind the future uses of a single, increasingly scarce, natural resource. In brief, I believe it does matter what point of view is used, the theory of general competitive equilibrium in a certain world notwithstanding.

Second, adoption of an ocean-rent-maximization point of view does not in itself, indicate what the bounds of the relevant ocean ought to be. Should there be one maximand for each of the Pacific, Atlantic, Gulf and Arctic ocean coastal regions? Or should the national ocean policy be drafted to maximize rent from one super-resource composed of bits of four oceans? Both extremes, and intermediate concepts too, are compatible with my suggestion.

Probably the four-ocean concept is best. Management of each ocean separately, with overall policies that differ in some respects because of special characteristics that distinguish one coast from another, would minimize the organization or transactions costs involved in that degree of national decentralization of ocean management. These costs would include those of management bodies in their administrative and political roles (including the costs of policy coordination with other neighboring jurisdictions to look after externalities and spillovers); and the costs of political action and compliance (including a range of ocean-user activities from lobbying to filling in statistical forms). Classified in another way, they would include the costs of information, management and enforcement to both administrators/politicians and to ocean-users/citizens. A proposition in the public choice theory of federal governmental structures states that the right number of units of jurisdiction is indicated by the number that is associated with the lowest total of government and citizen organization costs as just listed.

U.S. fisheries policy has recently been experimenting with the proper degree of decentralization. For reasons that are largely constitutional and irrelevant here, it has been necessary to transfer much fisheries' decision-making from the states to regional or coastal councils. For many fisheries this new point of view is a source of substantial improvement, though for some that are very localized and independent of conflicts originating elsewhere, the broader regional point of view is a source of compromise and unwanted fuzziness. I mention this innovation to suggest that it is possible to experiment with the organization costs of alternative scales of ocean management by examining not only hypothetical but also historical shifts in the scope of ocean jurisdictions. Such a process should help to overcome the indeterminacy of the relevant ocean unit for rent maximizing planning and policy. If the U.S. can make federalism work, it should not be beyond the wit of legislators to set terms of reference for ocean resource managers--and so for ocean economic researchers--that are a workable compromise between the organization costs of balkanized units and those of one centralized bureau.

A third difficulty is that the U.S. does not yet see itself as an ocean landlord, as is made clear by the limited scope of the powers it has transferred to NOAA: other federal agencies have even fewer and weaker powers, and the states with their agencies are confined locally. The U.S. external stance shows the same attitude in winning its broadened coastal powers the U.S. acted more in response to a variety of disparate internal pressures and external challenges than to a general seaward imperative. Thus it may be politically difficult to get consent to an ocean-rent maximizing concept.

This and the previous two difficulties however are not insuperable and, as I have suggested, they may not be new sources of difficulty at all. They are not serious enough to justify avoiding the ocean-rent approach as a basis for economic research. Making the best use of the oceans is analogous to the aims of other major programs, such as efficient development of outer space, the radio spectrum and inland boundary waters. Goals of this sort can become a means of assisting coordinations, indicating gaps and preventing excessive solicitude for interest groups. In reading the proceedings of the symposium, I noted other advantages to the ocean-rent maximizing approach. Blair Bower's remarks on the need for research into the economics of protection or enhancement of ocean activities suggest that the goal of maximizing U.S. ocean welath, if not pressed too far, could be a source of guidelines for investment. And Arlon Tussing's remarks on petroleum foreign policy suggest that the State Department's role in forming alliances with neighboring states could be assisted if cooperation and sharing were part of the nation's "ocean policy" rather than assorted extensions of existing diplomatic jobs.

V. Research

Apart from the likelihood that the "landlord" concept can help in procedures to assign priorities, can it assist in identifying particular research policies that might otherwise be missed? The general aim would be to construct a research agenda that identifies and compares those projects, policies or activities that make the best use of the oceans, when evaluated at their national or international shadow prices and examined in terms of their promised change in the total value of ocean spaces. This is of course a sort of benefit-cost analysis, with the ocean landlord as the referent group.

Among the papers in this collection, that by Dan Huppert provides the most convincing examples. The problems are sketched in Crutch-field's introduction. Huppert's notions on fisheries research include a central theme about the landlord: "As a sole owner, in effect, of the fishery resource the U.S. could seek to maximize the revenue collected..." from foreign fishermen. He then proposes research on the best level of fees to interact with existing effective tariff protection levels as an instrument of U.S. foreign trade policy. At another place, Huppert proposes that fee setting for foreign fishing be guided not only by revenue and foreign trade policy of objectives but also to its effect on U.S. fishermen's costs, presumably costs arising from pressure and congestion by foreign fleets. These are stimulating suggestions, although I would debate Huppert's tendency to ask administrators to try to incorporate all three differing objections. In particular, that fees should be discussed as part of U.S. foreign trade policy is an unnecessary complication. They are just fees. I also question the necessity for having the criterion for cost reductions only those costs borne by U.S. fishermen. Why not reduce all congestion costs by raising access fees until the payments willingly paid by fishermen from any port, domestic or foreign, produce a maximum revenue (annual rent)? If the answer is that national policies reveal that U.S. fishermen are to be preferred, such a preference could be made explicit in a rebate on fee payments by fishermen with U.S. nationality. This way of handling national distributional goals preserves the ideal that ocean rent, not fishermen's income, is the ultimate maximand.

More generally, Huppert's piece reminds us of an important truth about policies to protect domestic business or enterprise (including fishermen) from foreign users of a resource. If and when there are only domestic fishermen interested in a resource, public managers and their superiors can be relaxed about whether full rent is being collected. If it is collected, then it will be redistributed, probably to fishermen as some sort of transfer. If it is not, the beneficiaries are local citizens anyway. This is a corollary of the "we owe it to ourselves" maxim about the national debt. But when national and foreign fishermen share a resource, managers cannot afford to be relaxed. For fee-structure loopholes do not benefit "us," but are an unrequited gift of rent to "them."

Clifford Russell's paper on environmental management seems on first reading to be a challenge to the ocean-rent point of view. With the weariness of experience he warns against general-equilibrium models of the environment (including land-based activities) and more specifically against conceptually integrated marine environmental management models. He tells us why: we cannot escape our lack of information about natural interactions as the system or subsystem level. He then examines the tools of management and means of monitoring and enforcement that a comprehensive agency would have--they are the tools that RFF has been discussing and polishing since the early 1970s. He is of the opinion that expensive information would foil the efficient use of these "traditional" economic tools. After examining the NOAA strategy, sympathetically, he proposes a decentralized regional approach. This too he rejects and I leave it to the reader to study his analysis. My point is that this part of his discussion ranges from pole-to-pole, but then veers from a public solution to a private-enterprise marketable rights mechanism (of which more later). By pole-to-pole, I mean that Russell does a rough benefit-cost study of a centralized jurisdictional solution, run by NOAA, and of a decentralized solution of only, say, 400 square miles (no example is quantified)--but not of any intermediate size.

Although Russell may rightly feel that the whole idea of instituting a spatial management unit is a waste of time as a practical policy, it may be very practical when used as the central theme for economic research. Russell indeed seems to me to have lost sight of research while examining his polar policies. Disappointingly, therefore, he does not examine the public-administration idea consistent with his own work on public choice: that economists might contribute to research on the quest for the optimum scale of ocean management unit. His keen awareness of how the problem of information varies with size of management unit would have made his research suggestions valuable.

The magnitude of the information problem is apparent from Russell's initial remarks and from Blair Bower's accompanying comments. For Bower, an ocean region is a concept for dealing with conflicting uses, not a concept for maximizing rent or revenue. Although he does mention institutional research, Bower's excellent piece suggests to me that he would expect tradeoffs to be determined and administered in a technocratic benefit-cost framework, rather than a political one. The two papers complement each other well, Bower suggesting that he believes that information requirements are more daunting than other complexities of regional resource management, and Russell that he is in general disenchanted with discretionary management in any form. Bower's research suggestions, including one on the optimal time pattern of exhaustible resource management in a specific region, are surely part of the agenda that I believe would arise in the decision documentation of real-life regional agencies.

The useful paper by Gardner Brown, a model of its kind, cannot be cited one way or the other in connection with the approach I have suggested. Brown is strictly a professional here, concerning himself with the data of research methods more than with point of view. This means probably that he is not sympathetic with a suboptimizing approach and prefers to look for recreational outputs valued by national-goal standards. On the other hand, the methods he describes are chiefly concerned with ocean uses that conflict with recreation. This means that they are, in principle, value-free, adaptable to optimizing the utility or welfare function of any referent group from that of the country as a whole to that of a particular sole-owner of a bay or inlet. Certainly a management group maximizing rent for an ocean region would want to use Brown's research methods.

This brings us to ocean minerals. Comprehensive information is provided in Crutchfield's background paper, and also by Tussing, Kalter and Sebenius. Tussing's paper I find puzzling. Does he want research or not? He starts us off with some helpful remarks on measuring reserves in ocean deposits. But then he seems to be fighting a series of rearguard battles about supply and demand studies. With many of his remarks I agree, although a few seem to me to be critiques of studies or briefs that I have not been shown. With respect to research on leasing, one might deduce that Tussing would favor studies of reserves and offshore values if it could be shown by, say, theoretical modelling, that much good would be served by supplying the leasing authority with this information. This is certainly the right test. Tussing seems to feel that competition between bidders is the best we can ask for: public authorities cannot be expected to know as much as or more than the bidding firms. This observation suggests that Tussing views the authority as not maximizing anything and hence unmotivated to enter skillfully into taut bargaining with bidders. Perhaps he would give different advice if his client were a sheikdom, with purposes of its own arising from its conflicting opportunities over time and among users.

Kalter's paper, read with Tussing's, does provide a research agenda. I find its suggestions convincing, although I have no independent knowledge of the subject. From the point of view espoused in this paper, Kalter's agenda would be of service to a client at any level, From private owner to nation. His emphasis on compliance and administrative costs and lags is a useful one, suggesting not only that these might be reduced, but also that different levels of administrative body might have different levels of costs.

The Sebenius contribution on deep ocean resources is also a source of research ideas, although many of the questions he indicates would be asked by the international Deep Sea Authority rather than by member governments. However, the following applies to any mineral or hydrocarbon operation in the ocean:

> ...there are a series of questions about ocean mining that have received only rudimentary treatment. For example, given the apparent resource characteristics and the shape of the early industry, is the depletion rate likely to be optimal? Will there be a "common pool" problem? Are information externalities troublesome? How about pollution and interference with other ocean uses? Is claim-jumping likely in the absence of regulation? How does the unavoidable joint production of the minerals affect the analysis, if at all?

To conclude I examine the research agenda suggested by a single ocean-management point of view and a set of decentralized ocean management units whose quest for their own maximand would lead to an overall maximum. Research is needed to assist the decision about whether to encourage the formation of such units. Doing so was implicit in discussions of devolving the landlord's role to the states (Bower), among federal agencies, to contractors (implied I think in several papers), and to holders of individual rights or licenses (Huppert, Russell and Bower). The decentralized unit would then be charged with undertaking inventories, harvesting and gathering, using space as a store, monitoring and enforcing, collecting revenues, and coordinating with neighbors. Would their activities produce the information they require? Information about information may be the most pressing need. As Tussing asks, when does the administrator need information? Is it for distributional reasons only, or is it for efficient development and the avoidance of conflict? Will decentralized managers be able to produce the needed information? Will the flow of information improve with the rough NOAA approach described by Russell?

Among questions to be answered are the following: Can decentralization to the smallest units be coordinated by a combination of the
marketplace in entitlements with agency regulations? If so, how,
in detail? Can the system be set up without full knowledge, so
that with accumulating information actors can alter the system from
within? Can the system deal with resource-use conflicts by permitting other agencies to acquire and grant transferable rights so as
to reserve "parts" of the ocean for recreational, environmental or
future use? Can regional organizations or private rights systems
be tested in the small, before commitment to universal oceans'
systems? Research on these questions should probably be undertaken
immediately, before greater commitment to oil, fisheries or pollution rights is made.

Response to such questions suggests that concentrated multi-social-
science comparison of institutional alternatives is a pressing need.
Even the decision to reject these modes of decision-making needs
full inquiry. Too often discussion of the best "constitution"
for a resource is confused with discussion of the policies or
actions that would be provided by actors governed by constitutional
rules. This is wasteful: what is needed at once is comparison of
alternative units for making day-to-day policies about conflicts,
timing, quantities and qualities. Further economic research then
follows from the needs of the selected management unit: right-
holder firm, regional agency, or centralized government agency such
as NOAA.

List of Participants

Lee G. Anderson
College of Marine Studies
University of Delaware
Newark, Delaware

Dan Basta
Office of Ocean Resources
  Coordination and Assessment
NOAA
Washington, D.C.

Richard Bishop
Department of Agricultural
  Economics
University of Wisconsin
Madison, Wisconsin

Blair Bower
Resources for the Future
1755 Massachusetts Ave. NW
Washington, D.C.

Gardner Brown, Jr.
Department of Economics
University of Washington
Seattle, Washington

James A. Crutchfield
Department of Economics
University of Washington
Seattle, Washington

Robert Dorfman
Department of Economics
Harvard University
Cambridge, Massachusetts

Charles N. Ehler
Office of Ocean Resources
  Coordination and Assessment
NOAA
Washington, D.C.

A. Myrick Freeman, III
Department of Economics
Bowdoin College
Brunswick, Maine

Mason Gaffney
Department of Economics
University of California,
  Riverside
Riverside, California

Stephen R. Gibbs
Institute for Marine Studies
University of Washington
Seattle, Washington

John Gulland
Department of Fisheries
Food and Agriculture Organization
  of the United Nations
Rome, Italy

Dan Huppert
NOAA Southwest Fisheries Center
La Jolla, California

Robert J. Kalter
Cornell University
Ithaca, New York

Henry Lyman
Salt Water Sportsman
Boston, Massachusetts

Rogge Marsh
Exxon Company U.S.A.
Houston, Texas

Dan Nyhart
Department of Ocean Engineering
Massachusetts Institute of
  Technology
Cambridge, Massachusetts

Clifford S. Russell
Resources for the Future
Washington, D.C.

James Sebenius
Kennedy School
Harvard University
Cambridge, Massachusetts

Anthony D. Scott
Department of Economics
The University of British Columbia
Vancouver, B.C.
Canada

Robert Stewart
Pacific Marine Environmental
  Laboratory
University of Washington
Seattle, Washington

Arlon R. Tussing
Arlon R. Tussing and Associates,
  Inc.
Seattle, Washington

Conrad G. Welling
Ocean Minerals Company
Mountain View, California